"Jesus Rode a Donkey gives us an alternative to the current culture war that divides America and its faith communities. I can't think of a better Election Day gift for my Republican—and Democratic—friends.

—William McKinney, Ph.D., President,
Pacific School of Religion

"You do not have to be a Republican to be a good Christian. Dr. Seger's excellent book helps make it clear that there are several strategic Biblical issues in America in 2006 that are better addressed by Democrats. In the bright light of Scripture, many of us evangelicals, committed to its authority, truly dislike the forced dilemma between being a grieving Democrat or a frustrated Republican. Perhaps, as Dr. Seger reminds us, Jesus rode a donkey once, and his commands may become more clearly seen in the choices the present donkey makes for our future. Engaging some of the divine wisdom of this book could help make that happen."

—Paul de Vries, Ph.D., President,
New York Divinity School

"Linda Seger shows us a Christianity that overcomes divisions of liberal and conservative. But she also makes clear how liberal values are deeply rooted in the gospel message. Liberals need not think that their values are somehow less religious or Biblical than those of conservative Republicans. Seger does trenchant analyses of the conflicting values underlying conservative and liberal policy choices and asks which are closer to the values of Jesus, values rooted in love, compassion, and justice. This is an important book for this time in American life."

—Rosemary Radford Ruether, Ph.D., Professor of Theology,
Claremont Graduate University and Claremont School of Theology, and author of
Sexism and God-Talk and *Integrating Ecofeminism, Globalization, and World Religions*

"As a Baptist preacher's kid, Christian, and the only Democrat from El Paso County (an epicenter of Religious Right organizations), I am frequently compelled to point out the hypocrisy of Republican "value based" legislation. Linda Seger's book *Jesus Rode a Donkey* has given me reams of quotes, and I have used up at least one highlighter while reading it. It has also provided me with a strong defense against those who have at times called me "devil worshiper," "sinner," "evil," and—worst of all—a Democrat!"

—Michael Merrifield, State Representative,
District 18, El Paso County, Colorado State Legislature

"*Jesus Rode a Donkey* aptly demonstrates that no one secular political party has a lock on religious and Biblical authenticity and application. Those who are interested in this timely topic will admire Seger's effort to bring clarity and balance to American religious and political interaction."

—William Durland, Ph.D.,
author of *God or Nations: Radical Theology for the Religious Peace Movement*

"In this thoughtful book about crucial issues facing Americans today, Linda Seger calls for a new public discourse. Her perspective as a born-again Christian and a liberal Democrat challenges the right-wing stereotype that persons of deep faith are, or should be, conservative Republicans. *Jesus Rode a Donkey* also challenges left-wing Americans, especially liberal Christians, to affirm the vital connections between their personal faith and public policy."

— Lloyd E. Ambrosius, Ph.D., Samuel Clark Waugh
Distinguished Professor of International Relations and
Professor of History, University of Nebraska

"In a time when cultural awareness has become a requirement for effective global engagement, and a critical element in efforts to combat the growing threat of terrorism, Linda Seger offers a thoughtful treatise on tolerance and understanding among diverse religious traditions. While her book focuses on Christianity in the modern American political context, her approach is useful to anyone seeking understanding of different religions, customs, and cultural traditions."

—Colonel Thomas Dempsey, U.S. Army (Retired),
a regional studies specialist with experience in
conflict resolution in both the Middle East and Africa

"In *Jesus Rode a Donkey*, Dr. Linda Seger has taken on today's "story" of controversial partisan politics, government and religion, and the sensitive issues facing contemporary Christianity. Supported with excellent research and Biblical references, Seger provides us with a unique and fascinating critique of what it means to be a devoted follower of Christianity in America from a more liberal point of view."

—Kate McCallum, writer, media producer, and
founder of the Center for Conscious Creativity

"Linda Seger's book is an eloquent breath of fresh air in the political debate. *Jesus Rode a Donkey* is a clarion call for comity and peace-seeking dialogue. This book provides a well-marked path for those interested in removing the rancor and toxicity from our political discourse. In a rational world, every American President and Cabinet Secretary would be compelled to read it."

—Robert Grant, award-winning movie producer and writer

JESUS RODE A DONKEY

Why Republicans Don't Have the Corner on Christ

Linda Seger, Th.D.

ADAMS MEDIA
AVON, MASSACHUSETTS

Published by Adams Media, an F+W Publications Company
57 Littlefield Street
Avon, MA 02322
www.adamsmedia.com

ISBN: 1-59337-619-7

Printed in the United States of America.

J I H G F E D C B A

Library of Congress Cataloging in Publication Data
Seger, Linda.
Jesus rode a donkey / by Linda Seger.
p.   cm.
Includes bibliographical references and index.
ISBN 1-59337-619-7
1. Christians—United States—Political activity. 2. Christianity and politics—
United States. 3. Democratic Party (U.S.) I. Title.
BR526.S44 2006
261.70973—dc22
2006005208

Unless otherwise noted, the Bible used as a source is the *New Jerusalem Bible*, Doubleday &
Company (1973).

This book is available at quantity discounts for bulk purchases.
For information, please call 1-800-872-5627.

*Dedicated to my uncle, Dr. Norman Graebner,
who has taught American history and American diplomacy
for more than sixty years. His dedication to democracy,
and his dignity and grace, have been a model to me all my life.*

*To my researcher, Sue Terry, who knows where to find
everything—fast. I thank her for her generosity, care, and
spirituality. Without her, I could not have written his book.*

Contents

➤┤◆➤•O•◆┤◄

➤—⬧—○—⬧—≺

Acknowledgments

I n all my books, I ask readers to give me feedback before I send the book to the publisher. I have been particularly thankful to this group of readers. Thank you to my uncle, Dr. Norman Graebner, for adding quotes, giving me books, and checking facts for me. Thanks also:

- To my Quaker friend, Dr. Bill Durland, Ph.D. in politics and religion, who has guided me through several chapters; to my neighbor Tom Radcliffe, who has worked in the White House under several administrations and helped with the chapter titled "Secrets, Lies, and Deceptions"; and to William Flavin from the U.S. Army War College, who provided me with many papers and fact checks in the "War and Peace" chapter.
- To my fellow Christian Democrat readers, who gave me copious notes and wonderful insights: Pamela Jaye Smith, Kim Peterson, Cathleen Loeser, Bobbie Sue Nave, and Jim Nave.

- To my Christian Republican readers, who were so generous with their time, their insights, and their ideas about how to make this a book that Republicans would also like to read; in particular, thanks to Debra Weitala, from South Dakota, who read every chapter and kept me on track, answered many e-mail questions, and so lovingly proved how beautifully Republicans and Democrats can work together. And thanks to my Republican neighbor Steve Berendt for our ten-hour day filled with stimulating discussions of ideas and with his brilliant suggestions for honing the language of the book.
- To Dr. Cheri Junk for help with Chapters 1 and 2.
- To Kristin Howard for her help with Chapter 1.
- To Tirtza and Abe Weschler for help on Chapter 3.
- To Ann Grant Martin and Pam Jones for their comments on Chapter 6.
- To Devorah Cutler-Rubinstein for help with Chapters 7 and 8.

Many thanks to my researcher, Sue Terry, to whom this book is dedicated. I thank her for her brilliance, generosity, and support, and for always being there when I needed her.

Thanks to my agent, Janet Benrey, and thanks to the many people at Adams Media who have worked on this book. In particular, thanks to my editor, Paula Munier; development editor Larry Shea; copyeditor Kate Petrella; and book designers Paul Beatrice and Colleen Cunningham.

Many thanks to my assistant, Sarah Callbeck, for always being there when needed, for keeping her good humor and kind presence, and for being willing to deal with the many tedious details necessary. And for never letting me down! And to Martha Callbeck, for her good help on footnoting the chapters.

And thanks always to my husband, Peter Hazen Le Var, for reading chapters and for continuing to love me despite knowing what life is like when I'm writing a book!

Note: In order to be inclusive, my Biblical quotes come from the *New Jerusalem Bible,* which is used by Catholics and Protestants alike. Very occasionally, another translation is used.

Introduction

If you think about it—no one has a corner on God. Not Republicans or Democrats, men or women, black or white, Asian, Hispanic; nor any culture, nationality, or religious sect. If those of us who are Christians understand anything about the nature of Christ, we know he was a man for all seasons, a Son of God for all ages.

And yet, leading up to the election of 2004 and in the months following, I kept hearing about the Republican "values" vote as the "Christian vote." Supposedly, George W. Bush had the Christian vote, and those of us who were Democrats and Christians were not in line with core Christian values.

As someone who has always been religious, I became increasingly distressed by the growing divisions among Christians. I grew up Lutheran, the granddaughter of a Missouri Synod Lutheran minister. My mother was Lutheran, and my father was Presbyterian. It was not unusual for me to join my father to sing in the choir or to attend a Methodist church, because I liked their nonliturgical service. I became a born-again Christian my last year at Colorado College in Colorado Springs, helped in my own personal spiritual search by the evangelical Christian group, the Navigators, as well as by a Bible church located nearby. My first teaching job was at Grand Canyon College, a Southern Baptist college in Phoenix. Later, I taught at two Church of the Brethren colleges—McPherson College and University of La Verne.

I attended the Graduate Theological Union seminary in Berkeley, California, which is a consortium that includes Baptist, Lutheran, Episcopal, Presbyterian, and Catholic seminaries. My seminary, Pacific School of Religion, prepares ministers in both the Methodist and United Church of Christ. While there, I received an M.A. and a Th.D. One summer I did the Ignatian Exercises, which are the Jesuit exercises, usually done for five weeks by those entering the priesthood, but occasionally done by laypeople. These exercises included Bible reading, prayer, and meditating three hours a day on the life of Christ. This practice changed my life on many profound levels.

Throughout these years, I attended many different churches—Evangelical churches, Episcopal, Catholic, Methodist, Presbyterian, Lutheran, Baptist—but it took me some years to find my church home. One day in Phoenix in 1969, I decided to attend a Quaker Meeting (Society of Friends). I walked in, sat down, and knew I was home.

In 1993 I returned to graduate school to study feminist liberation theology. Although I recognize that anything with the "F" word is a red flag to some, I found that my studies brought me more deeply in touch with the liberating work of Christ. Much of my study previously had been in Biblical studies, church history, religion and the arts, and Christian mysticism, but I felt I had not brought my religion sufficiently into the social and political world. I did my internship with a Catholic charity in the Philippines (the Women's Economic Development and Earth Foundation—WODEEF). My time there changed my life, and the people I met and the work of WODEEF deeply touched me.

On the political level, I have also met the best of both conservatives and liberals. I come from an extended family that includes conservatives, fundamentalists, radicals, liberals, and mainstream Christians and find that we are all able to get along.

I grew up in a Republican household, although my mother switched to voting Democrat during the Vietnam War. My father was a staunch conservative—he liked things the way they were, and was a grounded, stable, and very kind man. He saw no need for change since he believed that our little town of Peshtigo, Wisconsin, was the center of the universe. He was content to go to his drugstore every morning, filling prescriptions for the 2,500 people from our town, most of whom he knew. He didn't confront. He didn't make waves. He played it safe, never took risks, never questioned. He didn't take stands, even when, at times, it seemed important to stand up and be counted. Yet, he was never hateful, never would willingly hurt anyone, and was one of the most generous people I've ever known.

My mother was a liberal in outlook. She was curious about the world around her and the world outside the boundaries of Peshtigo, of Wisconsin, and of the United States. She believed in possibilities, potential, imagination, what might be. She was willing to analyze and ask the Big Questions—about people, about values, about our lives. She was a problem-solver. If there was a way to make things better, she was willing to give it a try. She taught me to question and analyze and envision something better. Before I went to college, she told me, "It's all right to question your religion. If your religion can't hold up to questioning, it's not much good anyway." She believed Christianity was strong enough for any of my little but important questions, and by questioning, my faith would become stronger. She helped us understand that nurturing our potential and nurturing the potential of others was a worthy goal to make the world better. She wasn't afraid of change, but embraced it—and found the adventure of new experiences, new approaches, and creative ways to solve problems exhilarating.

I took after my mother. My sister took after my father.

I have seen the best of both. I know there is nothing inherently wrong with conservatives or liberals or fundamentalists or radicals. I know, because of my own family history, we can get along, and we can respect each other. I also know that our personalities and outlooks determine partly why we choose one party, or one approach to problem-solving, over another.

I have had, perhaps, a more ecumenical, and also a better experience with religion and with people of other political parties than many. I have met the best Christians of all types—from the most fundamentalist to the most liberal. I have found that none of them are so easily categorized. I have observed great faith and compassionate service from many people who are motivated by their faith and by their love of Christ.

In my discussions with Christians, I have always been amazed at how accepting and loving most are. I have found tolerance among the fundamentalists, and a commitment to Christ and the Bible in those considered liberal. My experiences have consistently moved me beyond stereotypes.

This is not to say there aren't differences among Christians, but I do believe labels aren't quite as neat as we like to make them. And until recently, I found that many of us could coexist as those who love Christ.

But something changed during these last few years. I noticed that the preaching from pulpits, the political ads, and the news from the television and newspapers expressed the view that somehow the Republicans owned God.

I began to feel that some Republicans actually believed that "Christian Democrat" was an oxymoron. When I attended evangelical churches, I felt insulted and offended by their negative comments about anyone who wasn't a Republican when I know, as do many Republicans, that Jimmy Carter, Al Gore, Bill Clinton, and John Kerry are all devout Christians.

What happened to our country? Instead of religion pulling us together to create a more just and loving society, it created malice, and even hatred, as if we Christians had become a dysfunctional family—unforgiving, and unaccepting of anyone who does not express themselves exactly as we do. It often seemed as if each Christian foot, hand, arm, demanded we be exactly like them. We had become dismembered, disembodied, incapable of moving together toward the society we kept insisting we wanted.

Instead of bringing about less judgment and more listening, we became blind to each other, and less respectful. Instead of working together to build a more just and loving society that acts in line with our Christian values, we built a less merciful and less compassionate society. Instead of bringing about a more peaceful and harmonious world, we brought about more dissension.

Non-Christians often told me they saw Christians as vicious, vitriolic, and at war with each other, like brothers and sisters having childish spats. How and when had we become so un-Christlike?

As a Christian who is also a writer, I realized I had to make a choice: either withdraw from the political scene for my peace of mind, or work to clarify my vision of how religion and politics can best work together. My spiritual journey for the last thirty-five years has been toward being a bridge-builder and a unifier. And yet, when asked to write this book, I realized I was taking on an intrinsically divisive topic—politics and religion. After much prayer, meditation, and discussion, I decided I was not only willing to do this, but desired to address an issue that needs to be resolved among Christians.

By no means do I believe that Democrats have some exclusive claim on God. To believe this would simply be adding more fuel to the fire. But it is time for Democrats to give an accounting of how Christian values are expressed through the Democratic Party. As Christians and as Democrats, we too are voting our values. We have a reason for our choices.

For those of you reading this book who are Republicans, I hope that it brings you new respect and understanding for your fellow Christians. For those of you who are Democrats, I hope that it helps you to articulate your values without feeling defensive or judgmental of others. This book may also speak to non-Christians; people of many faiths share the same commitment to mercy, compassion, unity, and peace. Many of us want to bring our values into the political arena. Virtually every religion includes a golden rule to guide our behavior. Most Christian values are universal values, and can, and should, provide a guide for moral and spiritual policies.

For those readers who are unsure about which party and which policies best express your values, perhaps this book will bring you to some new decisions about who you are, what you believe as a citizen of our country and of our world, and what actions you can take to help create a better world for us all.

Chapter One

How Would Jesus Vote?

*"[You] have neglected the weightier matters
of the Law—justice, mercy, good faith!"*

MATTHEW 23:23

Jesus and the prophets shared a vision for a people and a nation—that a nation would respond to its people with justice and mercy and good faith. These Christian values are also democratic values, asking us to come together to create a free, equal, and kind society that cares for all its citizens. As Christians, we are asked to help remove structures that oppress its citizens. Christian values recognize the redemptive potential and possibilities of humanity. Democracy provides a voice for the majority as well as the minority and promises freedom and protection for all. A democratic nation, founded on religious principles, struggles to create unity out of diversity, without compromising either one.

But how do we get there? In the vice-presidential debates in 2004, Dick Cheney was asked how his administration would bridge the divide to bring unity to the country. He said, "I believe it is essential for us to do everything we can to garner as much support from the other side of the aisle as possible . . . there are some Democrats who agree with our approach." For Mr. Cheney, unity meant the other side would agree with him.

If our country is dependent upon a one-party system, in which everyone thinks and believes and acts the same, we have no hope as a nation, for we will never find unity that way. We cannot, and will not, achieve unity if we continue to go about it as we have in the last few years. There have been many voices calling us to be a Christian nation, governed by Christian values with a Christian government; yet, in spite of all the Christians in government, we have not become a kinder and more just nation. Like the early Christians so often scolded by Paul for their divisiveness, we have failed to become a united people.

A House Divided Cannot Stand

We live in a divided nation. This is not just a division of Democrats versus Republicans. This is a division of Christians versus everybody else and Christians versus other Christians. The conservative Christians wonder if the more liberal Christians take the Bible seriously enough; they are concerned that the country will go to the dogs if the liberals get back in power, fearing that all of our values will be lost and that there will be rampant abortions and millions more homosexuals in our society. The liberal Christians fear that the conservatives will take away our democratic rights. They don't like the judgmental attitude of some of the more conservative Christians and are concerned that the conservatives don't care about important Christian issues such as poverty, war, ecology, and civil rights. Even though we profess the same faith, read the same Holy Bible, and try to be good followers of Christ, both sides, deep down, wonder if the other side is "suitably" Christian.

Why is it that the same Christians who are helpful, kind, and supportive of each other individually can be so vicious and vindictive when they enter into the social and political sphere?

I know many Christians, and am friends with a wide variety of Christians, who would call themselves fundamentalists, conservatives, Evangelicals, mainstream Christians, or liberal. (For a discussion of the different groups found within Christianity in this country, see the Appendix, "Christian Values and Christian Viewpoints.") On the personal level, I know I can call on any one of them if I'm in trouble. They are supportive of me, pray for me and for my friends and relatives who are sick, wish me well, and exemplify the love of Christ in their lives.

Yet, when I turn on the television, read the newspapers, read books written by some Christians, I find a level of nastiness, revenge, and downright hatred that astonishes me. My non-Christian friends have often told me they could never even consider exploring Christianity because of its public face. For them, Christianity means self-righteousness, pride, intolerance, and mean-spiritedness. And I must agree with their perception. If I weren't a Christian, and had to decide whether I would become one based on what I see from Christians who are the extreme public face of our religion, I'm not sure I could find my way to Christ. The vicious extremists, who seem to represent

Christianity because they have the loudest and most confident voices, have taken the love, kindness, compassion, and mercy out of Christianity and sounded their views with a passionate self-righteous fervor and vindictiveness that smack more of witch-hunting than of the egalitarian, embracing ideals that Jesus taught.

All of us Christians, whether conservative or liberal, have not done enough to denounce this viewpoint and let the world know this is not the face of Christ. Rather than banding together, we have divided and separated. We have allowed our faith to be distorted and misinterpreted. We would rather claim allegiance to a political party than to our faith.

This attitude has not only made us divided among ourselves, but divided from others around the world. The truth is, many people hate us. I have found, in my travels abroad, that most people don't hate individual Americans, but they no longer understand the attitudes of our country. They see Americans, collectively, as hateful, intolerant, and noncooperative with the world community. They see us as bullies in the world and condescending in our attitudes toward others. They see us as impossible to work with, with no respect for others, and little respect for each other. Many abroad are astounded by what our country has become. They don't understand our rhetoric about Christian values, because what they see doesn't strike them as values, or Christian at all. We have turned away from a gospel of love and a gospel of Christ in our politics, and have turned toward judgment, malice, and pride.

What is happening to us as Christians? Why do we keep attacking each other and demonizing each other, as if one party is the Great Satan that will bring down civilization and the other owns the Immaculate Heart of Jesus? Although Christians from both parties feel under attack, and both parties have attacked back, as a Christian Democrat I am appalled, puzzled, and offended by the constant attacks from Republican Christians, which come in the name of Jesus.[1]

A number of Republican Party spokesmen—including James Dobson from Focus on the Family; Senator Bill Frist; Representative Tom DeLay; and Tony Perkins, President of the Family Research Council—have said, in many different ways, that Democrats are "'God's people' haters,"[2] that they are enemies of Christianity, and that Democrats attack people of faith. Perkins has said the Democrats are working "like thieves in the night, to rob us of our Christian heritage and our religious freedoms."[3]

To say this, they have to ignore the Christian faith of most of the Democratic members of the Senate and the House. Are Patrick Leahy, John Kerry, Edward Kennedy, or Joseph Biden un-Christian, because they're Catholic? Is Hillary Clinton less Christian than Pat Roberts, even though both are Methodist? Would they tell us that President Carter wasn't Baptist enough? Would they reject Bill Clinton even though he was Southern Baptist, saying he didn't pass their litmus test? At what point do we decide, as Christians, that this kind of judgment about each other's souls is both un-Christian and un-American?

Protestant theologian C. S. Lewis said, "Democracy demands that little men should not take big ones too seriously; it dies when it is full of little men who think they are big themselves."[4] Perhaps it is time we denounce much of this rhetoric, for the sake of democracy, rather than embracing the walls that separate us.

We have become so divided that it seems issues no longer matter; all that's of importance is the party in which they're cloaked. Do we honestly believe this is how we create a good, just, and compassionate nation? When Christians start disdaining other Christians, there is no hope of working together toward a better society. Christians ask for a Christian nation, but now that we have a nation governed mainly by Christians, we find that instead of enjoying the fruits of the spirit and a more compassionate and effective society, we have, instead, become more divided than ever. Are we so out of sorts with each other that we honestly believe there is no way we can work together from across the political divide?

What we see is politicians using Christianity to manipulate their own agenda rather than using Christian values to guide our nation.

As a Christian who is also a Democrat, I have never felt hated by other Christians—until recently. The last three Evangelical churches I attended preached politics from the pulpit and made it very clear that Christians were expected to vote, or to have voted, for Republicans. I was offended by such an attitude and wondered why they didn't put a sign in the front that said, "Democrats are not welcome here!"

I have heard statements that vilify the Democrats, while praising George W. Bush with words that verge on worship and sometimes even idolatry.[5] I have heard prayers that thank God, fervently, that we have Mr. Bush in the White House, and that we now have this small window of four more years to "fix" everything, before the demonic Democrats have the chance of taking power away again.[6]

In Galatians 5, Paul says, "The whole of the Law is summarized in the one commandment: you must love your neighbor as yourself. If you go snapping at one another and tearing one another to pieces, take care: you will be eaten up by one another." Paul lists the problems when Spirit is not at work: "antagonisms, rivalry, jealousy, bad temper and quarrels, disagreements, factions and malice"—all the traits we read about almost daily in our newspapers and see daily on our television sets.

We have forgotten how to serve the Truth, the Just, the Good, and only gnaw at each other's belief systems and behavior. Is the Holy Spirit truly present in this behavior?

Which Is the Christian Political Party?

Both the Republican and Democratic parties and some of the others as well are made up of millions of Christians.

In the 2004 presidential election, many Republicans believed they knew exactly how Jesus would have voted— Republican. The Republican vote was called the "values vote." But the statistics and the actions tell us otherwise. Although the press implied that George W. Bush got the Christian vote, this is not true.

Although Mr. Bush received 78 percent of the Evangelical votes, that still left more than one out of five Christian Evangelicals who voted otherwise. The foremost evangelist of our time— Billy Graham—is a Democrat. Catholics, and other Protestants, on the whole, were almost equally divided between George W. Bush, who is a Methodist, and John Kerry, who is a Catholic.[7]

Even the breakdown of voters is not so neat. Some liberals voted for Mr. Bush; some conservatives for Mr. Kerry. Some people who are pro-choice voted Republican. Some who are anti-abortion voted for Kerry. Many who voted Republican confess to agonizing over their decision and finally voting for Mr. Bush because we were in the middle of a war and they felt we should stay with the same leader. Some of these have told me they now regret their vote.

Clearly, millions of Christians in both parties voted their values and their priorities.

Beyond Party to People

If we move beyond party to people, a Christian Democrat and a Christian Republican might agree on many issues. Sometimes they vote according to whom they feel they can best trust to keep promises. They vote for the person who seems to have the same priorities as they do, or the one they think can best exemplify these values in our government. Many vote for the issues, while trying to assess the character of the candidate.

Both democracy and Christianity are challenging. They challenge us to go against our seemingly natural human behaviors of hatred, intolerance, and self-righteousness and move toward an affirmation of equality. They ask us to find unity in a nation made up of diverse peoples.

On the surface, there do seem to be issues that are not easily resolved, because there seems to be an inner contradiction between Christianity and democracy. Churches often ask us to be homogeneous in our beliefs and actions. Churches have creeds, and dogmas, and statements of belief, and the members are asked to, at least verbally, agree with them. But our country is not homogeneous. From the beginning, settlers of our country came to America to find freedom, and soon found that there was a diverse group of others, all of whom wanted the same freedom for themselves. Early on, many of the early settlers decided they may as well respect that and create a democratic system.

All of us are constantly in a struggle between the desire to be inclusive and the desire to be exclusive. We are always being pushed between our natural suspicion of each other and the command to love our neighbor, even when the neighbor is someone far away, or someone we really don't like at all.

I have heard time and again that we are a Christian nation. But we are not a Christian nation—either in many of our actions or in the makeup of our citizens. No matter how much we might like to be homogeneous in religion, we are not. We are a diverse nation, made up of Christians, Jews, Buddhists, Muslims, Hindus, Wiccans, Hare Krishnas, Sikhs, New Agers, atheists, agnostics, and a few Zoroaster followers, among others.

There are many people other than Christians who have values. Many of those values are similar to ours—among them, the values of freedom, equality, honesty, justice, mercy, compassion, and the golden rule. Many people besides Christians see America as the land of opportunity, the land where they can achieve their dreams. Although there may be more of "us" than "them," and although our country may have been founded mainly (but not entirely) by Christians, our country has strived from the very beginning to give freedom and justice to all. As

Christians living in a democratic nation, we have to remember that what we desire for ourselves must be available for all. Suppressing another's freedom is not the answer.

I have heard that everything would be fine if we just followed Christ. Of course, if we all were more Christlike, things would be much better. We would see the fruits of the Spirit all around us—love, joy, peace, patience, kindness, goodness, faithfulness, gentleness, and self-control.[8] But we're not as Christlike as we would think. Unfortunately, our sinful and flawed and imperfect nature keeps getting in the way.

Was Jesus Political?

On the surface, it might seem as if Jesus was not a political person but was someone who focused, instead, on individuals and individual relationships. He certainly did not live up to the Jewish hopes for a political Messiah. The Jews in Jesus' day imagined a militant Messiah who would lead an army, overthrow the oppressive rule of Rome, and establish a religious kingdom.

We can, however, see some of the political viewpoints of Jesus through the actions he took and those he didn't take. Jesus didn't identify with any of the political structures of the day. He rejected the Sadducees, the conservatives who were willing to go along with foreign domination provided it didn't compromise their position. He confronted the Pharisees, who observed religious practices in great detail, made hundreds of oppressive religious laws, and also supported the established powers of the day. He never joined the Essenes, who rejected political involvement and took no part in any of the religious ceremonies because they considered them impure. They formed a separate sect, and moved to Qumran by the Dead Sea. He was not part of the Zealots, one of the most politically active groups. They were nationalists, who wanted a radical transformation of existing political institutions through violent revolution.

Many of Jesus' followers were from different political parties with different political and religious beliefs. Simon, called the Zealot, would have either been a revolutionary or a sympathizer with the group that desired to overthrow the Roman government. Matthew, the tax collector, worked for the oppressive government that Simon wanted to overthrow. Yet, there's no evidence that Jesus tried to change their political parties, or even their religion. He wanted to change their hearts and their actions.[9]

Was Jesus Conservative or Liberal?

The labels of conservative and liberal have been so overused they have become almost meaningless. One side hates the other side, even though those considered to be liberals often hold conservative values, and those considered to be conservative often hold liberal values.

The word "conservative" comes from the word "conserve," which can mean "to preserve." Generally, conservatives want to preserve the status quo. They prefer to maintain existing habits and views and institutions. A true conservative usually wants government to have a limited role in social and economic affairs. At their best, conservatives ground our country by recognizing the ideals of the past and giving us a solid foundation on which to stand.

At their worst, conservatives can be inflexible, rigid, legalistic, and immovable. They are sometimes fearful of risks and distrustful of change. Because they are often unable to imagine other possibilities or to believe that change can lead us to a better society, conservatives are less apt to envision new ways to solve social problems.

Liberal is a word coming from the Latin *liberare*—to set free or to liberate. Liberals tend to advocate reforms that would achieve greater freedom for citizens. To achieve that, they are more apt to criticize the status quo, imagine new possibilities, and ask how it can be done better. They are willing to be unconventional and untraditional in order to solve a problem.

At their best, they tend to be tolerant of others and want to remove restraints to the freedom of all citizens, not just for themselves. They are progressive, wanting to improve the social welfare of others. The word "liberal" often means generous and bounteous and open-handed, as used when someone gives liberally to charity. At their most extreme, liberals can become so freedom-minded that their actions lead to excess, anarchy, and a lack of restraint that can become destructive.

Both of these positions need to be more balanced. Lacking balance, either position can lead to the vicious extremism that we see in almost all political parties and religions—ranging from the fundamentalists who will kill in the name of their party or their religion, to the radicals who destroy property and create anarchy in the name of freedom.

Like most of us, Jesus exemplified both conservative and liberal values. There were certain values he wanted to conserve; there were others that he wanted to liberate from a rule-oriented culture in order to reinterpret, broaden, or change them.

The Freedom to Love God

The most important value that Jesus wanted to conserve was the commandment to love the Lord your God with all your heart, with all your soul, with all your mind, and all your strength.[10] Love of God is above all things and is the guiding principle throughout the entire Bible. How to love God has been one of the thorniest issues our country has ever confronted.

Our nation was founded by many who loved God. Before the Constitution was written, the early colonies tried to legislate the love of God. They became repressive when they tried to impose laws about how this love was to be shown. The Massachusetts Bay Colony persecuted any who didn't love God in the same way they did. They banished those who didn't agree with them, particularly the Quakers. Besides banishment, Quakers were imprisoned, whipped, branded, burned, and enslaved; some had their ears cut off and their property confiscated; several were put to death for insisting on the right to worship in their own way.[11]

Puritan minister Roger Williams (who later helped found the first Baptist church in America) was banished from Boston because he believed that everyone had the right to think and worship as he pleased. In his pamphlet called *The Bloudy Tenent of Persecution, for the Cause of Conscience*, published in 1644,

Williams said, "How ghastly and unbelieved . . . was the damage done and the number of innocent human beings slaughtered in the effort to make men and women worship God in some certain way."[12] He believed in separation of church and state, so neither could control the other, and complete toleration by the government of all sorts of religion, even the religion of the Indians. Williams, the Quakers, and other tolerant Christians established freedom of worship and freedom from a state-sponsored religion.

The writers of the Constitution didn't want to legislate religion. They recognized that democracies cannot be ruled by prayer. As a result, the Constitution was designed to try to channel these motives in the direction of the public good.[13]

One of the clearest definitions between the Republican and Democratic values lies with the question of what part religion should play in a nation. The Democrats have had a fairly consistent policy to protect our religious freedoms. The Republicans have, during some previous administrations, been protective of religious freedom. However, the last few decades have seen the rise of the Moral Majority and the Religious Right within the Republican Party, which itself has become increasingly influential, potentially threatening freedom of worship.

Who Are the Dominionists and What Control Do They Want?

Within the Republican Party is an influential group of Christians called the Dominionists, who believe they are called to have dominion over the government. Their goal is to expand their political influence in the Republican Party, and therefore, throughout America. It is estimated that about 35 million Christians, almost all of them Republicans, subscribe to these theories.[14] Christian Democrats are particularly concerned about our country going backward and becoming less democratic, rather than more so, as a result of the increasing power of this group within the Republican Party.

The movement was begun by D. James Kennedy in Florida in 1959. (Kennedy also helped found the Moral Majority in 1979, along with the Rev. Jerry Falwell and others.) Kennedy says, "Our job is to reclaim America for Christ, whatever the cost. As the vice regents of God, we are to exercise godly dominion and influence over our neighborhoods, our schools, our government, our literature and arts, our sports arenas, our entertainment media, our news media, our scientific endeavors—in short, over every aspect and institution of human society." There is nothing wrong with bringing values into every aspect of our social and political life. That's what we would want in a country that tries to serve the Good. But Kennedy is not talking about trying to make Christianity more prevalent in American political policy; rather, he is promoting the sole use of the Dominionist brand of Christianity in making public policy—to the exclusion of not only other faiths, but also other interpretations of Christianity. This kind of exclusion and lack of protection for those unlike themselves is unconstitutional and unjust.

Another Dominionist, David Limbaugh, brother of Rush Limbaugh, says, "We have a right, indeed an obligation, to govern." They believe that the government's work is to proselytize, to protect property rights, and to promote homeland security but not to promote social change. They want to restore school prayer, put a Bible in each classroom, and criminalize the homosexual lifestyle. In addition, they want anyone who protests American policies to be arrested for treason.[15]

Some in this group want all citizens to pay "tithes" to church organizations, which are to become social-welfare agencies for the government. Others want the death penalty for so-called moral crimes such as blasphemy, sodomy, witchcraft, and apostasy. They are upset about a court ruling that said that executing minors was unconstitutional. The Family Research Council, which is made up of Dominionists and is one of the most influential and radical Christian Right lobbying groups, has taken a stand against teaching tolerance and diversity.[16] With the Dominionists in charge, all other voices, except a certain brand of conservative Christians, would be silenced.

What would this mean for you and me? Let's take the controversial subject of school prayer. In a state-sponsored religion, whose prayer would prevail? I can think of a number of prayers that would be counter to my own belief systems, as well as the belief systems of many others.

I can imagine a prayer from a teacher or preacher that says, "Our Lord and Commander, we ask that you give your power to the troops in Iraq and help them to overcome the enemy as we fight this great Crusade to lead us to truth."

I have heard prayers like this. To me, it's a self-righteous prayer that makes nationalism the religion, rather than Christianity. It sees the Other as the enemy, rather than as the Neighbor, and it implies that there will be hundreds, if not hundreds of thousands of the enemy killed in the name of Jesus. As a pacifist, I find no room for my own Christian belief system in this prayer.

I also can imagine another kind of prayer, which would be anathema to most conservatives, and perhaps to millions of other Christians as well: "Our Ground of all being, Mother Earth, Father Sky, embrace our bodies and bring us into unity with you."

Although this may be a more loving prayer, it is so vague and unspecific that it would be meaningless to many. Yet, I have also heard prayers such as this.

I can imagine nationalist prayers that would insist on our complete loyalty to our president, even when he is lying and covering up treasonous or illegal or immoral activities. Do we really want to be saying state-sponsored prayers that keep us from questioning Watergate? Or the Iran-Contra illegal deals? Or the prisoner abuse in Iraq, Afghanistan, and Guantánamo Bay?

What about classrooms in which most of the students are not Christian but Jewish, or Buddhist or Muslim, or not religious at all? Does the majority rule? Will we all be asked to chant? Will the non-Christians be forced to pray "in Jesus' name"?

What Else Would Be Changed?

In gathering everything in the United States under one belief system, the Dominionists would also change the courts. James

Dobson, Tony Perkins, and former House Majority Leader Tom DeLay discussed what to do with courts that are not conservative enough: de-fund them. DeLay said in April 2005, "We set up the courts. We can un-set the courts. We have the power of the purse."

Perkins explained what he meant by de-funding the courts. Instead of going through a process of impeaching judges, which can take a long time, Congress, through the Appropriations Committee, could just "take away the [judge's] bench, all of his staff, and he's just sitting out there with nothing to do." Which courts are they talking about? The courts that are not conservative enough for them—such as the Ninth Circuit Court of California. As Dobson explained, "Very few people know this, that the Congress can simply disenfranchise a court . . . They don't have to fire anybody or impeach them or go through that battle. All they have to do is say the 9th Circuit doesn't exist anymore, and it's gone." Dobson claimed they had the right to do this, because the GOP won the election. "We've got a right to hold them accountable for what happens here." But winning an election does not give anyone a mandate to tread on the rights of the minority.

The Dominionists are against any voice for the Democrats or for other Christians. But they're also against what they call "squishy" and "weak" Republican senators who are not always in agreement with them. This includes Republican moderates such as Senators Olympia J. Snowe, Susan Collins, Lincoln Chafee, Arlen Specter, Chuck Hagel, Mitch McConnell, and George Allen, all of whom the Dominionists felt needed to be shaken up. Dobson was personally affronted that they didn't follow everything he said: "Sometimes it's just amazing to me that they [these senators] seem to forget how they got here."[17]

The Dominionists seem to forget about our democratic rights to free elections, the protection of the minority, and the right to diverse voices in government. They deny and defy the Founding Fathers' system of checks and balances, wherein the executive, the legislative, and the judicial branches of government are kept in integration and balance so that none obtains overwhelming power or influence over the others. They apparently see the executive branch as a ruler and want to be sure the other two branches fall in line or are paralyzed. Our government was set up to guard us against the power of a group such as this. Even though this group lays claim to democratic and Christian values, it practices neither.

George W. Bush sought the blessing of the Dominionists before running for president, and he continues to consult them on matters of federal policy, in some cases on an ongoing basis. Pastor Ted Haggard, head of the National Association of Evangelicals, speaks weekly to President Bush or to one of his advisers, as does Rev. Richard Land, the top lobbyist for the Southern Baptist Convention.

The Dominionists' troubling vision for our country is not shared by all conservative Christians. Some are embarrassed and dismayed by this group's views. Many conservative and fundamentalist Christians, as well as mainstream and liberal Christians, are not comfortable with this extreme theocratic vision for our country or with this expression of our faith.

Luis Palau, an evangelical preacher who is close to Billy Graham, bristles at the coarseness of these calls for absolute power.

Palau is concerned about the ways this influential Republican Christian group belittles homosexuals, "effete" intellectuals, and secular humanists. Palau says, "If we become called to Christ, we will build an effective nation through personal ethics. When you lead a life of purity, when you respect your wife and are good to your family, when you don't waste money gambling and womanizing, you begin to work for better schools, for more protection and safety from your community. All change, historically, comes from the bottom up."[18]

Other evangelical Christians are equally concerned about this movement. Senator Mark Pryor, an evangelical Christian, says, "It is presumptuous of them [the Christian Right] to think they represent all Christians in America, even to say they represent all evangelical Christians."[19]

As Christians, we have to come to terms with what kind of government we want. Personally, I don't want it run by the flawed and imperfect theology of the Dominionists, any more than I want to run the nation with my own flawed and imperfect theology. I know, for sure, that I don't have a handle on God, or a corner on knowing the perfect will of God. I know, without a doubt, that some of my interpretations of Bible verses may not be considered accurate. I am absolutely convinced that God is far bigger than anything my limited mind can contain and that I am far from showing the perfect love Jesus has commanded us to show each other. I also know, with certainty, that the Dominionists are no different. Like all of us, they are sinners and flawed. Do we want them running our country? If not them, then whom can we trust? Neither the Dominionists, nor the conservatives, nor the liberals, nor the humanists. We should trust the voice of the people.

C.S. Lewis, the Protestant writer and theologian, said he believed in democracy "because I believe in the Fall of Man. I think most people [want democracy] for the opposite reason. A great deal of democratic enthusiasm descends from the ideas of people . . . who believed in democracy because they thought mankind so wise and good that everyone deserved a share in the government. The danger of defending democracy on those grounds is that they're not true . . . I find that they're not true without looking further than myself. I don't deserve a share in governing a hen-roost, much less a nation. Nor do most people . . . The real reason for democracy is . . . Mankind is so fallen that no man can be trusted with unchecked power over his fellows. Aristotle said that some people were only fit to be slaves. I do not contradict him. But I reject slavery because I see no men fit to be masters."[20]

Some might think that a sort of theocratic rule is fine, since those governing are religious. But Thomas Jefferson believed that our nation would encounter the same problem if one group of people determined the religion of another group. He said, "Difference of opinion is advantageous in religion. The several sects perform the office of a censor . . . over such other. Is uniformity attainable? Millions of innocent men, women and children, since the introduction of Christianity have been burnt, tortured, fined, imprisoned; yet we have not advanced one inch toward uniformity. What has been the effect of coercion? To make one half of the world fools and the other half hypocrites."[21] This conservative value of religion and love of God only works when it is liberally given to all its citizens and each can freely choose how to exercise it.

Upholding True Conservative Values

Another value that Jesus affirmed is the value of accountability and responsibility. Leaders are to rule justly, not be beholden to the rich, the powerful, the influential.[22]

Both political parties have had a number of presidents, and members of Congress, who have lied, deceived, and tried to get away with breaking laws. It is a right and righteous act to hold these people accountable. Yet, the scandals of the Republican Party since 2000 have often involved those who demand accountability from others, but not for themselves. When House Majority Leader Tom DeLay was first being investigated for breaking various ethical laws, the Republicans tried to change the ethics rules to protect him, until an outcry forced them to stop. When he was indicted on several counts, including breaking laws that carried a prison sentence, the Republicans blamed the Democrats for making ethical breaches a political issue. Instead of truth-telling, blaming became the focus of the discussions.

The value of holding each person accountable for his or her actions, as taught by Jesus and the prophets, is a conservative value. Justice transcends political parties.

The Bible also begins with a commandment that none of the prophets, or Jesus or Paul, have overturned—the commandment to tend the environment that God has given us. Although this is a conservative value, it has been adopted by those considered liberals. We are asked to conserve, preserve, and care for the world that God has given to us. Noah went to considerable trouble, under God's command, to make sure that the animals didn't become extinct. Jesus extols the beauty of the lilies of the field and the birds of the air, telling us that God will care for us, as He cares for nature. If there is one Christian value that should transcend political parties, it should be our care for the environment.

Fiscal Responsibility

Fiscal responsibility is usually considered a conservative value, although the Democratic Party has been more fiscally responsible than the Republican Party for more than twenty-five years.

There is a great deal said about money in the Bible—much of it about giving money to the poor and about letting our money work for us.[23] Our country rarely follows these values—spending more than it has, not caring enough for the needy, only rarely creating surpluses.

We love money. It defines us as powerful and comfortable and important. We use it to gain political favor and to increase our clout. We spend it easily. We deny it to some, give a great deal of it to others. We hide and waste a great deal of it.

Jesus tells a story about the boss who gave money to his various servants and went away for a week. When he returned, he was pleased with the servants who used the money to increase the master's wealth. He punished the servant who hid the money and did nothing with it. Jesus told the story of the prodigal son, who was wasteful with his money. Although he was forgiven and accepted back into the family, misusing his inheritance led to great misery.[24]

Have we been good stewards? The Republican Party used to be considered the party of fiscal responsibility, but this has not been true since Ronald Reagan's presidency. President Reagan ran up the national debt to historic proportions, followed by President George H.W. Bush and now George W. Bush.

When Bill Clinton entered office, there was a budget deficit of about $250 billion, which he inherited from the spending practices of both Mr. Reagan and George H.W. Bush. When Clinton left office, he had turned this deficit around, and left George W. Bush with a budget surplus of around $523 billion.[25] According to House Minority Whip Steny Hoyer, over a ten-year period, this was a projected surplus of $5.6 trillion.[26]

This did not last long. George W. Bush has run up the largest debt in American history. By 2003, Mr. Bush had run up a budget deficit of $378 billion. The 2005 budget deficit is expected to exceed $427 billion.

What is the consequence of this deficit? David Walker, the comptroller general of the General Accounting Office, says that without reform, the economy could slowly grind to a halt. "We could be doing nothing more than paying interest on federal debt in 2040 if we don't end up engaging in some fundamental reforms of entitlement programs, mandatory spending, discretionary spending and tax policy."[27]

Some of this debt comes from mismanagement and from a lack of foresight to prevent or to better deal with catastrophes. In the cases of Iraq and the damage from Hurricane Katrina and Hurricane Rita, warnings that would have prevented tragedy were ignored. The U.S. government was warned by both the U.S. Army Corps of Engineers and the Southeast Louisiana Urban Flood Control Project that the levees would break if there were a category 4 or 5 hurricane. They asked for some millions of dollars to repair them, which was denied. The levees did break, and now it's costing billions.

Although George W. Bush had been warned about the problems that would ensue if he went into Iraq without a well-thought-out plan for rebuilding the country, he went in anyway, without the plan. In spite of billions of dollars put into the country, much of the money goes for security, and for repairing, and repairing again, what continues to be blown up by insurgents.

When we had a surplus, Mr. Bush refunded money, including large amounts to the people who least needed it—the upper middle class and the rich. Although repealing the tax cut for the very rich would help matters a great deal, Mr. Bush has refused to do so.

The Liberal Values of Jesus

Although both the Republican and Democratic Parties contain conservatives and liberals, the Republican Party has increasingly sided with its more conservative members. The Republican Party has made "liberal" a dirty word.

Yet, our country was founded on liberal and liberating values. The Founding Fathers were willing to change the status quo, overthrow an oppressive government, and create a new form of government by the people, of the people, for the people. Many Christians in the early years of our country's history questioned the laws of the time, and changed them, in order to create a freer, more just society.

All men are created equal under God, but in the period of time leading up to 1860, they were born into an unequal system. Only white men who owned property enjoyed inalienable rights. Blacks were considered three-fifths of a person. Married women had almost no civil rights at all. Many Christians, but not all, supported this idea, quoting the Bible to justify slavery and oppression of women. Many Christians limited and resisted extending equal rights to others.

How did this change? Through the work of other Christians. Most of the first abolitionists were Christians—mainly Quakers, Methodists, and Congregationalists. Over time, the impulse to liberate women grew also from Christian roots.

The most recent and extraordinary example of this process was the civil rights movement in the twentieth century, led by a Baptist minister, Dr. Martin Luther King Jr. The movement was conceived in African-American churches and sustained by Christians of all racial and ethnic groups. Many Christians have been, and continue to be, at the forefront of the fight for the civil rights of others.

Throughout the Gospels, we see the portrait of Jesus as a man who questioned the prevailing religious and social establishment. Many actions that Jesus took, and stories that he told, were about liberating people from legal, religious, and governmental oppression. Rather than demanding adherence to religious dogmas and the hundreds of religious laws, he questioned the way things were, and followed the freer Law of Love.

Jesus transcended sexism when he talked to a woman at the well in Samaria.[28] He affirmed Mary's desire to listen and to learn, rather than Martha's playing of the traditional woman's role.[29] Women followed him around the countryside and he accepted them, even though this would have been against the social customs of his age. Women became some of his most beloved followers, and some of the leaders in the early Church.[30]

He challenged the racism of his day by telling a story about a man he perceived as good and righteous—a Samaritan, one of the most hated people.[31] This would be similar to telling a Klansman a story about a good and righteous African-American.

He challenged classism, by associating with the lowlifes of society—the rejects, the prostitutes, the tax collectors, the outcasts, the sick, the lepers, and the untouchables, even eating with them and saying that they would enter the kingdom before the religious leaders of the day.[32] He pardoned the repentant thief on the cross, telling him that he would join Jesus in Paradise.[33]

The Democrats have had a long history of backing equal rights and overcoming unequal laws. It was a Democratic president—Lyndon B. Johnson—who signed civil rights legislation to bring equal rights to ethnic minorities. The Democrats, to the chagrin of many Republicans, have been consistent in their desire to see equal rights for all people—women, ethnic minorities, those of other religions, and those of different sexual orientation.

The Democratic Party Platform for 2004 begins by offering its vision of America—"an America that offers opportunity, rewards responsibility, and rejoices in diversity . . . We will honor the values of a strong American community: widening the circle of equality, protecting the sanctity of freedom, and deepening our commitment to this country. We recommit to the ideal of a people united in helping one another, an ideal as old as the faiths we follow and as great as the country we love."

Liberating the Law

Jesus, as well as Paul, brought liberal values to the idea of marriage. A Jewish man and woman were supposed to marry and to have children. Jesus was single, and didn't fulfill the appropriate social and religious customs of his age. Paul clarified that it didn't matter if a person were single or married; each was to be valued.[34]

Jesus was against capital punishment, a position that is considered a liberal value. He forgave the woman caught in the act of adultery, and freed her, even though the religious law of his time proclaimed that she be stoned to death.[35]

Jesus rethought the idea of forgiveness, clarifying that no longer should one seek revenge through an "eye for an eye"; nor should one forgive another only seven times, but rather seventy times seven.[36]

In many ways, Jesus was far more radical than are the most liberal members of Congress, asking us to act in a way that we often find impossible and impractical.

He changed the way we were to think about the enemy. We are to make friends with our enemies, recognizing that to not do this would cause nothing but trouble.[37] Jesus expanded our idea of the neighbor, telling us that we are to think of our enemy as our neighbor, and he added a new commandment: to love our neighbor as ourselves. This doesn't mean that we are naive about evil, but that we don't add fuel to the fires of hatred. Rather than demonizing and attacking the enemy, we should use diplomacy, which is far more in line with the values of Jesus.[38]

Jesus practiced nonviolent resistance to oppressive laws. He suggested that we love our enemies—feed them, clothe them, care for them, and "offer no resistance to the wicked." This turns the enemy into a friend. He also suggested a subversive tactic that is often used in nonviolent resistance. If the person of his day were asked for his coat, he was to give the cloak as well. If he were asked to go one mile, he was to go two miles.[39]

Why is this nonviolent resistance? If a person in Biblical times gave up his coat and cloak, he would be naked, thereby shaming the person who asked him. It wouldn't take long for the Romans to decide that this was embarrassing and not effective.

A Roman was allowed to ask his subject to carry a burden for one mile, but not for longer. If someone started to walk the second mile, the Roman would be breaking the law. It wouldn't take long for the Romans to stop asking, once they realized that they couldn't stop their subjects from walking that second mile.

Overturning the Social Structures

Jesus and the prophets rethought the social structures that generally rewarded the rich and powerful and asked us to change our focus to the poor and the needy. The prophets asked for a compassionate nation, and Jesus asked for a compassionate people. Who do we particularly need to care about? Those people who cannot give back to us, but who are in need of our care.

Jesus challenged us to give respect, care, and our help to others, even those unlike ourselves, and even those we might hate. How has our country responded? Racism, sexism, and ageism have continued to be ingrained in our national laws and our national identity. Any challenge to these policies is met with resistance. Republican policies have continued to resist affirmative action policies to help those who have been left out and left behind.

Jesus asks us to be fair in our dealing with others. How have we responded? Over and over again, our government has rewarded graft, corruption, and dishonesty. No-bid contracts have been given to the powerful—those close to the Bush and Cheney families—to rebuild Iraq. When these companies, such as Halliburton and Bechtel, were brought before congressional investigation committees to explain their overbilling, overcharges, and lack of effectiveness, Mr. Bush continued to reward them by giving them another contract—to help rebuild New Orleans. Whose money is being misspent? Yours and mine.

Jesus rode a donkey, not an elephant. Elephants were ridden by the rich ruling classes. Jesus didn't identify with the rich ruling classes, but with the people. He was with the people and for the people and of the people—a core value of both democracy and Christianity.

The Ethics of Jesus

Jesus asked us to go beyond the letter of the law to the spirit of the law. Christian values go beyond simple rules to difficult ethical questions.

When Jesus picked corn on the Sabbath, and healed on the Sabbath, the letter of the law said this was wrong.[40] Jesus raised the ethical question—"Does this benefit or harm others?" If it benefits others, we may need to change the law.

Our country has many difficult ethical problems to consider. Does stem cell research hurt or harm? Is it better to use stem cells to save lives, considering that the cells will be thrown away and wasted otherwise? How are we to handle the ethical dilemma of abortion, knowing that without *Roe v. Wade*, some women will continue to have abortions, the difference being that the rich will have safe abortions and the poor will have unsafe abortions? How are we to handle terrorism and the proliferation of nuclear weapons? And what about the wide-ranging effects of a global economy? What should we do about climate change and health care and education? The Bible gives us no clear guides on many issues, except to be willing to confront ethical problems, guided by the Holy Spirit and the Law of Love.

Vote the Golden Rule

Why do so many Christians vote Democratic? Because they see their values best expressed in the Democratic Party and they see that many of the actions and policies of Jesus are at the center of Democratic policy.

Many of us bring together our practice of religion and democracy by voting the Golden Rule. What we want for ourselves, we are also willing to give to others. We vote for the rights of others that we would also want for ourselves. We give the same protections, care, and respect to others that we would want for ourselves. For this reason, we care about the Others' rights with the same passion that we care about our own.

What would Jesus be doing in our society? As the Prince of Peace, he would be questioning our wars, which kill tens of thousands of civilians and leave tens of thousands of children homeless and as orphans.

As the One who accepts and loves, he would be rebuilding homes, instead of blowing up abortion clinics in the name of God. He'd be caring for AIDS victims instead of limiting the rights of homosexuals. He'd be volunteering at soup kitchens rather than granting tax cuts to the rich. He'd be planting trees instead of strip-mining national parks. He'd be working to take care of those who have trouble surviving in our society, rather than rewarding the rich.

He would continue to question authority, knowing that power and privilege can easily corrupt. We are told by Republicans that we must not critique our government, must not question the actions of George W. Bush. If we do, we are unpatriotic and un-American. Yet Jesus consistently questioned, critiqued, and denounced the establishment of his day. He recognized the potential that power had to become oppressive.

Jesus went beyond labels to people, beyond party to people.

Democracy asks us to debate and discuss issues to find the best solutions. It asks many of the same questions that Christianity asks:

What are the most important issues the government needs to address?

What is the goal of a Good Society?

What are the means to reach this goal?

How do we bring justice and mercy into a society, and create a society in which all of us, together, work for the Good?

Chapter Two

The Poor, the Needy,
Widows, and Orphans

"The spirit of the Lord is on me, for he has anointed me to bring the good news to the afflicted. He has sent me to proclaim liberty to captives, sight to the blind, to let the oppressed go free, to proclaim a year of favour from the Lord."

LUKE 4:18–19

This was Jesus' first mission statement. It is often called the Social Gospel, because it proclaims his intent to move people from captivity and oppression to freedom. This is not only spiritual freedom, but proclaiming the Kingdom of God among us, within the society in which we live, and throughout the earth.

When Jesus quoted from Isaiah in this passage, he left out the last phrase of the second sentence—"and a day of vengeance for our God."[1] He put the emphasis back on the people we are supposed to care about. This is a challenging message. Many of us in America do not know people who are poor or destitute. If we do, we might believe their problems are of their own making and God really does help those who help themselves. Many Americans have lived in such privilege we turn our eyes away from the homeless, blame the AIDS victims for their disease, try to justify why the poor are so poor, and claim God's blessing to explain why we're so comfortable.

Our country is powerful and rich. We easily envy power and wealth, and try to get it for ourselves, forgetting that Jesus and the prophets ask us to change our perspective, and to take the side of the poor—to care about those without means, those who need healing.

The Command for Compassion

There is much disagreement about exactly what we, as Christians, should be changing in our nation. The Bible tell us nothing about many of the issues that confront us in contemporary society—whether we should talk to or negotiate with terrorists, whether our country should honor living wills, what kind of health care or educational system we should have. But there is one area in which the Bible is absolutely clear—we are to help the poor, the needy, the broken-hearted, the oppressed. The entire Bible, beginning with the stories in Genesis and throughout the Hebrew Scriptures and the New Testament, testifies that those who oppress the poor and the needy are not in God's good graces.

In Isaiah, God says "Shame on you . . . you who make unjust laws and publish burdensome decrees, depriving the poor of justice, robbing the weakest of my people of their rights, despoiling the widow and plundering the orphan."[2] God promised that he would bring justice to them and that He would crush their oppressors.[3]

While protecting the poor, God warns the rich: "In prosperity people lose their good sense, they become no better than dumb animals. So they go on in their self-assurance, right up to the end they are content with their lot."[4]

In Amos he condemns the rich "for crime after crime of Israel I will grant them no reprieve because they sell the innocent for silver and the destitute for a pair of shoes. They grind the heads of the poor into the earth and thrust the humble out of their way."[5]

The Bible tells us God is a stronghold for the oppressed and he will not desert them. He listens to the laments of the brokenhearted. He fills the starving, and rescues those in chains and misery from hard labor. He gives the hungry a home, where they sow the fields, and blesses them with a bountiful harvest. God provides a refuge for the weak and seeks justice for the poor.[6]

Throughout the Bible, the words for the "poor" are not neutral ones, but expressions of the suffering and misery they endure. The poor person might be *ebyon*, "the one who desires, the beggar, the one who is lacking something and who awaits it from another," or *dal*, the "weak one, the frail one," or *ani*, "the bent-over one, the one laboring under a weight, the one not in possession of his whole strength and vigor, the humiliated one" or *anawy*, "humble before God." In the New Testament, the word *ptokos* is used, meaning "one who does not have what is necessary to subsist, the wretched one driven into begging."[7]

It is the duty of the rich to help the poor, and the strong to protect and bring justice to the weak.[8]

The Kings and Judges of the Hebrew Scriptures were commanded to find ways to equalize that which was unequal. They had authority over the nation, and woe to them if they only honored the rich! They were told not to cheat the poor. The poor were given the right to glean the edges of the fields for food, so they would not starve in a land of plenty. A tithe was to be collected every third year for them. The rich were not to make a profit from the poor, or charge them interest on a loan, or treat them as slaves. There were special compensations for the poor so they would not appear before God empty-handed. In the year of Jubilee, the poor could return and claim their ancestral lands; the injustices of the past would be ended and they could start anew.[9]

If God had to choose sides, whose side would He be on? The needy. The suffering. Those without means. Those who have need of a loving Savior. The expected order is turned upside down in the Bible. It is not the rich and powerful who are blessed, but the poor.

Protestant theologian Karl Barth, in his *Church Dogmatics*, says the Christian community "explicitly accepts solidarity with the least of little ones . . . with those who are in obscurity and are not seen, with those who are pushed to the margin and perhaps the very outer margin of the life of human society, with fellow-creatures who temporarily at least, and perhaps permanently, are useless and insignificant and perhaps even burdensome and destructive . . . these men are recognized to be brothers of Jesus Christ . . . and therefore the community confesses Jesus Christ

Himself as finally the hungry, thirsty, naked, homeless, sick, imprisoned man . . ."[10] As we do unto the least of these, we also do unto Christ.

If there is one command in the Bible that seems absolutely clear from beginning to end, it is to help the poor. It is the greatest litmus test we can apply to any governmental policies. If we had to choose only one issue that addresses the place where Christian values and political policy clearly come together, it wouldn't be abortion, or homosexuality, or stem cell research, or even education, protecting the environment, or employment—it would be to help the poor and the oppressed. We, as Christians, are called upon to allow the light of Christ to shine on the sadness that is at the core of the human condition, and to be part of God's redemptive work on earth.

Can We Agree on Helping the Poor?

When setting out to write this book, I had presumed that this was one issue where we could find agreement among Christians. I was wrong. Although there are more than 2,000 verses in the Bible about the need for individuals and nations to help the poor and the oppressed, there is a powerful group of conservative Republican Christians that does not believe the Bible on this issue. They believe individuals and churches are asked to help the poor, if they so desire, but not nations. They believe charitable giving should only come from those who wish to give.

I must admit I was shocked to learn this. After all, this idea is coming from conservatives and fundamentalists who say they take the Bible literally. I started to question several of my colleagues who were conservative Republican Christians about this issue in order to understand it more clearly. I promised not to use their names in this book if they would clarify this issue for me.

I was told, by one conservative Christian, "We are called to help, not to force others to help or to use our mob power to steal from those who do not want to help." Another Republican Christian said liberals believe in helping the poor in various social programs. He saw the liberal Democrats as giving far too many handouts, and the government shouldn't be in that business. In his view, conservatives believe that "the church, not the government, should be involved with helping and caring for the poor."

I e-mailed him back, asking who the church is most apt to help. Certainly they are most apt to help fellow Christians. Where does that leave the immigrant who has just received citizenship but has few resources? Or the Muslim, who lives in a poor community? What about the workers who have been hurt by the Enron or WorldCom or Adelphia scandals, left out in the cold while the CEOs have made millions of dollars? What about the drastic needs that come from communities hit by a hurricane and left with billions of dollars in damage? Or from the tsunami that has washed away hundreds of thousands of people and hundreds of communities, leaving needs far beyond what one church, or two or three, or even one denomination, can handle?

One of the Christians said we should not be forced to give money to causes that we don't believe in. He is also a pacifist, so he said he didn't want to fund the war. I agree. I don't either. If George W. Bush had listened to us, and millions of other people who didn't want this war, we wouldn't have to. But if we take that reasoning to its logical conclusion, it seems the government would abandon any compassionate policies. People who adhere to this reasoning might think, I shouldn't have my tax dollars go to funding education, because I don't have any children and I'm finished with my own schooling. I shouldn't have to fund Medicare at this point in my life, because I won't have to worry about my retirement for a few more years and Mom and Dad are dead. I shouldn't have to fund the roads in Iowa, because I haven't driven on them for many years. When did we become so selfish we forgot about the common good? If we followed this policy, it would divide the nation into prideful interest groups with only their own selfish desires at heart.

Many Evangelicals do not see the necessity of helping the poor because they believe that they must focus on their individual relationship with Christ. After hearing this idea a number of times, I asked one of my Republican Christian friends, who is a Baptist, if she agreed with this. She said she did not. She answered, "There are plenty of lost, lonely, and deserted people within our borders to keep both church and state busy, so I fear that the statement that churches should fix the problem is a veiled form of greed. I don't see that the churches are responding, and therefore our disenfranchised people will be out in the cold, literally. Which is truly heartless."

She continued, "Of course, churches should be stepping up and out for our own faith, but that does not mean we should eliminate government assistance. I don't see how anyone in their right mind can think that churches can replace Medicaid, or take care of all our health needs, or education and job improvement programs. There is a huge difference between soup kitchens and shelters and the long-term needs of people with mental and physical disabilities."

After hearing from the many Republicans who do not agree with my friend, I wondered if I had misread my Bible. Perhaps I was wrong. Perhaps the Bible was only talking to individuals. I soon found more than 500 passages addressing nations. I reread the book of Jeremiah, the prophet appointed by God to talk to the nations. God said, "I brought you to a country of plenty to enjoy its produce and good things; but when you entered you defiled my country and made my heritage loathsome."[11] There are many loathsome acts that the nation did: "The very skirts of your robe are stained with the blood of the poor."[12] "There are wicked men among my people . . . they set traps and they catch human beings. Like a cage full of birds so are their houses full of loot; they have grown rich and powerful because of it, they are fat, they are sleek . . . they have no respect for rights, for orphans' rights, and yet they succeeded! They have not upheld the cause of the needy. Shall I fail to punish this, Yahweh demands, or on such a nation to exact vengeance."[13] God tells the nation they must "treat one another fairly . . . not exploit the stranger, the orphan and the widow . . . not shed innocent blood."[14] He scolds the nation and its leaders for having "eyes and heart for nothing but your own interests, for shedding innocent blood and perpetrating violence and oppression."[15]

If we are commanded to help the oppressed, we need to know who the oppressed are and why they're oppressed. Is it their own doing, or part of the wages of sin, or does oppression come from the rich and the powerful and the social structures that support the privileged?

What Is the Human Condition?

To understand oppression, a number of theologians begin by looking at the human condition and by looking at the wages of sin. What is wrong with us? Why is there inequality and oppression? Why did Jesus come to save us? What, and how much, needed saving? Does our Fallen Nature, which is explained by the story of Adam and Eve, express why life has to be this difficult? What can be done to bring us back to the blessings of the Kingdom?

Genesis contains many interpretations of the meaning of the Fall. Some say it's the fall from obedience to disobedience, from innocence to corruption, from unity to separation. An interpretation that is particularly meaningful to me comes from Protestant theologian Paul Tillich. He points out that when Adam and Eve were in the Garden of Eden, everything was in harmony and in unity. They were in harmony with each other, in harmony with the Garden, in harmony with the animals, and in harmony with God. They walked in the cool of the evening with God. Obedience was not a problem. They had what they needed. It was, truly, Paradise.

The Fall, then, was the fall into disharmony, or what Tillich calls separation or estrangement from God. The curse Adam and Eve received, and therefore we all receive, was alienation on every level. No longer would the plants easily grow when Adam tilled the soil. After the Fall, he worked by the sweat of his brow. No longer were Adam and Eve in harmony with each other. He dominated her, and yet she couldn't escape her desire for him. No longer were they in harmony with God. They were exiled from the Garden, where they had once walked so easily and closely with God. Immediately after the Fall came the violence of brother against brother, when Cain killed Abel. Then came disharmony in families, disharmony as societies began to form. There was violence over territory, violence over imposing one law over another, disobedience both relationally and socially. On every level, we were no longer free, complete, fulfilled, and joyful.

With the coming of Christ, we were given the opportunity to move back into harmony with God. Our alienation and separation were overcome. The atonement brought us back into at-one-ment with God, through Christ. We are moved to express our regained freedom and joy by allowing Christ to work in our lives and by responding to others, as he responded to all of us.

Every part of our lives, and therefore every part of our society, can be touched by Christ—if we work toward allowing it to be. In fact, many Christians would say that when the Holy Spirit works in our lives, we are continually and naturally moved into compassionate action with everyone around us—in our relationships with others, in our relationships with our neighborhoods, our cities, our states, our country, as well as globally. Christ is not limited. In an ever-expanding circle of life, we are called into the national and international arena, to express our faith in our world, to create justice, and to bring mercy.

Fighting Oppression Within and Without

Oppression happens individually, relationally, socially, and politically. Individually, we are in bondage to sin. We are burdened and weighed down. This can be expressed in many ways. We might feel restless, as if we can find no peace within ourselves. Everything irritates us. We are impatient; we are afraid. We feel hopeless, unloved, uncared for. We are in a state of alienation and cannot get connected. We are having trouble finding our way.

For many of us, salvation begins on the individual level. In my own experience, I began to find peace through daily reading of the Bible and other spiritual works. I began to feel connected to something bigger than myself and felt a Presence that could guide me and comfort me. I found a particularly helpful Bible verse to be: "Seek ye first the Kingdom of God, and all these things will be yours as well."[16] I began to feel that unless I found inner freedom and peace, I would continue to have trouble relating to the world and contributing to the world.

As I moved my faith into relationship, I struggled with pride and envy. I competed with others. I was jealous of everyone who had more than I did, or who seemed to have an easier life. I began to find freedom as I entered more actively into a religious community. As a student at Colorado College, I began to attend

Bible studies with the Navigators, a conservative Christian group. Later, my Quaker community, both locally and internationally, nurtured me into moving my faith into the world. Quakers believe, when we pray, meditate, and wait and listen to the Holy Spirit, we will naturally be moved into social action.

For each of us, that social action will take different forms—whether to visit the prisons, to feed the homeless, to help educate others, to help the jobless learn skills and find jobs, to build homes for others, to start recycling centers, to plant trees, to care for animals, to change the laws of our land to better help others—the list is, of course, endless.

For many of us, there is a point in our spiritual journey when we realize we need to make changes in our world in order to help the oppressed. Oppression can come from oppressive organizations, laws, social structures, or governments. We might find we can't help the homeless because an oppressive government won't let us. We can't help the prisoners who are tortured or executed, because we'll be imprisoned ourselves. We watch the innocent victims of oppressive governments and of war, and realize we can no longer work individually, but need to do something to address the root of the problem at the political level. We become nationally and internationally involved.

I'm not sure there is much a nation can do to nurture one's individual spirituality, except to stay out of the way and not interfere with our seeking and finding God. Our Constitution guarantees us the right to freedom of religion and freedom to worship in a way that best expresses our relationship to God. I certainly don't want my country legislating my spiritual journey and telling me where it's supposed to take me. Although some

Christians believe there is one True Church (although there is no agreement about which one it is!), people find their church home in different places. People have been killed for religious freedom, and their martyrdom has helped lift the oppression that once allowed only one denomination, and only one form of worship. As Sojourner Truth once said when speaking about women's rights, "All I ask is that you take your foot off my neck!" Sometimes that's all we want from government on the individual level—to keep out of our way so we can work out our own salvation.

Working for God's Kingdom

A number of Christian denominations interpret the work of Jesus as being political and social work, not just work for the individual soul. This is true among the mainline and more liberal Christian churches, which have tended to be more attentive to the poor and needy, but increasingly, also, among the more conservative churches. In 2005, the National Evangelical Conference called for "greater Christian involvement in society including: poverty, human rights and justice." In "For the Health of the Nation: An Evangelical Call to Civic Responsibility," which is the paper put out by the National Association of Evangelicals, there is a list of a number of specific issues Evangelicals are called to address: "disaster relief, refugee resettlement, and the fights against AIDS/HIV, human rights abuses, slavery, sexual trafficking, and prison rape." It goes on to list the "protection and well-being of families and children, of the poor, the sick, the disabled, and the unborn, for the persecuted and oppressed, and of the rest of the created order."

The paper recognized we are called to work for God's kingdom,[17] which would be a kingdom marked by "justice, peace, forgiveness, restoration and healing for all." We are to "demonstrate God's love for all, by crossing racial, ethnic, economic, and national boundaries."

More liberal denominations probably would add to this list, by clarifying that we are to work for gender equality and to show God's love for homosexuals as well.

The conference document calls for churches "to model good race relations." It encourages governments to use their militaries only for a "just war" and only after pursuing peace nonviolently.

The conference also cautioned its members to "act with humility, civility and integrity in the process and to not become shrill or hateful."[18]

The Southern Baptist statement of faith also calls upon its members to follow the Social Gospel: "In the spirit of Christ, Christians should oppose racism, every form of greed, selfishness, and vice . . . We should work to provide for the orphaned, the needy, the abused, the aged, the helpless and the sick. . . . In order to promote these ends Christians should be ready to work with all men of good will in any good cause."

The media were surprised by this nonpartisan approach at the National Evangelical Conference. But not everyone at the conference agreed with this focus. Tom Minnery, vice president of public policy for Focus on the Family, said, "The issues of marriage, the issues of pro-life are the issues that define us to this day . . . do not make this about global warming."

I have noticed, in my conversations with a number of Republican Christians, the deciding factor for their vote is much like the Focus on the Family emphasis. They have tended to make their political clout felt with two political issues—abortion and homosexuality. Ecology and caring for the poor are not part of their agenda. However, the conference wanted to change this focus. It calls on Christians to work for the transformation of "both individuals and institutions," although it does not address any specific legislation.

Historically, mainline Christian churches have been more apt to emphasize the Social Gospel than have the more conservative churches, and traditionally Democrats have had a stronger platform to help the disadvantaged. The document presented by the Evangelicals is a very good sign; it may be the beginning of some unity among denominations as they work toward a common goal.

Liberation Theology: Transforming the World

We take the Gospel into society and ask, "What can the Gospel tell us about the best choices to make when we're creating laws and public policy? What does it mean to be a Christian in society? How do we best express our Christian values and our faith in public?"

In 1968, a number of Catholic priests, bishops, and laypeople met at Medellín, northwest of Bogotá, Colombia, and began questioning how to be more effective in their work with the poor in Latin America and South America. They began by recognizing that the poor are often kept in poverty by social and political structures. They looked at ways the government, the Church, and the wealthy colluded to make the rich richer, and the poor poorer. The participants wanted to understand how they could be effective in changing social conditions that would also change the abject poverty and misery of millions of lives.

In 1973, Gustavo Gutiérrez wrote a book called *A Theology of Liberation*. Liberation theology is a practical theology, addressing the practices necessary to transform the world into a more just, caring place. Gutiérrez believes "communion with the Lord inescapably means a Christian life centered around a concrete and creative commitment of service to others."[19] This theology seeks to build "a world where every [one], no matter what his race, religion, or nationality, can live a fully human life, freed from servitude imposed on him by other men or by natural forces over which he has not sufficient control."[20] It seeks a society "based upon justice, respect for the rights of others, and human fellowship."[21]

The theology questions and critiques the role of the Church with society and governments, particularly when the church takes the side of the rich and powerful, rather than protecting and helping the poor and the needy. It asks, "Is the Church fulfilling a purely religious role when by its silence or friendly relationships it lends legitimacy to a dictatorial or oppressive government?"[22]

Liberation theology critiques government policies that keep the poor countries poor because of the policies of the rich countries, which keep the poor ones from growing out of their poverty. It seeks to empower the oppressed, so their liberation is not done *to* them or *for* them, but *by* them.

The concepts of liberation theology spread to other areas of the world. The work of liberation theology, through the efforts and struggles of such Christians as Desmond Tutu, helped rid South Africa of apartheid. In the 1970s and 1980s, liberation theology also expanded to include liberation for other groups of people. There is black liberation theology, Latino liberation theology, Asian liberation theology, and feminist theology. There also has been, particularly during the 1970s and 1980s, a male liberation movement, only partly inspired by religion, which focuses mostly on men's needs to liberate themselves emotionally and free themselves from the way society defines them.

Our American history is filled with social progress as Christians took their faith into the nation. Many times, it was the socially activist Christians who changed the country, in spite of being beaten, imprisoned, and killed. Christians fought for freedom of worship, and died for it. They fought against slavery, and after more than a hundred years of the abolitionist movement, they eventually prevailed. They fought for civil rights, for women's rights, for the rights of children. They fought for laws that would protect a child against incest and abuse and that would protect women from the human trafficking industry. They fought to raise consciousness about rape, fighting for better laws to protect women and prosecute rapists. They fought for a woman's right to inherit property, and to follow her calling into the profession of her choice, including the ministry. They tried to pass laws that would give women equal pay for equal work. They fought for the rights of workers, and the right to unionize. They fought for affirmative action, for ways to equalize the playing field for women, and for ethnic minorities, who had been discriminated against for centuries. And although most of these problems are not yet resolved, Christians and non-Christians alike continue to try to work against oppression.

Feminist theology asks two questions when judging a law or a public policy: "Who does it benefit and who does it harm?" If a law benefits the rich at the expense of the poor, or harms the poor and the underprivileged, then that law has to be carefully assessed, because it probably is an unjust law. For instance, some companies only use part-time help so they won't have to pay the employees' health care costs. This benefits the corporate officers, who gain more profits, but harms the employees.

What Have We Done to Help the Poor?

We know what we're asked to do. How have we done as a nation? It depends on the year. The Democrats have been known as the party that responds to the oppressed, and they have a good history of making social change that helps the lower rungs of our society.

When our country was in the depths of the Depression, President Franklin Delano Roosevelt created the New Deal, a set of social programs that addressed unemployment, unfair distribution of income, and corruption in government. It offered relief, recovery, and reform. People were put back to work cleaning up the national parks, building barracks for the military, providing programs for scholars and artists. The Republicans criticized the government for interfering, but the Democrats realized that the system wasn't working and needed help from the government.

In the first 100 days of Roosevelt's presidency, a tremendous amount of legislation was passed to try to fix the problems. In 1935, the Social Security Act was passed. Then the Labor Relations Act, which gave labor the right to organize, a right that had been taken away from them during previous Republican administrations. Monopolies were broken up and price fixing outlawed in order to treat the poor fairly. Democrats passed laws for Medicare and Medicaid, in spite of opposition from the Republicans.

During Lyndon B. Johnson's administration, the Civil Rights Act of 1964 was passed, which gave greater protection to those suffering from discrimination and racist policies. The Voting Rights Act also was passed, abolishing the poll tax, which had interfered with the voting rights of the poor, particularly blacks. President Johnson declared a War on Poverty, to help the poor.

How are we doing now? Not too well. Martin Luther King Jr. said we can judge a nation not by how it coddles the rich, but by how it cares for the poor. Our country is definitely coddling the rich.

Helping the Super-Rich

During his presidency, Bill Clinton raised taxes on the wealthiest taxpayers, and expanded tax breaks for the working poor.

George W. Bush did the opposite. He created more tax cuts during his presidency. Although he has said most of the tax cuts have gone to low- and middle-income Americans, that is not true. Most of the tax cuts, 53 percent, go to people with incomes in the top 10 percent, and more than 15 percent of the tax cuts go to the top 0.1 percent who make up the super-rich.

In fact, the only taxpayers whose share of taxes declined in 2001 and 2002 were those in the top 0.1 percent (or one-thousandth) of our population who make at least $1.6 million a year. These people are the fastest-growing group of income earners, making two and a half times more than they made in 1980. In the new budget of George W. Bush, the merely rich will still carry some of the tax burden, but the super-rich will give very little.

The taxpayers with the highest incomes pay the same percentage of income, Medicare, and Social Security taxes as those making $50,000 to $200,000.

We might say, "More power to them!" We might find no problem with this because we too hope to be wealthy. Or we believe being super-rich shows how much God loves us. Or we might believe the wealth of the rich will trickle down to us. Not true. Not at all. The yearly incomes of the super-rich have increased. There have been increases in their investments and returns (except for those who are going to trial or jail for their corruption—and even they still are able to keep their fancy houses and some of their profits). But the lower 90 percent of the taxpayers aren't getting any. From 1950 to 1970, for every additional dollar earned by the bottom 90 percent of taxpayers, those at the top earned an extra $162. Guess how much they're getting now? From 1990 to 2002, for every additional dollar earned by the bottom 90 percent, the top taxpayers earned an extra $18,000.

The rich are not just leaving everyone else behind, they're leaving us way, way back in the dust.

Some say the richer getting richer is just fine. They believe their accumulation of wealth means more investments and innovation and more growth. Tim Kane, an economist at the Heritage

Foundation, says "lower taxes and lower marginal tax rates are leading to more growth. There's an explosion of wealth. We are so wealthy in a world that is profoundly poor." Well, maybe he is, but if you are a poor or middle-class or "merely rich" person reading this book, think back to your last four years, and ask whether you are living in a world of great wealth.

Economic growth has not been good. The stock market has been on a roller-coaster ride. Unemployment has risen, then fallen a little, then risen. Jobs are not secure. Billions of dollars are being spent to fight a war that is unpopular with many Americans. We're trillions of dollars in debt.[23]

Others do not think these differences in wealth are a good idea. Some of the wealthiest Americans, such as Warren E. Buffett, George Soros, and Ted Turner, are concerned this concentration of wealth can turn our society into an aristocracy. Ted Turner said, "The growing gap between the super rich and the middle class in the USA and around the world disturbs me. In the USA, the richest 11% of the population owns almost 40% of the wealth . . . More alarmingly, the five richest people in the world are worth more than the combined annual net worth of 63 countries. Extreme economic disparity works against the interests of freedom and democracy. I don't believe the richest Americans need more tax breaks . . . Believe me, they don't need it."[24]

Nearly Everyone Left Behind

On paper, many of the ideals of the Republicans sound good. The 2004 Republican Platform, for example, emphasizes ownership for our citizens—each citizen having more control over Social Security, over health care, and over their financial well-being in general. The platform talks about building assets in the stock market, about savings and making it easier to save more for retirement, about encouraging more home ownership, about helping small businesses with lower taxes, about lower taxes in general. These are all ideas that can be helpful to the middle and upper classes, but not to the lower classes, who have no health care to begin with, no assets in the stock market, no money to save, no retirement pensions, and no businesses, and who already may be paying minimal taxes. There is very little in the platform about the poor and needy.

The 2004 Democratic Platform affirms a commitment to the middle class and the poor, seeing this commitment as democratic and religious: "We recommit to the ideal of a people united in helping one another, an ideal as old as the faiths we follow and as great as the country we love. To those who are threatened, we pledge protection; to those who are victims, we promise justice; to those who are hopeless, we offer hope." What specifically did they pledge? They pledged to stand up for the middle class, to reform health care, improve education, and protect the environment.

Democrats wanted tax reform. They said they would roll back the tax break for the top 2 percent of the richest Americans. The Democrats would not give tax breaks for companies that send American jobs overseas. They wanted fair labor standards in their trade agreements to stop child labor abuse, and they wanted to insist on maintaining environmental standards. They wanted to protect workers' rights, including the right to organize a union; to support programs for workforce development;

and to require companies to give employees at least three months' notice before a planned shutdown.

That was the Democrats' plan. George W. Bush's plan for the future, in contrast, has many provisions that will negatively affect the middle class and underclass. If elderly people sign up for the new Medicare prescription drug benefit, hoping the cost of their medicine will decline, they may lose some of their food stamps. When asked why, members of the Bush administration explained "older Americans will spend less of their own money on drugs and will therefore have more to spend on food, reducing their need for food stamps." Of course, these government officials have never had to decide whether to buy food or medicine, nor do they recognize the cost of simply living in our society.

Here's how this bill would work with a hypothetical case. Mrs. Smith, who receives $798 a month in Social Security, pays $147 a month for medical expenses and does not receive Medicaid. Under the new plan, she will spend $105 a month, for a savings of $42. Her monthly rent is $421. So Mrs. Smith pays out $568 a month just in rent and medical expenses, which leaves her with $230 per month for food, basic supplies, clothes, utilities, and transportation costs. She doesn't have the money to buy a book or a magazine, get cable television, go to a movie, or travel to see her grown children. She is living on the edge, and if anything goes wrong in her life, she could easily be out on the street. The government considers her savings of $42 per month in medical expenses to be a whopping gift to her, so they reduce her monthly food stamp allotment from $27 to $10. So Mrs. Smith will have to tighten her belt, and just eat less. This we call "social services."[25]

Although we had a No Child Left Behind policy, the No Child Left Behind education initiative is reduced by $806 million for the 2006 budget. No Child Left Behind will put some additional money into testing children, but not into educating them.

Although we say we're for education, $100 million was cut in support of the Corporation for Public Broadcasting, including support for a number of educational programs for children, such as the Ready to Learn Program and *Sesame Street*.[26] Republican Rep. Ernest Istook (R-Oklahoma) said "Big Bird and his friends can fly on their own." Or not fly at all. Republicans may say they don't want to leave children behind, but their actions say ensuring this is not a priority. Forty-eight educational programs will be terminated, including ones for college-readiness training.

It isn't just small children who are left behind, but college students also. The U.S. government will cut almost half a billion dollars from the education budget, eliminating many of the grants and loans that help middle-class and poor students get a college education.[27]

The latest Republican budget also affects benefits for veterans, those people so highly praised by Mr. Bush during his campaign, when he said he'd never do anything to hurt them. The new budget increases the veterans' copay by 214 percent. They now have to pay much more for their medications.[28]

There also are cuts affecting job training, rural health care, low-income schools, and people lacking health insurance.[29]

In addition, although there has been no increase in the minimum wage for eight years, George W. Bush rejected a measure to raise wages for the workers on the lowest rung of the economic ladder.

The Energy Department's budget will be cut by about 2 percent, which will reduce cleanup of sites. And the Environmental Protection Agency will be cut by about half a billion dollars, including cuts for water quality protection programs, for land preservation, for the building of sewage and water treatment plants.

Almost half a billion dollars will be cut from the Center for Disease Control and Prevention, which provides preventive health care and bioterrorism preparedness.

Money for the National Park Service would be cut. The Office of Violence Against Women's budget would be cut by $19 million.

At the Democratic Convention, the soon-to-be Illinois Democratic senator, Barack Obama, recognized that positive change can only be achieved through our ability to empathize with those in need: "I am my brother's keeper, I am my sister's keeper . . . If there is a child on the south side of Chicago who can't read, that matters to me, even if it's not my child. If there's a senior citizen somewhere who can't pay for her prescription and has to choose between medicine and the rent, that makes my life poorer, even if it's not my grandmother. If there's an Arab American family being rounded up without benefit of an attorney or due process, that threatens my civil liberties . . . I am my brother's keeper."

Caring for the Sick

Although we're the richest nation in the world, we still have no national health care program. Between 46 million and 69 million Americans don't have health insurance. They can't afford it. Yet, they're unable to find cheaper ways to get the medications they need, because looking for a source of prescription drugs outside of America is prohibited. The cost of drugs in the United States is sometimes two to three times as much as the same drug in Europe or Canada.[30] The natural alternative—to buy drugs abroad—is illegal, even if it means it could save our lives and even though other countries have the same quality control as we have.

How many of us have relatives or friends who are struggling because their health care needs aren't taken care of? How many of us know someone who has to decide between food and rent or medicine? Just ask around, and chances are you know someone who is struggling with this issue. One of my friends pays $850 a month in health insurance, even though her income is only $900 a month from her husband's disability, which she started receiving after his death. I asked her about her expenses beyond the normal health insurance costs. The medications the insurance doesn't pay for cost about $300 a month, even after her co-pay of about $30 or $40. She can't work, because of the pain and problems that come from two hip replacements and two knee replacements from arthritis. She isn't yet eligible for Medicaid or Medicare. She has now gone through almost all of her resources from her husband's life insurance policy and soon may have to move out of the one-bedroom apartment she loves. She lives in almost constant terror, not knowing what will happen to her.

This would not be happening to her if she lived in most European countries, and even in some non-European countries.

Former House Majority Leader Tom DeLay, who was very active in the very public fight to save Terri Schiavo and have her feeding tube reinserted, voted to cut Medicaid by $15 billion, an action that resulted in denying money to care for poor people in nursing homes, some of whom also are on feeding tubes.[31]

The new Social Security proposal, which has been so ardently advocated by our government, does nothing for the poverty of millions. Although George W. Bush has said it will help the poor, it doesn't. It gives them only 50 percent of their current poverty-level wage when they retire. They can barely make it now. How can they expect to make it on half as much money?

Budget Cuts Show Our Priorities

In the budget cuts that passed in 2005, we can see the priorities. Who will win with this new budget? Homeland Security. NASA, for further space exploration. The Department of Defense. The Department of Homeland Security.

The Bible says, "For wherever your treasure is, that is where your heart will be too."[32] We know what the government treasures by seeing who gets the money. We might say we can't afford these many services, but if all of Mr. Bush's tax cuts were repealed, our government would have enough revenue to take care of many of our social problems. Instead, we are told we can't afford to address the poor, or global warming, or education, because we can't afford it. Nor does there seem to be the moral will to address these problems.

Who do these policies benefit and who do they harm? George W. Bush is considered to be the "strong Christian president" who upholds Christian values. But his policies, time and again, favor the rich and punish the poor. Who will inherit the trillions in debt? Our children, grandchildren, and great-grandchildren. Who will suffer from his Social Security policies? We will. Who will have a problem with the lack of health care? We and our friends and relatives will. Who will suffer because students can't afford to go to college, or are deeply in debt from loans? Our country. We say we want to keep up with other industrialized countries, whose children score higher in science and math tests, but we don't favor educational policies that help achieve these goals. We say we don't want any child left behind, but we have left behind children, teenagers, college students, adults, and retired people.

What Do Many Christians Say about These Policies?

George W. Bush's economic policies have been criticized by leaders of five mainline Protestant denominations, who find the 2006 federal budget "unjust." Leaders of the Episcopal Church, USA; Evangelical Lutheran Church in America; Presbyterian Church (USA); United Church of Christ; and United Methodist Church referred to Luke's Gospel story of the poor man Lazarus lying at the gate of the rich man, who ignored his needs. The poor man went to heaven, the rich man to hell, for his lack of compassion. The leaders said, "In telling this story, Jesus makes clear that perpetrating economic injustice is among the gravest of sins . . . Like many Americans, we read our daily newspaper through the lens of faith, and when we see injustice, it is our duty to say so . . . The 2006 Federal Budget that President Bush has sent to Capitol Hill is unjust. It has much for the rich man and little for Lazarus."[33]

The Most Rev. Frank Griswold, presiding bishop of the Episcopal Church, USA, said there are three questions that should be asked about the budget: "Is the budget compassionate? Does the budget strive to serve the human family, both at home and around the world? Does the budget serve the common good?"[34]

Expanding Our Neighborly View

When Jesus was asked which was the greatest of the Ten Commandments, he said there were only two that would encompass all others: "Love the Lord your God with all your heart, mind and soul, and your neighbor as yourself."

But who is my neighbor? Jesus challenged us to expand our view of who we are directed to care for. It is easy for us to be kind to the neighbor next door, the person we like, the one who goes to our church, who is of our own race, and even the same gender. Of course, that person is our neighbor, and as people in community, we should be neighborly toward each other. I have witnessed great kindnesses done by churches and communities that care for their members in need—bringing food every week or every day, setting up prayer circles, taking the sick to the doctor, doing their laundry, cleaning their house. When non-Christians complain about Christians, I often tell them these stories of how Christian communities have responded to those in need among their members, and what a kind, gracious, and compassionate Face of God they present in their good works.

In the Good Samaritan story, Jesus expanded our concept of our neighbor. Jesus deliberately chose, as his main character, a Samaritan—a member of the group of people hated by Jews. When a man had been robbed and left for dead on the side of the road, everyone walked by—the priest, the Levite, the people known as the "good religious people." Who helped the wounded man? A Samaritan, who paid for the injured man's healing and thus showed himself to be the true neighbor.

Protestant theologian Karl Barth, quoting Kierkegaard in his book *The Epistle to the Romans* says, "But the neighbor is—everyman. A man is not thy neighbor because he differs from others, or because in his difference he in some way resembles them. A neighbor is the man who is like unto thee before God. And his likeness belongs to a man unconditionally."[35]

Who is your neighbor? Those whom you like and even those you don't like. If you're a Republican, your neighbor is Hillary Clinton, Joseph Biden, John Kerry. If you're a Democrat, your neighbor, whom you are not to hate, is Karl Rove, Donald Rumsfeld, George W. Bush. For all of us, our neighbor is also the most hated man in the world—Osama bin Laden. If bin Laden were to ask for a cup of cold water, we are to give it to him. If he were wounded, we are to help. It is a radical Gospel, and that is what Christianity is—simply radical! It stretches us, and asks us to think differently, to think against our human nature, which says, "No way! That's not what it means! I wouldn't lift a finger to help that man!" We are asked to think of those we hate as our neighbor, and to set social policy that deals compassionately, and justly, with them.

That means we are asked, as a society, to look out for the dispossessed and the needy, whomever they may be. The Muslim who has been jailed, perhaps for being at the wrong place at the wrong time. The terrorist—yes, even the terrorist who is being treated inhumanely. The homosexual who may be the victim of hate crimes. The non-Christian, whom Christians sometimes demonize, as if such a person has no values and no place in what they consider a Christian nation. The hurt and the helpless. The person who can't afford health care. The battered woman. The abortion doctor who is reviled and even shot at for doing a job that is legal in the United States. Make your list of the people you hate. Those are the people you're asked to feed and clothe, and to whom you are to show fair treatment, justice, and mercy.

The Gospel is a radical and challenging Gospel. It forces us to do great acts of mercy, compassion, and kindness. William James says in *The Varieties of Religious Experience*, "The best fruits of religious experience are the best things that history has to show . . . the highest flights of charity, devotion, trust, patience, bravery to which the wings of human nature have spread themselves have been flown for religious ideals."[36]

Chapter Three

Beautiful Savior, King of Creation

*"Yahweh God took the man and settled him in the
Garden of Eden to cultivate and take care of it."*

When we first meet God in the beginning of Genesis,
we meet God the Creator of the natural universe. It is
described as beautiful. He calls it Good. For thirty-one verses,
the Bible tells us of the wonders of God's creation. The Glory of
Creation is recounted again in the Psalms, in Job, in Proverbs 8,
in John 1, in Colossians, in Revelation.[1]

Both the Apostles' Creed and the Nicene Creed begin with
the image of God the Creator: "I believe in God the Father
Almighty, Creator of Heaven and Earth" and "I believe in One
God, the Father Almighty Creator of Heaven and Earth and of
all things visible and invisible." After God created the world, He
committed what some might think was a foolish act. He gave us
dominion over His creation. He told us we were in charge. He
told Adam and Eve they were to be fruitful and multiply and

subdue the earth. Many people on our planet have interpreted that to mean they can do with the earth what they please. It's ours, to serve us. We can take from it what we need and more. We can rape and exploit the earth if we want to.

But what does this really mean? There are two important words used in these first verses. An entire theology is created out of how we understand and interpret the words "subdue" and "dominion." If we get these meanings wrong, we get our theology wrong and our actions wrong and we cause irreparable damage to God's Creation.

The word "subdue" in the Hebrew is *kadash* (sometimes spelled *kavash*). The word implies a hierarchical relationship, in which human beings are given control and power over the earth. Sometimes it's used in relationship to military conquest, or to one forcing another into a subordinate position such as slavery or rape. It also is sometimes used to show an abuse of power.[2]

Radah (or the Hebrew root, "rdh") is the word for "dominion." It means "to rule as God rules"[3] or "the right and responsibility to rule, to govern the rest of creation."[4] We are asked to care for the earth, as God cares for it.[5] *Radah* does not itself define whether we are to rule benevolently or malevolently. The word is used in several different contexts in the Bible. Sometimes, it implies a kind and humane rule. Other times, it implies an antagonistic relationship, as when ruling over enemies.[6] When put into context, it seems that dominion and subjugation were understood as "a call for restraint in the rule over material and animate creation, for self-limitation, and for harmony both with fellow human beings and the rest of the world." We see some of this benevolent rule by looking at Genesis 1:16–18, in which the sun and moon are given authority to rule, or to "control and order," rather than exploit, the day and night. It is not about brute force, but about harmony and dependence.[7] Dominion becomes stewardship on behalf of God. Sin is excess, disharmony, and rebellion caused by appropriating God's authority for ourselves. Except for Genesis 1 and Psalm 8, the theme of human domination is not found in the Hebrew Scriptures. But even here, our rule is accountable to God. We are to be responsible. We are to exercise control, and to order and maintain and protect.

Genesis 1:28, says theologian Walter Brueggemann, "emancipates man and sets him over nature and makes him responsible for 'nature' entrusted to him. Nothing in this text supports the contention that it authorizes the kind of action which has issued in our current ecological crisis."[8]

If we are to rule as God rules, we can ask, "Does God oppress or liberate? Does God imprison or release? Does God beautify the earth, or destroy it?"[9]

When we look at the context of the time in which Genesis was written, we see that population growth was needed, it was not easy to replenish the earth. There was great hardship trying to grow crops on the rocky slopes of the hill country in Palestine. The crops were dependent on rainfall, which was unpredictable. The land had to be dominated and controlled and subdued to provide even a meager existence. This idea of dominion comes not from an idea of our power, which we now have with technology, but from our powerlessness, which would have been the experience of the people of that age.[10]

Before the Fall, we could have dominion over the earth because we had kept our relationship to God. After the Fall, we were estranged from God, estranged from each other, and estranged from the earth. God could no longer trust us. With the eating of the forbidden fruit, we had become "like God," and had surpassed our authority. If we had been allowed to live forever, we would be a rival to God.[11]

The Fall tells us that we cannot be trusted to obey, to be good stewards, to be responsible over what God has given us. We only have to look at many of the ecological catastrophes on our earth to know that harmony and responsibility have been lost. All that had been so wonderful and perfect in the Garden was marred, destroyed, taken away from Adam and Eve. No longer were they masters, but slaves. No longer were they in relationship with God, but cut off and separated.

From Dominion Theology to Dependence Theology

Christians who believe we are to have dominion over the earth and subdue it often take their theology from before the Fall, from Genesis 1 or Psalm 8. But there is another theology, the one that is emphasized in Genesis 2 and for most of the rest of the Bible. In Genesis 2, Adam, the human being, is made out of topsoil. The word *Adamah* is sometimes translated as "earth person" or, we might say, the "earthling was made out of the earth" or the "human was made from humus."[12] Adam was created much like plants and animals were created. The divine breath blown into the nostrils of Adam is the same breath by which the animals live and breathe. Here the role of the human is to "serve"[13] or "to till," and this is the work of slaves serving their masters and humans serving God.[14] Adam is told to cultivate and to take care of the garden. Here the idea is not of lordship, but of servanthood.[15] It is a theology of dependence rather than domination.

Which theology do we choose? Domination or service? Theodore Hiebert, professor of Hebrew Scripture studies, says both theologies "capture the paradox of human existence." On the one hand, we believe ourselves to be powerful and in control, a view expressed in Genesis 1, which has led to our ability to destroy the human race entirely through our misuse of our resources.[16]

"On the other hand, we know ourselves as humans, as does Genesis 2, to be only a single species in a large and complex web of life we do not entirely understand and can never really control. . . . Our only hope of survival in fact, is in recognizing our dependence on this web of life and adapting our behavior."[17] "Special attention to the dependence theology of Genesis 2 is important . . . because our greatest temptation as individuals and as a race is to think more highly of ourselves than we ought to think. Indeed, it may not be an oversimplification to say it is just such a proud and self-centered perspective that has allowed us to exploit nature for our ends and has brought upon us the ecological crisis we now face. . . . Perhaps what is most needed in our day is not a new view of power . . . but rather a new humility . . . by which we read our texts and live our lives from the point of the view of the whole creation rather than from our human perspective alone."[18]

Seeing Ourselves in Relationship

If we look at nature, we can see we are part of a system that interacts with animals and with the earth. If we see creation as relationship—relationship with each other, relationship with the earth, relationship with God—this brings some to an experience of love and awe for God's work, which leads them to live more responsibly with the earth.[19]

St. Francis of Assisi, Teilhard de Chardin, and many of the saints understood this relationship. Conrad Bonifazi, in his *A Theology of Things*, says nature is not a mass of stuff, but vibrant and responding to our human existence.[20] "Matter may weigh us down or uphold us, degrade or ennoble, threaten life or sustain it, become a source of weariness or exuberance, but its 'nature' and effects will be determined by our relation with it."[21]

We are warned, however, to be careful of any theology that puts us so in harmony with and dependent on nature, because that can be as dangerous as a theology that puts us as having final authority over nature. Theologian Walter Brueggemann says our misunderstanding might come from a misunderstanding of our power and freedom. Jesus made clear what true dominion means: "You know that those who are supposed to rule [have dominion] over the Gentiles lord it over [subdue] them, and their great men exercise authority over them. But it shall not be so among you; but whomever . . . would be first among you must be slave of all."[22] We are not to abuse others, or abuse the earth, but to serve it. Other verses in the Bible clarify this idea of subjection and authority. Subjection between children and parents, and slaves and masters, has to do with harmony without threatening. 1 Peter declares that we are to tend the flock of God in our charge, "not as domineering over those in your charge but being examples to the flock."[23]

Setting Limits

After we were told to have dominion over the earth, that commandment began to be clarified.

In Chapter 2 of Genesis, we are told to cultivate and take care of the garden. We are given the ultimate responsibility—to work the garden, to dress it, to keep it as it was created—to keep it good. Throughout the Bible, there are other commands given to us about how to treat God's creation:

We are to guard and protect the animals. Noah was asked to save two of every species, so they wouldn't become extinct.[24]

In Proverbs and in Deuteronomy, we are told to show compassion to animals.[25] "If you see your brother's donkey or ox fall over on the road, you must not disregard it, but must help your brother get it on its feet again."[26]

We are to guard and protect any animal that is hurt, wounded, or vulnerable. "If, when walking, you come across a bird's nest, in a tree or on the ground, with chicks or eggs and the mother bird sitting on the chicks or the eggs, you must not take the mother as well as the chicks. Let the mother go; the young you may take for yourself."[27]

When we work with animals, we are to treat them properly: "Thou shalt not plow with an ox and an ass together."[28] Plowing with animals of two different sizes would be a hardship to them.

We're told to protect the trees that bear fruit: "If, when attacking a town, you have to besiege it for a long time before you capture it, you must not destroy its trees by taking the axe to them; eat their fruit but do not cut them down."[29]

God gave us a legacy and a command—to take care of the earth. What have we done in return? We've contaminated the lakes, rivers, and streams. We've polluted our skies. We've scarred the land through strip-mining. We've allowed thousands of species to become extinct. We've bombed and raped millions of acres of land. Worldwide, there are land mines in more than sixty-seven countries, which makes it impossible to farm the land without the danger of loss of life and limb. We've changed the climate of the earth, causing droughts, floods, hurricanes, and global warming.

Many of these problems are coming from developed countries and developing countries. It is often "the rich minority which consumes the most resources and causes most of the pollution, especially by increasing technology."[30] Our acid rain floats across the border to do harm to Canada. The industrial pollution from Germany has killed some of the forests of Norway. The nuclear accident at Chernobyl continues to cause problems not only in the Ukraine, but also in surrounding areas.

But it's not only the rich countries that are to blame. There are also the slash-and-burn policies of Brazil and Indonesia and clear-burning in Africa for farming, as well as overfishing in remote Pacific islands. Our footprints on the earth have not made this earth better. We have not been good stewards. We have not cared enough.

The Cosmic and Mystical Christ

Every religious interpretation of Creation expresses the glory of God found in creation. Those Christians who believe in "Intelligent Design," or in Creationism, can see God's genius in His creation. Others, who believe in evolution, see the wonder of the creative process set in motion by God's divine spark, which continues to evolve into beauty and wonder.

There is a theology called Creation Theology, which believes we have been given an Original Blessing with the creation of human beings and with the creation of the earth. This theology sees our lack of caring and our unwillingness to be good stewards as an affront to the Holy Spirit and to the Mystical or Cosmic Christ, who exists within creation.

This way of seeing Christ and the Holy Spirit in creation is not new. Many saints and other Christian writers have said that their spiritual journey has moved them toward learning to see God in everything, including nature. God is both immanent, within the earth and within all of us; and transcendent, beyond the earth and beyond us. This is not pantheism (worshipping nature), but a way of seeing the Divine within, about, and around us.

St. Mechtild of Magdeburg (1210–1285) said, "The day of my spiritual awakening was the day I saw, and know I saw, all things in God and God in all things."[31]

Meister Eckhart said, "Everything that is, is bathed in God, is enveloped by God, who is round-about us all, enveloping us . . . We must learn to penetrate things and find God there."[32]

In the twentieth century, several theologians began writing about Creation Theology. Matthew Fox, who has a number of books and articles about this theology, calls it "a way of seeing the world sacramentally."[33] Hildegard of Bingen says "All of creation is a song of praise to God."

This viewpoint sees nature as more than a "thing" God has given us to play with, work with, and use as we want. It is closer to the idea that the Spirit of God infuses all creation with its Presence, and is without limits in our world.

As a born-again Christian, I understand that when I accepted Christ as my personal Savior, I received the Holy Spirit. The Spirit is within me, not just somewhere "out there." I recognize the "within-ness" of the Holy Spirit. Julian of Norwich says, "We are in God and God, whom we do not see, is in us."[34]

Quakers say, "There is that of God in everyone"; sometimes they call it "The Christ Within, the Seed, the Light Within." Others speak of a sense of the Presence.

Although most Christians probably agree that the Holy Spirit can exist within people, some may find it more difficult to believe that the Holy Spirit can also be within other physical matter.

Yet, every time we take Holy Communion, we are attesting to this fact. Some churches believe that when the bread and wine are blessed before the Lord's Supper, they *become* Christ. Matter has become Spirit.

Catholic theologian Pierre Teilhard de Chardin, in *Hymn of the Universe*, goes a step further, believing that Christ penetrated all of matter when he became incarnate in a physical life. He believes that Christ is not limited by the physical body; the love and delight that God has for creation, the love that God has for matter, causes matter to have a spiritual dimension. He says, "To be pure of heart means to love God above all things and at the same time to see him everywhere in all things. The just man . . . will have eyes only for God. For him, objects have lost their surface multiplicity . . . God may truly be laid hold on."[35]

In Creation Theology, we learn to see beyond the surface of matter, believing that a spiritual dimension exists throughout all creation.

According to Matthew Fox, the concept of sin in Creation Theology consists of "injuring creation and doing harm to its balance and harmoniousness, turning what is beautiful into what is ugly."[36]

In Creation Theology, all is potentially redeemed by Christ. As Revelations tells us, there is, and will be, a New Heaven and a New Earth.

Whether we see God and Christ *within* creation, or creation as a gift from God to us, it is still blessed. It is still declared as Good.

Poet Elizabeth Barrett Browning wrote, "Earth's crammed with heaven, and every common bush afire with God; And only he who sees takes off his shoes; the rest sit round it and pluck blackberries." God is here and everywhere, if we only but see.

Becoming Aware of the Sickness

We can't resolve any problems if we deny them. With any sickness, we begin the cure by admitting that the sickness exists. Then, we decide to do something about it.

In order to understand the state of the sickness of our environment, it might be helpful to use an analogy of a sick person who is trying to get well.

In 2004, my sister was diagnosed with ALS (the affliction also known as "Lou Gehrig's Disease"). Often, when people first get sick, there are a variety of reactions. In the case of my sister, the doctors didn't take it seriously for more than a year. They ignored it, saying, "It's nothing! You'll feel better soon. It's just a little cold or flu. You're just a little under the weather!"

At some point, sometimes when it's too late, it becomes clear to everyone that this person is very ill. In some cases, the seriousness of the disease makes people want to distance themselves from the person who is sick. Doctors may not have time to see her, or may only suggest some stopgap measures that do very little to treat the disease. In some cases, friends desert the person, not wanting to be too close to the illness, or not knowing what to do or how to help.

Others get realistic about the disease and begin to assemble their resources. People who knew my sister began to recommend doctors, and tried to think of everything they knew and everything they could possibly do to help her get better. They sent her articles about various medicines, various treatments, about people with the same illness. Because my sister is a Christian, there have been many prayer groups formed to pray for her. In my sister's case, a Christian friend had a Christian friend who knew a Christian doctor who had also been diagnosed with ALS and then rediagnosed with Lyme disease. He went on a regimen that healed him. Because of his miraculous recovery, he began to focus on studying this disease and then opened a clinic to treat it. My sister was retested and it began to seem that she had Lyme disease, not ALS. This Christian doctor then began treating my sister. (Unfortunately, the treatment didn't work and she was rediagnosed with ALS in summer 2005.)

All of us who want her to get better know the value of her life—to herself; to her siblings and her relatives, who treasure her good spirit; to her coworkers, who adore her and respect her work as a microbiologist; to her church community, which has rejoiced in her musical talents for well over twenty years; and to her Bible study groups, which are supported by her kindness. Her health is of concern not just to her, but to all of us who love her.

This same analogy holds for how we think about the earth. Many people don't believe there's a problem. They believe there is no proof of global warming, of an increasingly contaminated water supply, of low food production, of pollution. They don't see the sickness, and continue to carry out policies that lead to further sickness. They discount the problem. It doesn't matter to them how many scientists identify and define earth's sickness; it just doesn't seem important enough to them. Some of our government officials have set themselves up as little gods in their ivory towers, refusing to see the problem, refusing to create policies that would protect us.

Some know there's a problem but aren't worried, because it doesn't seem as if it will affect them personally. They believe that any major problems won't come to fruition for at least another fifty years, and by then they'll be dead.

Others see the sickness, but think the wonders of current technology will solve all the problems when the problems get bad enough. They believe that somehow something, from somewhere, will come to the rescue. They don't think about how long it takes and how much money it takes to develop workable technologies. It's a bit like telling a dying person, "Don't worry. In another ten years, there'll be a cure for your disease. You just have to wait a bit!"

There are those Christians who believe these environmental problems are evidence that the end of the world is nigh, and they say, "bring it on!" They see no reason to do anything about the environment because the problem will be over and done with soon; at least it will be for all Christians, when we're all raptured up to what is, we hope, a more environmentally pure heaven.

Armageddon is on its way, along with the Second Coming of Christ. They figure the worse it gets, the sooner we'll see Jesus.

This thinking terrifies me. To think some so-called Christians are playing with God's creation in order to manipulate a Second Coming seems foolhardy and un-biblical, as if anyone but God can cause the Second Coming. As long as we're here, we're responsible. And do we really believe that God will call us good and faithful servants if we abdicate our responsibility, even for an hour?

Some see the sickness, and see it isn't just a sickness that hurts one or two people, but affects billions all over the earth. They recognize that we have the power to kill others, either quickly or slowly, by ignorant or repressive environmental policies. They recognize that we are hurting our neighbor, whether it's the person nearby, or the people in the next town, in a neighboring country, or far across the sea in another land. We forget we are to be Good Samaritans in all things, no matter where our neighbor may live.

Defining the Problem

It is difficult to solve a problem until we define it. What is the sickness of our planet? Most scientists can agree on these points.

Water tables are dropping. Half of the world's population lives in China, India, and the United States; these three countries supply more than half of the world's grain. Because of droughts and misuse of land and water in these countries, water tables are falling and wells are running dry. When water levels fall, the level of grain production also falls, which, in turn, leads to famine. This leads to higher prices for grain, which leads to farmers overworking the soil in an effort to get more crops, which leads to soil erosion and desertification of land that was once rich and fertile.

When food and water are scarce, violence often occurs between villages and nations as they fight over these necessities. When the water level goes down, clean water is difficult or impossible to find. A third of all the people on earth do not have access to clean water. Contaminated water leads to diarrhea, cholera, malaria, and sickness and death, especially in children.

When we have less water, corporations seize the opportunity to take control of the scarce water supplies and begin selling water. They privatize water, depriving people of their access to water.

Some economists see water as the oil of the future, and predict that countries with enough fresh water will market it to countries where water is in short supply. Although on the surface it might seem that moving clean water would be helpful for water shortages, much of this water is marketed as bottled water, which only the middle class and wealthy can afford.[37]

Sometimes governments manipulate the agricultural harvest. Much of America's wheat land is kept fallow each year. It may be possible to feed everyone in the world, but when farmers are paid subsidies not to grow certain crops, it further contributes to the problem of hunger.

Temperatures are rising. Increasing temperatures are affecting our food supply. Some might say that we shouldn't be concerned just because it's a little warmer this year. Not true. We should be very concerned. The International Rice Research Institute in the Philippines and the U.S. Department of Agriculture indicate that for each 1.8-degree Fahrenheit rise in temperature during the growing season, we can expect a 10 percent decline in fields of wheat, rice, and corn. In 2002 and 2003, the intense heat produced a drought in India and in the United States, and every country saw its grain harvest decline. During these two years, thirty-five thousand people in eight countries died from effects of the record-high temperatures. The Intergovernmental Panel on Climate Change, made of up 1,500 scientists organized by the United Nations, projects that average temperatures will rise more than 10 degrees Fahrenheit during this century. If we don't do something about climate change, millions of people will die as a result of the drought, famine, and the violence that comes from the struggle for scarce resources.

Food prices are rising. The scarcity of food leads to rising food prices. Grain production in China rose in the early 1990s, but began dropping in 1998 because of water shortages, conversion of cropland to non-farm use, and paving over farmland for roads, as more of the population bought automobiles.

The resulting rise in grain prices will destabilize governments in the many countries that have very little money but must import a substantial amount of grain. Without China's important grain production, there will be more need to import from the United States and India, which will not be able to fulfill the need.

Food is being polluted. Not only does our food supply become scarce because of our environmental policies, but many of those policies make the food we have unfit to eat. We're told not to eat tuna because of the mercury content. We're told not to eat salmon because of pesticides. Acid rain and pesticides also make other fish and other food products inedible.[38]

Earth in the Balance

Al Gore, former senator, vice president, and presidential candidate, wrote a book in the early 1990s titled *Earth in the Balance: Ecology and the Human Spirit.* I originally read this book shortly after it was published, and then reread it in preparation for writing this book. Gore's book provides some of the best scientific and religious thinking on the environment. It approaches environmental and energy issues from the viewpoint of Scripture, ethics, morality, and spirituality, while also bringing together a tremendous amount of scientific information.

Gore looks at our confusion about environmental issues by also looking at our confusion, as Christians, about how we are to relate to the earth. Christians have been of two minds about this throughout history. For some, we are separate from the earth, and independent of the earth. What we do, in our own little moral universes, has little bearing on what happens on the earth. Our thoughts are about eternity, and about being heavenly minded. Of course, some Christians are so heavenly minded that they're no earthly good.

Other Christians see this differently. They believe we are entrusted with the earth by God. As good responsible stewards, we recognize that what we do has consequences, and just as we wouldn't destroy a church, or kill our neighbors, neither would we desecrate the earth, which was given to us as a gift. We are integrally connected to the earth, not separated from it. Consider this miraculous statistic. The percentage of water in our bodies is the same as the percentage of water on the earth.[39] The percentage of salt in our bodies is approximately the same as the percentage of salt in the oceans of the world.[40] We are unified with the earth physically, as well as spiritually.

The earth is a living system. Just as God breathed life into us, the earth itself lives and breathes. Just as God saved us during Noah's flood, so did he save the animals, two by two. God's care for living creatures is not limited only to us.

In fact, we are so connected that what each of us does in our own part of the planet affects the other side of the world. Famines, floods, fires, hurricanes, or any natural or unnatural catastrophes can change our individual lives, and they can also change our society. Gore recounts a number of these connections in his book, but one that particularly impressed me occurred in the 1930s—the Dust Bowl years.

In the 1920s, the mechanization of the tractor, the combine, the one-way plow, and the truck led to unwise land use. Farmers, as well as other experts, mistakenly believed that repeatedly plowing the land until it was smooth and pulverized made it better able to absorb and hold rainwater. For a few years this worked well. There were record crops, and the early signs of the danger of wind erosion were ignored.[41] Then, in 1932, strong winds began to blow, taking away some of the topsoil. Then came rain, and flooding, which further eroded the soil. When this was followed by a dry winter and spring, the big dust storms began taking more of the topsoil, leading to a drought. In 1934,

Secretary of the Interior Harold Ickes told the people of Oklahoma to leave their homes. By that time, only 15 percent of the acreage of Texas and Oklahoma was useable.

Dirt and dust were everywhere. The earth was barren. Emergency hospitals were set up to treat "dust pneumonia" and other respiratory diseases caused by inhaling the dust. The dust and dirt blew all over the West, and even to the Atlantic Ocean. As a result, farmers could not make a living in their own states. They were without work and lost all of their land. So what did they do? They started moving into other states, such as California, which could not absorb this vast migration of people. This led to unemployment and hunger. There were food riots. There were long bread lines. Finally, legislation was passed to help those who suffered, requiring millions of dollars of government money, specifically for Franklin Roosevelt's New Deal legislation.[42] Who suffered? Our entire society. Our lack of environmental policies can cause consequences not just for the earth, not just for individuals, but for many parts of society.

Gore clarifies in his book that this is not just a scientific problem, but a moral problem as well. Many Christians feel a moral obligation to respond when we hear that mankind is slashing and burning one football field's worth of rain forest every second, and destroying half of the living species on earth in the space of a single lifetime. We grieve, and decide to do something about it, when we hear that more than 376,000 children under the age of five die from starvation every day because of failures of crops and failures of our politics. Yet still we pump millions of tons of pollutants into our environment, threatening the earth's climatic balance.[43] We continue to build gas-guzzling trucks and

SUVs and cars, which benefit the oil companies in the short run, but don't serve the many of us who ask for better mileage.

Where do we see God? In a dead bird? In sick animals? In polluted water? In polluted skies that cause sickness for us and our children?

In December 1989, Pope John Paul II addressed his "brothers and sisters in the Catholic church, in order to remind them of their serious obligation to care for all of creation. . . . Respect for life and the dignity of the human person extends also to the rest of creation, which is called to join man in praising God."[44] Are we creating a world that praises all creation? Are we becoming good stewards? Or don't we care?

Learning to Care

The Bush administration has not made the environment a priority, in spite of repeated pressure from scientists, Christians, and the voting public. Republican pollster Frank Luntz said, in 2003, "The environment is probably the single issue on which the Republicans . . . are most vulnerable."[45]

This lack of response to the environment by Republicans has been an ongoing problem under Ronald Reagan, George H. W. Bush, and George W. Bush. When a number of people protested Mr. Reagan's policies, which were going to destroy hundreds of redwood trees, he shrugged off their concerns, saying, "If you've seen one redwood tree, you've seen them all."

When many people protested drilling for oil in the Arctic National Wildlife Refuge, even former Secretary of the Interior

James Watt, known for his pro-development stands, agreed that the region was too sensitive for drilling. Some people responded to the environmentalists' concern by asking, "Who cares about the caribou?" Perhaps some don't care, but Noah cared, and God cared, and some of us also care.[46]

Former head of the Environmental Protection Agency, Republican Christine Todd Whitman, recounts a number of other ways that her own party has continued to discount environmental concerns.

In her book *It's My Party Too*, she quotes Vice President Dick Cheney, who said, "Conservation may be a sign of personal virtue, but it is not a sufficient basis for a sound, comprehensive energy policy."[47] If conservation and care for the environment is not a basis, then what is?

The United States, which has 4 percent of the world's population, emits 25 percent of the world's carbon dioxide.[48] We refuse to sign any international environmental treaties, such as the Kyoto Protocol, because we would then be asked to join the international community in doing our share to protect the environment.

Some Republicans handle these problems by denying there are any problems at all. Whitman mentions that many Republicans said they would be happy to see the "United States completely disengage from the rest of the international community on the climate change issue—which many of them thought was really just a hyped-up Trojan horse effort to use a false concern about a nonexistent problem to weaken U.S. economic strength."[49]

When press secretaries for House Republicans were given talking points to use about environmental problems, they were told to say: "Global warming is not a fact." "EPA data . . . is falsely exaggerated"[50] In other words, they were told to go against all scientific evidence, and against the desire of the 80 percent of Americans surveyed who wanted the government to address pollution.[51]

At times it seemed that the Bush administration wanted to protect the environment, but changed its mind due to pressure from other Republicans.

During his first bid for the presidency, George W. Bush promised he would diminish carbon dioxide emissions. Christine Todd Whitman, as the head of the Environmental Protection Agency during Mr. Bush's first term, took these promises seriously. In 2001, representing the United States, she met with her environmental counterparts from the G8 countries Great Britain, Italy, Canada, France, Germany, Japan, and Russia to discuss energy policies. Before leaving, she checked with Condoleezza Rice, Mr. Bush's national security advisor, to make sure that Bush would abide by his campaign promise to reduce carbon dioxide emissions, because she knew that representatives from other countries were becoming increasingly skeptical and concerned about his environmental decisions. Rice reassured her—George W. Bush would keep his promise. When Whitman returned from the conference, she learned that the pressures from businesses to let up on regulations convinced Mr. Bush to change his mind. He went back on his promises, embarrassing Whitman, who had to figure out how to spin the news so that the United States did not look arrogant or unconcerned. Of course, we really were arrogant and unconcerned, but it was imperative that we pretend that we weren't.

As other pro-environment policies came up for review, Whitman found they were struck down, over and over again. She recounts the opposition in Congress by Republicans on the Senate Environment and Public Works Committee as well as the House Energy and Commerce Committee. She pointed out, in particular, Jim Inhofe (R-Oklahoma) who was chair of the Senate Environment and Public Works Committee, and Representative Billy Tauzin (R-Louisiana),[52] who used their positions to "bottleneck some important environmental proposals," including their opposition, "in the months following 9/11, to giving EPA much-needed regulatory authority to require thousands of chemical facilities around the nation to assess and address their vulnerability to terrorist attack."[53] Members of the Republican Party have not only tried to keep any new bills from passing, but have tried to roll back regulations that protect the environment.[54] "Numerous businesses and trade associations, often represented by powerful Republicans, spend millions of dollars each year lobbying against virtually any new environmental regulation."[55]

As Whitman sees it, the problem was not with Mr. Bush, but with the Republicans in Congress and with the Republican-run businesses that not only didn't want any new regulations, but even wanted to weaken the current regulations. It seemed, to her, that the Republican corporations had the power, and they put considerable pressure on Mr. Bush to protect them against any policies that would hurt their profit margin, or demand environmental responsibility.

As I see it, the administration has a choice—to create a sound and moral environmental policy, or to cave under pressure from Republican businesses and corporations. In this case, there was no environmental leadership from the administration.

George W. Bush's decisions continued to show he had little concern for the environment. In 2001, he appointed Philip A. Cooney as Chief of Staff for the White House Council on Environmental Quality. This was a strange choice for someone who wanted to protect the environment. Cooney had previously worked as a lobbyist for the American Petroleum Institute, leading the oil industry's fight against regulations that would limit greenhouse gasses. In his position on the Council, he repeatedly edited government climate reports to play down, and dismiss, the links between the environmental problems and greenhouse emissions. His actions led one of their employees, Rick Piltz, to blow the whistle on Cooney's practices. Piltz eventually resigned from his position, because he saw that Cooney's editing was tainting information.[56]

Bush's lack of concern was further reinforced when he appointed Dick Cheney, his vice president and the former CEO of one of the largest energy companies in the country, to oversee the Energy Task Force. This is somewhat like asking a ten-year-old cookie-lover to be in charge of guarding the cookie jar. Cheney certainly was not an objective leader for this job—and he proved it. He denied access of environmental groups who wanted to discuss their findings and to discuss environmental policy. Instead, he welcomed meetings with energy companies.[57]

Whitman tries to spin this information, either by mentioning other past accomplishments of Republicans (there were some!) or by mentioning the lack of cooperation from some

Democrats with moderate policies (that also did happen). She
wonders why the Republicans have so little concern for the
environment. She admits that the business interests clearly
overrode almost all policies, even though she believed that the
two need not be incompatible.

As a result of the lack of a strong energy policy in the
United States, gas prices have soared. Rules have been rewrit-
ten to allow more than 20,000 facilities to spew more smog,
soot, and mercury into the air. More arsenic has been allowed in
the water. Asthma has reached epidemic proportions, some of it
due to environmental hazards.

"It's no wonder so many people today feel they have reason to doubt the party's commitment to the environment" says
Whitman.[58] Whitman believes that the Republican Party has
moved away from environmental policies in order to secure its
base with business. In spite of what the American people want,
business clearly is getting its way.

During 2005, George W. Bush delivered his energy bill,
which had been stalled for four years. Mr. Bush wanted a bill
that asked for $6.7 billion dollars—which would be about the
cost of one month of the war in Iraq. Congress passed a bill that
cost twice as much—$12.3 billion. The bill will give about $4
billion in tax breaks and relief to companies in the oil and gas
industries (which are already making record profits), and about
another $4 billion in tax breaks to the coal industry to promote
clean coal technologies. It will provide loan guarantees and
other subsidies so the nuclear industry can build new reactors,
even though we don't yet know how to make a reactor safe, or
how to store nuclear waste safely.

George W. Bush's recommendations for dealing with the climate crisis include voluntary rather than mandatory reduction targets and timetables. Since no corporation has yet been willing to voluntarily cut its profits in order to help the environment, there is no reason to think that voluntary responses will help.

Mr. Bush discusses developing new technologies to solve the problems, rather than asking us to make any changes in our lifestyle. But what technologies does he have in mind, and how much money has he put aside to develop them? There seems to be no plan.

There will be a few tax breaks and subsidies for alternative energy sources, such as wind turbines and the geothermal and solar industries. The bill will double the use of corn-based ethanol. It will require new efficiency standards for appliances such as air conditioners and refrigerators.

Utilities will have to meet federal standards for the electricity grids, so we won't have another blackout like the one we had in 2003. It expands daylight savings time by one month, adding three weeks in the spring and a week in the fall, but this won't start until 2007, almost two years after the bill was passed.

What the Energy Bill Won't Do

George W. Bush's energy bill won't have any immediate effect on diminishing our use of gas and oil. Many Democrats reluctantly voted for the legislation, even though they didn't believe it did enough to reduce our consumption of oil—which is about 20 million barrels a day, more than half of which is imported.[59] Even the sponsors of the bill said it would have little impact on today's energy prices and would not curtail the nation's use of oil.

Democratic Senator Bill Nelson of Florida said, "The bill does little to nothing to reduce our dependence on Middle East oil." Although a "modest provision" was added to the bill to try to reduce our oil use by one million barrels a day by 2025, it did not pass the Republican-controlled House of Representatives because it was considered a backdoor way to impose tougher standards on automakers. The bill puts no stringent standards on either the oil and gas industry or the automakers.

Most of the tax breaks will go to the traditional energy industry—such as gas, oil, and electricity. Many Democrats criticized the billions of dollars in subsidies given to the oil companies, which already have plenty of money thanks to the high price of gasoline. Democratic Representative Edward Markey of Massachusetts said, "These are the wealthiest companies in America. We shouldn't be subsidizing them."[60]

Democratic Senator Jeff Bingaman of New Mexico wanted to see more emphasis on renewable fuels and wanted a provision that would require utilities to generate at least 10 percent of their electricity from renewable fuels. But the Republican-controlled House would not pass that either. Democrats Henry Waxman, Hilda Solis, Lois Capps, and Edward Markey wanted to see more government support for new technologies. Programs for greater efficiency and conservation will get $1.3 billion, but that's only a third of what the Senate wanted.

Jill Lancelot, the president of Taxpayers for Common Sense, says, "The bill is filled to the brim with massive giveaways for mega-rich energy companies. By stuffing the measure with so much pork, [they] will have attempted to buy off enough votes to guarantee passing a so-called energy bill."[61]

Overall, the bill has been criticized for doing virtually nothing about our two greatest environmental and energy issues: our dependence on imported oil, and global warming, which is caused by the fuels the bill so generously subsidizes.[62] What is missing are standards for fuel consumption, which can come from encouraging automakers to develop vehicles that will not be dependent on gasoline imports. Because transportation accounts for two-thirds of our oil consumption, any movement forward would diminish our dependency on foreign oil. Alternative fuel would also reduce emissions from carbon dioxide, which is the main cause of global warming.

The United States has no lack of good ideas for how to reduce emissions, how to reduce global warming, how to reduce energy consumption. We have plenty of American ingenuity to create more hybrid cars, which already have a long waiting list of buyers who clearly want alternatives. But little is being done by the Congress or George W. Bush to listen to these voices. A group of military and intelligence experts, including Robert McFarlane, James Woolsey, and Frank Gaffney Jr., "implored Mr. Bush as a matter of national security to undertake a crash program to reduce the consumption of oil in the United States."[63]

Republican Senator John McCain calls the president's approach to the issue "disgraceful." Columnist Kai M. A. Chan from Princeton has called George W. Bush's response indefensible and says it should lead to moral outrage. Chan says, "The Bush Administration has the gall to claim that the US cannot afford to risk any harm to its economy! The richest country in the world whines that it *cannot afford* to limit its emissions."[64]

Outside of Washington, there is a great deal of consensus on the need to reduce our consumption, and how to do it. The Energy Future Coalition, the Rocky Mountain Institute, the National Commission on Energy Policy—bipartisan or non-partisan groups concerned with the environment—have issued major reports about energy policy and energy efficiency. We are simply not turning to the best minds in our country to help us create strong policies in one of the most important areas facing us today.

George W. Bush gives a very general analysis of the problem, saying that the issue is one "we've got to deal with," and that human activity is "to some extent" to blame. This analysis is much too general to lead to any kind of wise and informed policy, particularly because none of the policy decisions seems to truly deal with the problem, or our human responsibility.[65]

The government's refusal to deal with global warming has been costly. We have already suffered many of the effects, and can only expect to have more tragedies in the future. Climatologists have studied the effect of global warming on our oceans and see a connection between the rising water temperatures and the intensity of hurricanes of the last thirty years. Ruth Gorski Curry, research specialist from the Woods Hole Oceanographic Institution says, "As carbon dioxide levels climb to levels unprecedented in the last 400,000 years, the planet is warming, its ice is melting, and evaporation/precipitation patterns are changing. . . . Most climate simulations agree that greenhouse warming will enhance the frequency and intensity of hurricanes and typhoons in the coming century."[66] The number of category 4 and 5 hurricanes, such as Hurricane Katrina and Hurricane Rita, has almost doubled since the 1970s. Scientists see this pattern connected to the steady increase in water temperatures, which have risen 1 degree Fahrenheit in the last thirty years. Although scientists don't see evidence of more hurricanes as a result of global warming, they see evidence that the warming of the oceans is producing hurricanes of greater intensity. The intensity has also created greater rainfall from the hurricanes. Even the Environmental Protection Agency (EPA) is recognizing the connection. The EPA acknowledges that "the Earth's surface temperature has risen by about 1 degree Fahrenheit in the past century, with accelerated warming during the last two decades" and it recognizes that most of this is due to human activity.[67] Our unwillingness to be visionary, to plan for the future, to care about our environment, to take care of problems before they get out of control, is now forcing us to spend billions of dollars to rebuild cities ravaged by Hurricane Katrina and Hurricane Rita.

Denial becomes more and more expensive. George W. Bush said on an ABC television interview, "I don't think anyone anticipated the breach of the levees." But that is not true. He was repeatedly warned about this problem but refused to take any action. In 2004, the *New Orleans Times-Picayune* said, "For the first time in 37 years, federal budget cuts have all but stopped major work on the New Orleans area's east bank hurricane levees, a complex network of concrete walls, metal gates and giant earthen berms that won't be finished for at least another decade." The article predicted that if there were a strong hurricane, the area would "fill up with the waters of the lake, leaving those unable to evacuate with little option but to cluster on rooftops—terrain they would have to share with hungry rats, fire ants, nutria, snakes, and perhaps alligators. The water itself would become a festering stew of sewage, gasoline, refinery chemicals, and debris." And it all happened exactly as predicted.

The tragedy from Hurricane Katrina did not take us by surprise. It was a tragedy waiting to happen. George W. Bush's repeated refusal to fund the drainage systems and the levees magnified the disaster. He repeatedly slashed funding requests from the Army Corps of Engineers. When the Corps asked for $26.9 million, Mr. Bush asked Congress for $3.9 million, which delayed seven contracts that would have improved the levees that hold back Lake Pontchartrain. When the Southeast Louisiana Urban Flood Control Project asked for $62.5 million, the White House proposed $10.5 million. When former Republican Congressman Michael Parker protested the lack of proper funding, he was forced out as head of the Army Corps of Engineers. Former Louisiana Senator John Breaux, a pro-Bush Democrat, said, "All of us said, 'Look, build it or you're going to have all of Jefferson Parish underwater.' And they didn't, and now all of Jefferson Parish is underwater."[68]

Adlai Stevenson, former Democratic presidential candidate and later ambassador to the United Nations, said in 1965, "We travel together, passengers on a little spaceship, dependent on its vulnerable supplies of air and soil; all committed for our safety to its security and peace, preserved from annihilation only by the care, the work, and I will say, the love we give our fragile craft."[69]

Environmentalist Barry Commoner says, "We live on the surface of a planet. Everything we need, everything we use comes from the skin of that planet—the layer of air, soil, and surface waters on the earth's surface, and minerals that lie beneath it. This is the source of all of our resources—food, oxygen, and raw materials. We speak of this thin layer as the ecosystem—the network of biological interaction between living things and their environment that sustains life on the planet."[70] Our policies are not only destroying others; they are destroying us, too.

The Democratic Platform on the Environment

Because the Democrats are not the majority in the current government, they don't have the voice to change policies. However, we can look to various other sources to see what they would do. Certainly Al Gore's book and his analysis give us some indication of alternative policies, as do the Democrats' response to the current energy bill. The 2004 Democratic Party Platform also clarifies how the party would reprioritize these environmental problems.

The Democrats begin their policy statement by drawing on the idea that we have dominion over the land and must therefore use it wisely. "For generations, Americans of all political beliefs have understood that the protection of our environment and the stewardship of our land are vital to the strength of our nation. God gave America extraordinary natural gifts: it is our responsibility to protect them."

The Democrats recognize that our environmental policies also affect the economy and the family. "The health of our families, the strength of our economy, and the well-being of our world all depend upon a clean environment."

The Democratic Party Platform for 2004 calls for an environment where "children can safely play in our neighborhoods, our families can enjoy our national parks, and our sportsmen can hunt and fish in our lakes and forests."

How will they do this? In a variety of ways.

The Democrats are committed to "promoting new technologies that create good jobs and improve our world."

They see the necessity of "working with our allies to achieve these goals and to protect the global environment, for this generation and future generations."

They want to "strengthen the Clean Air Act by controlling all of the top pollutants and offering new flexibility to industries that commit to cleaning up within that framework." This means reducing mercury emissions, smog, acid rain, and water pollution that originates from factories, large corporate farms, stormwater runoff, and sewer overflows. It also means cleaning up the polluted sites, such as the nuclear waste dump in Nevada. The Democrats also want companies that lease lands to restore them to their original state when the lease runs out.

The Democrats want to preserve wildlife, and protect the lands and rivers used by hunters and fishermen.

Because they recognize that the global environment impacts the American environment, and vice versa, they would work with others overseas to address these concerns, including the concerns of climate change and global warning.

Democrats recognize that our environmental policy and our energy policy must work hand in hand. We must gain independence from foreign oil. In the 2004 platform, they say, "No strategy for American security is complete without a plan to end America's dependence on Mid-East oil. Today, the American economy depends on oil controlled by some of the world's most repressive regimes. This leaves our economy dangerously vulnerable to nations that do not share our interests. America too often is silent about the practices of some governments because we depend on oil they control."

From this policy statement come specific action statements:

Harness the natural world for energy—sun, wind, water, geothermal and biomass sources, and our crops.

Give tax credits to those whose companies use more energy-efficient methods.

Create energy-efficient vehicles, including hybrid cars and hydrogen cars.

Improve fuel standards.

Seek more diverse sources of oil, including areas already under exploration, such as Mexico, Russia, Canada, and Africa.

What's the Effect?

Our lack of a strong environmental policy doesn't just pollute our country. Nor does it just pollute other countries. It has far more dangerous effects.

Our dependence on natural resources affects the state of the world. We are overly dependent on oil. On one level, this affects us superficially. We can't go on as many vacations because the price of driving or flying is too high. We can't afford other things, because a greater percentage of our income is going to gasoline, instead of education, leisure activities, food, and rent. For the poor, these extra cents per gallon determine whether they can get to work easily, or whether their children will have enough food.

But this also affects us on a far more profound level. The countries that are rich in natural resources, particularly oil, hold us hostage. Their regimes become increasingly more oppressive to their citizens as governmental leaders get richer, live more lavishly, and rule with an iron fist. These oil-rich countries become more dependent on only one industry. Those who work for that industry get the benefits. Those who don't, become poorer. When the citizens try to protest, they're killed; all of the weapons and all of the power lie in the hands of the small group that controls this one resource.

Ultimately, this leads to war. It's no accident that our last three wars have involved countries that are rich in oil—Kuwait— or well located for lucrative energy pipelines—Afghanistan and Iraq. This is where many of the problems are, and they exist on many levels. We get involved in the repressive regimes that have oil—invading and occupying their land—but don't get involved in the genocide in countries that have little oil and don't serve our own national interests.

Through this long chain of connections, our policies perpetuate the social injustices in our own country and in other countries in the world. The rich get richer, because they're associated with oil. The poor get poorer, because the resource is scarce and they have to pay more for it.

There is a Native American saying that has been borrowed by many religions—we are to recognize that our actions will affect the seven generations that follow us. If we were to think of our actions in terms of their long-term consequences to future generations, we might have drastically different policies.

We have been tempted, in our dominion over the earth, to play the despot rather than the benevolent king. St. Basil, Bishop of Caesarea, created a prayer in the fourth century to acknowledge, and expand, our sense of stewardship: "O God, enlarge within us the sense of fellowship with all living things, our brothers the animals to Whom Thou gavest the earth as Their home in common with us. We remember with shame that in the past we have exercised the high dominion of man with ruthless cruelty, so that the voice of the earth, which should have gone up to Thee in song, has been a groan of travail. May we realize that they live not alone for us, but for themselves and for Thee. That they too love the sweetness of life."

Chapter Four

The Ethical Dilemma of Abortion

*"Make your view heard . . . on behalf of all the unwanted;
. . . defend the cause of the poor and the wretched."*

Proverbs 31:8–9

There is one thing we probably can all agree on: a loving marriage with happy and healthy children is a great blessing.

But life doesn't always work out this way. Women marry and are abused, battered, threatened, and killed. Many children are neglected, and live in unsafe and unhealthy environments. In other periods of history and other parts of the world today, the women and children would not have any recourse. They would be forced to stay in an unhappy family situation. In some religions, the woman would be told that under no circumstances should she divorce. She might be allowed to leave, but certainly not start a new life. Matthew, Mark, and Luke are very clear "everyone who divorces his wife . . . makes her an adulteress; and anyone who marries a divorced woman commits adultery."[1]

I don't hear either Christian Democrats or Christian Republicans arguing about divorce anymore. It seems to be a secular law most religions accept as part of our national laws, even if they don't accept it for their own church members. But in order to understand various Christian attitudes toward abortion, it might help to understand attitudes toward divorce and how they exist side by side with secular laws.

When I was twenty-two, and shortly after I had become a born-again Christian, I married. Naive about relationships, filled with romantic illusions, I married a man I didn't know well. Even before the wedding, I was more and more uncertain about this relationship, but I didn't know how to break it off, nor was I at all sure that it wouldn't work. In my religious innocence, I figured God would make everything all right. I just had to trust and have faith.

Quickly, I realized I had married an emotionally abusive man. He was controlling, picky, and critical. He stole without any remorse; nothing big, but our little apartment was furnished with chairs and tables he took from the Army base where he worked. This behavior caused a deep conflict within me. On the one hand, as a fundamentalist Christian, I figured I was stuck for life. But because I was a person who was deeply spiritual, something seemed wrong with this interpretation.

Several times he threatened my life. Not by holding a gun to my head, but by telling me, "I might kill you some day. I wonder how I'll do it. There's a gun in my closet but I might do it while you sleep by smothering you with a pillow."

As a fundamentalist, I kept telling myself, "I just have to be more loving." But it didn't matter how loving I was. Clearly this man did not love, cherish, or respect me. In fact, I knew, deep inside, that he didn't even like me! I soon realized I did not have the strength to live in this lifestyle without it having severe consequences in many different levels of my life.

In one of my prayers about what to do about this, I told God I didn't understand. I said, "If I'm not allowed to get divorced, then marriage to an abusive man is the only sin that can't be forgiven. I could kill someone, serve my time, and come back into society as a changed person and go on to try to live a happy life. But if I marry someone who is abusive, I can't ask forgiveness and start again. I am stuck. And my only alternatives are insanity, suicide, getting killed, or getting a divorce and suffering the condemnation of my Christian community."

As I thought further about the situation, I realized I was becoming more and more depressed and immobilized. I had recently finished graduate school. I had studied hard for a career, and knew that I had contributions to make. But I would be unable to make them in this situation.

I realized the fundamentalist interpretation of the Bible allowed me to leave him, but not to get a divorce. Therefore, neither of us would ever be able to marry again, until one of us died. Since I was only twenty-three, I didn't see death for either of us as a possibility unless he carried out his threat to kill me. Nor did I understand how a mistake at twenty-three should determine the happiness or unhappiness of my entire life.

After more struggle and reflection, I realized this view of God was uncaring and uncompassionate and did not reveal the loving God I had begun to know. I also realized it was imperative I leave, since it would be unfair to bring a child into this situation. Because no birth control could be trusted 100 percent, there was no way I could be sure I wouldn't get pregnant. I feared for my physical life and my emotional life if I continued to have any ongoing relationship with this man. I knew when I left, I had to make sure he wouldn't know where I had gone.

I did leave, and eventually got a divorce. I told all of our mutual friends to write to me through my parents, who would forward the letters. I couldn't trust these well-meaning friends to keep my location a secret.

Although I felt that my religion would not support my decision to divorce, my country's laws did. I was allowed to get a divorce, and start life again, as a wiser, more careful person.

I was offered a teaching position at a Southern Baptist college, where I revealed to the dean and the president (but not to students or other faculty members) that I was divorced, thinking that they might not accept me into the faculty. Though they did accept me (I later learned that both of them also got divorced), I kept my divorce secret for a number of years, expecting to be censured by religious people. Keeping the secret kept me from finding some resolution to my divorce and from getting on with my life. Seventeen years later I remarried, and found the love and spirituality that I so desired in a relationship.

As the years went on, most churches began to acknowledge divorce as a solution under difficult circumstances.

Soon after my divorce, I started looking at other churches that weren't as fundamentalist and legalistic. I did further study of divorce, and began to understand that divorce had originally been forbidden as a way of protecting women from a man who could simply say "I divorce you" three times and throw her out on the streets. I also saw how these same verses could be used to control. When the verses against divorce are combined with the verses in Ephesians 5 about the woman being submissive to a husband, they could justify the oppression of the wife—including beating her, not allowing her to see anyone or do anything without the husband's permission, keeping her tied to him with a very tight rope. I have met women who are in unhappy and oppressive marriages and whose misery shows through in their faces and in every movement they make. They have not been freed by God, but are in complete bondage to a husband who cannot, or will not, change.

I began to realize, experientially, an overly legalistic interpretation of the Bible can get in the way of our relationship with a loving God and the guidance of the Holy Spirit.

From this experience, I began to see how very flawed our decisions can be and how very difficult and complex many relationship issues are. I recognized my church and my country might disagree about how to resolve this and other issues. Certain churches would not recognize my right to a divorce. My country did.

The Right to Life and Liberty

There are issues in our country in which the pursuit of life, liberty, and happiness and the rights of the individual conflict with certain religious beliefs. American citizens struggle with how much the government should be interfering in our lives. Should the government be legislating individual morality? If so, does that mean that police will be peering into our bedrooms to see what we're doing? Will they be checking to see what books we're reading, who we associate with, what marches or parades we take part in, and where we're traveling? Some extremists would like to peer into our private domain, but make it clear we are not to peer into their domain of the banks and the boardrooms.

The government struggles with determining which issues are of interest to the state, and which are not. Government regulates many areas that might seem a personal decision—such as the seat-belt laws, child restraints in the car, the helmet laws, food-labeling laws, zoning issues, no-smoking laws, and so on. We accept these laws because not doing so would cause negative economic consequences to our society. When people don't use seat belts or helmets or proper child restraints, police drag out the battered and the dead from accidents. This leads to more money spent on medical needs that could have been prevented.

We try to understand how far to go with legislating what seem to be personal freedom issues. Should we legislate sex, since the cost of sexually transmitted diseases, pregnancy, and abortions can also be a drain on society? And if so, do we legislate against a person who has sexual relations with anyone other than a monogamous, healthy spouse? Or do we go too far when we have to peer into everyone's sexual practices to decide who is moral and who is legal?

Many issues in our country divide us as we struggle to understand which issues are of interest to our country, and at what point our government interferes too much with our individual freedoms.

The Hot-Button Issues

Two of the most divisive issues in our country are abortion and homosexuality. Why are these issues, which seem to involve individual rights and choices, of such concern to Christians? What is the government's interest in these rights? Why is there so much disagreement, among legislators and among Christians, about what to do about them?

There are some issues, such as the environment, or our treatment of the poor, in which it seems that Scripture, morality, ethics, and spirituality lead us to the same conclusion about how we are to act. We are to care for the earth. We are to be protectors of the poor.

The issues of abortion and homosexuality do not seem to line up quite so nicely. Each side believes that its views are the right ones, but to reach these views, each side has to focus on one set of Christian values, and ignore the others.

There are no clear Bible verses about either of these issues. There is not one verse in the Bible that mentions abortion. Christians use Bible verses that imply a certain religious stance on these issues, but the verses can be interpreted in different ways. Some who try to take a literal interpretation of a verse may have to ignore the spirit of other verses. Some who take an overall spiritual or theological view of certain Scriptures may have to ignore the strong implications of other passages.

Is it possible for us to find some clarity about these issues, so we aren't constantly dealing with seeming contradictions? Have we, perhaps, misinterpreted some Scripture, in the same way we formed new interpretations about what the Bible had to say about slavery and women's rights? Will these issues continue to divide Christians for many years to come, or might we find some common ground that will help us resolve them?

A Woman's Right to Choose

One of the most divisive issues in our country is abortion. Conservative Christians tend to be against abortion; more mainstream and liberal Christians tend to be pro-choice. The Republican Party has taken a stand against abortion. The Democratic Party has taken a stand on the woman's right to choose, following the U.S. Supreme Court decision of *Roe v. Wade*. Both parties, however, have members who are pro-choice and anti-abortion.

But that is simplifying a complex issue. We can probably safely say that all Christians—in fact, all Americans—are against abortion. No one chooses to have an abortion because it's fun, or easy, or a good form of birth control. If we could make abortion unnecessary, we all would all be grateful.

Conservative Christians have taken the strongest stand against abortion. Focus on the Family considers it one of the most important issues facing Americans today (along with homosexuality). There is a concerted effort by many conservative Christians to back appointment of U.S. Supreme Court judges who will seek to overturn *Roe v. Wade*. Many Democrats see this as creating negative consequences for our society. This will lead to more unwanted children, a higher crime rate, and more women on welfare. It will take us back to the years of back-alley abortions, with more women dying from self-induced abortions and from botched abortions performed by incompetent doctors. The rich, of course, won't have to be too concerned because they will be able to fly to another state or country for a safe abortion. If *Roe v. Wade* is overturned, the individual states will again have the right to make their own laws concerning abortion. This means, for example, that abortion might then be illegal in Texas but legal in California. Currently there are laws against transporting a minor across state lines for an abortion without the parent's permission. This law won't affect the adults who can drive across the state lines on their own, but it will affect the pregnant minor. The law will have two consequences: either there will be more unwanted children who will need to be cared for in some way by the state, or there will again be the illegal abortions that have, in the past, resulted in the deaths of thousands of women. As usual, the burden will fall on the poor.

Very conservative Christians base their stand on abortion on the Scriptures. But what do they find in the Scriptures specifically against abortion? Nothing. Jesus never mentioned it. Nor did Paul. Nor did any of the prophets, nor any of the writers in the New Testament.

In the Hebrew Scriptures, there are several verses that are used to justify the stand against abortion, although none of them specifically mention abortion. They are, however, strong and clear passages about God's love for us, and protection of us, including the unborn. They talk about how God has made us,[2] formed us in the womb,[3] called us before birth.[4] We are created before birth by a loving Father.

The Bible tells us that God protects the pregnant woman, and is wrathful toward anyone who hits a pregnant woman. For this abuse, He will demand an eye for an eye, a life for a life.[5] If we question whether a child who is deformed or retarded or blind, deaf, or mute should be aborted, the Lord says we are not to question why we are made deaf, or mute, or blind. We are not to question God about his children.[6] The child is the Lord's, not the mother's or the father's, so a woman should not have control over her own body.[7] The Bible does not, however, tell us who is to control a woman's body when difficult ethical problems need to be resolved. The state? The national government? The doctors? A local pastor? The husband? The family?

Some fundamentalist and conservative Christians believe abortion should be illegal under all circumstances because the Scriptures referenced here imply we must never abort a fetus. They see these Bible verses as clearly saying that God has formed us, and we must not take away the life that He has created in the womb.

This causes some difficult ethical problems. If the mother is dying and she could be saved by abortion, some fundamentalists would say the doctors must not, ever, save the mother. They must allow her to die, and try to save the fetus. In this case, they make two moral decisions: First, it means they believe taking action that will result in a death (of the fetus) is worse than taking no action at all and allowing death to happen (to the mother). Second, they believe this group of growing cells, whether still an embryo within the first few weeks or a fetus, has exactly the same rights to live as the mother, and in fact even more rights, whether or not it would be able to survive on its own outside the womb.

These Christians believe even if the fetus is damaged in some way, or can't be carried to term, or would not live more than a few months after birth, abortion would still be considered wrong.

Clearly this is one of the most difficult ethical issues for Christians to face. On the one hand, as Christians, we are to care for all living beings. Certainly from conception there is movement and cells multiplying and life beginning to form into a human being. I do not question a moral judgment on this subject. Any kind of killing of anything and anyone that has movement and life demands complex moral judgments. When is it all right to kill? In war? When attacked in our home? Is it all right to kill someone who has committed a crime, or someone who is brain dead and who has left a living will, or a fetus that is not yet a fully developed baby? Our country accepts these other justifications for killing, through laws established by the courts.

It is, of course, easy for some of us to decide what someone else should do. When problems in pregnancy become personal, and there's danger to someone we love, how does that change our ethical decisions?

Love Can Change Decisions

A few years ago, a good friend of mine, who I'll call Jane, was happily pregnant. She had married recently, and was eagerly anticipating a baby. Soon after she became pregnant, the doctor told her there was something very wrong with the fetus. He couldn't diagnose it exactly, but suggested abortion. Since Jane and her husband were against abortion, they prayed for a miracle. As the months went by, the doctor became clearer about the problem. She told Jane her baby would die in the womb. Again, the doctor recommended an abortion, since the pregnancy was still in its early stages. Jane and her husband decided to allow the process to take its course. Jane called several of us to keep us informed about what was happening.

Jane's mother, who is a conservative evangelical Christian and would never consider herself pro-choice, made a pro-choice statement—"Whatever you decide, your father and I support you." Since I'm pro-choice, I made a similar statement: "Whatever you decide, you have our support. But I do have some questions that are important for you to think about. Are you in danger by carrying this fetus? Could this be a danger to your life? Could this lead to an inability to have other children?" My husband, who is also pro-choice and who works in medicine, mentioned to Jane, "It's very dangerous for you to have dead matter in your body. If you decide to carry the fetus until it dies, make sure the doctor supports this decision and will remove it immediately." We both advised her to make sure the doctor would support her decision; otherwise, she should get another doctor. My husband and I both admitted our concerns about her health, but put no pressure on her to get an abortion. This was her choice, but above all, we wanted her to be safe and to not hurt her health. It was clear, from everything the doctor had said, that there was virtually no hope for this fetus to live.

After five months, during a checkup, the doctor discovered there was no longer a heartbeat. Instead of removing the fetus immediately, the doctor waited four days and sent her to an abortion clinic. Shortly after Jane returned from the clinic, she began bleeding and was then taken to the hospital, where she stayed for several days. Clearly, there was more danger than had been expected.

If *Roe v. Wade* had been overturned, Jane would not have had the choice of whether or not to have an abortion. Because she wasn't the victim of rape or incest, and because it didn't seem that there was immediate danger to her health, she would not have had the freedom to choose to carry the fetus until it died. The law would have deemed there was not sufficient danger to her health to justify an abortion. Yet, in retrospect, there was serious danger.

Jane's story is filled with ethical dilemmas. At what point does one give up hope? How does one judge the danger, when no one can possibly know all the possible medical problems? Whose rights should take precedence in this situation—Jane's or those of the fetus? If Jane had been working full-time, what consequences would there be for her health and her job and her welfare, knowing she would not be able to bring the child to term? Who should make the judgment about how to handle this difficult dilemma—Jane or the government?

Jane's decision to stay the course deepened her spiritual life. She and her husband felt close to God as they struggled with the decision. She believes it strengthened her marriage. For her, there was clearly a positive spiritual side to her decision, in spite of the dangers. And that's what pro-choice is—allowing each person to make the choice as she is so guided. I, personally, would not want George W. Bush, or Clarence Thomas, or Antonin Scalia, or the minister down the street, or the person next door, to be deciding Jane's fate. I would want Jane to make an informed decision, perhaps with the help of her family and her family doctor and her pastor, or perhaps through prayer and meditation and reflection.

Without *Roe v. Wade*, it would not be her decision, but someone else's.

The abortion issue is filled with ethical dilemmas. Without *Roe v. Wade*, how will the victims of rape be treated? And what about the victims of incest? Will the girl be forced to have a baby who may be beaten and abused by the father as well?

Of course, not all unwanted pregnancies are this catastrophic. Some result from failure of birth control, which has never been 100 percent effective and has not improved in its effectiveness since the 1960s. Some are caused by foolhardy behavior and passions unchecked. There are those who would say these girls and women should be punished, and even deserve to suffer for their behavior, although these same people rarely mention punishing the man, who may just be "sowing his wild oats," or so overcome with passion he couldn't help himself. Who suffers? The mother and the child.

It isn't just teenagers who are getting pregnant. What are the married people to do if they can't afford another child? Are they to be celibate?

The Social Consequences of Abortion

Unwanted children present problems to society, and this leads to other ethical dilemmas. Has abortion increased or decreased certain social problems, such as crime? In the book *Freakonomics*, Steven D. Levitt and Stephen J. Dubner explored the ways in which unwanted children affect our society. They noticed crime had been at an all-time high until it began to fall in the early 1990s with a suddenness that surprised everyone.

The rapid decrease seemed unexplainable. They began to study what might have caused it. They looked at the aging of the population, tougher gun-control laws, the increased number of police, a stronger economy. They discovered, after careful examination, that these factors had very little or no effect. Then they looked at the issue of abortion.

After 1973, women could have an abortion if they had an unwanted pregnancy. The authors wondered if this could have had an effect. To analyze this, they began by looking at other societies, such as Romania, where abortion was declared illegal in 1966. This had an immediate effect on the society. The birth rate doubled within one year, and as the unwanted children grew older, they did worse in every way: they tested lower in school, they had less success in the job market, and they were more likely to become criminals.[8]

Before 1973, there were several states that allowed abortion. In that year, *Roe v. Wade* made abortion legal throughout the United States. Justice Harry Blackmun wrote the majority opinion, clarifying the harm to the mother, and to society, that can result from denying women a choice. "Maternity, or additional offspring, may force upon the woman a distressful life and future. Psychological harm may be imminent. Mental and physical health may be taxed by childcare. There is also the distress, for all concerned, associated with the unwanted child, and there is the problem of bringing a child into a family already unable, psychologically and otherwise, to care for it."[9]

The authors go on to say, "The Supreme Court gave voice to what the mothers in Romania . . . —and elsewhere—had long known; when a woman does not want to have a child, she usually has good reason. She may be unmarried or in a bad marriage. She may consider herself too poor to raise a child. She may think her life is too unstable or unhappy, or she may think that her drinking or drug use will damage the baby's health. She may believe that she is too young or hasn't yet received enough education. . . . For any of a hundred reasons, she may feel that she cannot provide a home environment that is conducive to raising a healthy and productive child."[10]

The authors saw that the most important impact from legalized abortion was the impact on crime. In the early 1990s, which would have been the time some of the unwanted children would have become rebellious teenagers starting on a life of crime, the rate of crime fell. And it continued to fall. "Legalized abortion led to less unwantedness; unwantedness leads to high crime; legalized abortion, therefore, led to less crime."[11]

The authors admit their research can lead to many reactions—disbelief, shock, revulsion, and objections. They rechecked their research by comparing how crime rates fell in the states that legalized abortion before *Roe v. Wade*. They looked again at Romania and the effect of abortion on its society. They looked to see if states with the highest abortion rate eventually had the lowest crime rate. They looked at studies in Australia and Canada to see if they also affirmed this link. They saw the negative ramifications in a society that forbids abortion.

They reached the conclusion that "when the government gives a woman the opportunity to make her own decision about abortion, she generally does a good job of figuring out if she is in a position to raise the baby well. If she decides she can't, she often chooses the abortion."[12] They were also aware of the moral ramifications: "One need not oppose abortion on moral or religious grounds to feel shaken by the notion of a private sadness being converted into a public good."[13]

What does this mean? They discovered, from a purely social viewpoint, the good of abortion outweighed the bad. Abortions helped society by leading to a lower crime rate; less cost for trying, convicting, sentencing, and housing criminals; and less cost to families, schools, and society for all the problems unwanted children bring.

What does this mean from an ethical viewpoint? If the Republicans are going to overturn *Roe v. Wade*, they will also need to pass bills, create programs, and legislate policies that will make up for the negative effects unwanted children can have upon society. If they're going to force women who can't afford children to have babies, they're going to have to put aside money for better prenatal care, better health care, better job training for the fathers and mothers who have another mouth to feed, better pay in the form of raising the minimum wage, better child care for the children when the parents are at work, better funding for schools—many of which are now drastically underfunded— better after-school programs for the children whose parents are working during those hours, better housing so parents can better shelter their children, better educational programs for the children, and more jails, more policemen, and more judges to handle the increased crime rate in case all the other social programs don't work. They will need to create better adoption programs, making sure that their fellow Christians do not only adopt healthy white babies, but also babies from other ethnic backgrounds, as well as crack babies, and other babies with mental or physical disabilities. Since the Republicans have never before made these issues priorities, there is no reason to think that they will do so now.

We not only have to be realistic about the consequences; we also have to be realistic about the political situation. Republicans have not had a history of emphasizing or creating social programs that address these issues. In the last few years, the moral code of the Republicans has blinded many a legislator to the reality of the problem. Birth control is not taught to teenagers, because it would be immoral for them to have sex. They have sex anyway, and as a result, there is more AIDS, more of other venereal diseases, and more unwanted pregnancies. Condoms are not given to teenagers, because it would be immoral to use them. As a result, more teenagers have unprotected sex. Are we really serving society by not recognizing what is effective, and what is not? If we are to create a better society that truly handles its problems, we have to be willing to look the problem square in the eye, and decide to do something about it.

Reframing the Argument

Democratic Senator Hillary Clinton tried to change the face of the argument. In 2005, she reached across party lines, believing "people of good faith" can find "common ground in this debate."

She looked for the issues we could all agree on—"increasing women's access to quality health care and reducing unwanted pregnancy. . . . We should all be able to agree that we want every child born in this country and around the world to be wanted, cherished, and loved. The best way to get there is do more to educate the public about reproductive health, about how to prevent unsafe and unwanted pregnancies."[14] She said, "We can all recognize that abortion in many ways represents a sad, even tragic, choice to many, many women." Both Bill Clinton and Hillary Clinton have said abortion should be "safe, legal, and rare." In his article about the speech, Andrew Sullivan says, "Hers is . . . a broadly pro-life position. Not in an absolutist, logically impeccable fashion—which would require abolishing all forms of legal abortion immediately—but in a pragmatic, moral sense. In a free society, the ability of a woman to control what happens to her own body will always and should always be weighed in the balance against the right of an unborn child to life itself."

Sullivan asks, How can we change? "Clinton's approach is the right one. Acknowledge up front the pain of abortion and its moral gravity. Defend its legality only as a terrible compromise necessary for the reduction of abortions in general, for the rights of women to control their own wombs, and for the avoidance of unsafe, amateur abortions. And then move to arenas where liberals need have no qualms: aggressive use of contraception and family planning, expansion and encouragement of adoptions, and a rhetorical embrace of the 'culture of life.'"

When discussing Clinton's speech, Sullivan says, "Clinton did one other thing as well. She paid respect to her opponents. She acknowledged the genuine religious convictions of those who oppose all abortion. She recognized how communities of faith have often been the most successful in persuading young women to refrain from teenage sex. She challenged her pro-choice audience by pointing out 'seven percent of American women who do not use contraception account for fifty-three percent of all unintended pregnancies.' She also cited research estimating that 15,000 abortions per year are by women who have been sexually assaulted—one of the several reasons, she said, that morning-after emergency contraception should be made available over the counter. By focusing on contraception, she appeals to all those who oppose abortion but who do not follow the abstinence-only movement's rigid restriction on the surest way to prevent them."

What was the Republican response to Hillary Clinton's effort to find agreement and reach across party lines? She was rebuffed. Rather than trying to resolve this serious issue, Republicans refused to even discuss it. Many Christian Democrats see this as denial, not effective policymaking to help solve a social problem.

Some Christians are willing to broaden this whole debate about abortion, believing that to be pro-life means, truly, to be pro-life. They look for what they call a consistent life ethic. In 1987, some of these people—Catholics, mainline Protestants, and Evangelicals, as well as interfaith and non-religious members—formed a group originally called the "Seamless Garment," based on John 19:23, which describes Jesus' garment as "seamless, woven in one piece." This group, now called Consistent Life, believes if one is against abortion, and is pro-life, this stance has to be consistent for all life. Most of the group's members are Christian Democrats who see a connection between the Democratic Party's stance of defending the life of the poor and the weak and the logical conclusion they would also defend the life of the unborn child. They see a contradiction between a pro-life statement that defends the life of the unborn, calling it a "culture of life," but then allows policies that result in the death of hundreds of thousands through war, and execution of inmates on death row. The Seamless Garment Network calls this a "most egregious example of Republican double-speak."

Consistent Life sees that a change in thinking is urgently needed, because there is so much violence in our society—increases in the death penalty, violence in the military, structural violence, and the high number of abortions. Its members' stance on life brings together other stands that relate to peace, justice, human rights, and reverence for life.

Democrats for Life

The Democratic Party has started to address these issues, realizing that its rejection of pro-life members is not consistent with the party's ideals of inclusion. Not every Democrat is pro-choice. Not every Republican is pro-life. But the Democrats had not been welcoming to women who were pro-life—until recently. The Democrats for Life of America, which was founded in 1999, recently issued its "95-10" initiative, which includes fifteen different policy programs that set out to reduce the number of abortions in American by 95 percent in ten years. These programs include funding to increase public awareness of alternatives; comprehensive sex education that includes a discussion of abstinence but also includes education about contraception and sexually transmitted diseases; abortion counseling and education for college students; and tax credits for adoption and domestic violence prevention. The group's policies are aimed at helping women as well as protecting unborn children.[15]

Democrats for Life was formed as a response to the extreme positions both parties have taken, which have not been effective at reducing abortions. The Republican Party Platform of 2004 said, "We oppose using public revenues for abortion and will not fund organizations which advocate it. We support the appointment of judges who respect traditional family values and the sanctity of innocent human life." The Democrats' 2004 platform said the party stands "proudly for a woman's right to choose, consistent with *Roe v. Wade*, and regardless of her ability to pay. We stand firmly against Republican efforts to undermine that right."[16] However, neither party platform has been in line with the majority of party members. Most Republicans and Democrats take a middle ground: 60 percent of Democrats would outlaw abortion in some cases; nearly 70 percent of Republicans would allow abortion in some cases.

What is being done to confront this difficult issue? NARAL Pro-Choice America, the leading advocacy group for abortion rights, is trying to help pass a bill called Prevention First, which would increase funding and access to contraceptives and family planning. The bill is supported by Democratic Senator Harry Reid, who opposes abortion rights, and Senator Hillary Clinton, who supports them.

The pro-life approach of Democrats for Life differs from the Republican viewpoint, which endorses abstinence-only programs; such programs have been found to be ineffective, because they withhold information about sex education. Democrats for Life criticize the Republican Party platform on abortion, comparing it to "having a bunch of tin cans tied to your back bumper—it sure makes a lot of noise but is not very pretty and certainly doesn't accomplish much."[17]

They further criticize the Republicans' gag rule that denies U.S. family planning aid to foreign health-care providers. If someone who is working for our government or in the military overseas wants an abortion, even though one would be legal in the United States, that person is not allowed information about where or how to get one.

A new bill, sponsored by Democratic Senator Barbara Boxer and Republican Senator Olympia Snowe, was passed 52–46 to overturn the Global Gag Rule. The consequences of the gag rule have been catastrophic for certain countries. In Kenya, clinics have closed, leaving tens of thousands of poor people without services. In Ethiopia, contraceptive supplies have run out, leaving thousands at risk of sexually transmitted diseases and unwanted pregnancies. In fact, rather than preventing abortions, the Global Gag Rule has made unsafe abortions more likely because contraception is inadequate.

Women who are poor need help in paying for contraceptive services, as well as help in understanding their alternatives. Keeping them ill-informed and misinformed, although it may sound morally right to some, does not help stop unwanted pregnancies.

Although abortion is not risky with women who go to a professional abortion provider, 68,000 women die every year in countries where abortion is illegal. Making abortion illegal does not stop it. In fact, the abortion rate in countries where abortion is illegal, such as Chile, Peru, Nigeria, and the Philippines, is higher than in the United States. Abortion rates are lowest in Western Europe, where abortion is legal and covered by national health insurance, and unwanted pregnancies are fewer.

Belgium has the lowest abortion rate. Abortion is legal, but there is sex education that recommends abstinence, stresses responsibility, and also teaches teens how to use contraception. Belgians recognize that not all teenagers are going to follow abstinence-only programs—so it's imperative they are educated for when they don't.

The Abstinence-Only Approach

The abstinence-only curriculum, which was created as part of the Republican program, was analyzed by Representative Henry A. Waxman. His report found that 80 percent of the curricula contained misleading, false, or distorted information. Abstinence-only programs say condoms are not effective at preventing HIV or STDs, and pregnancy occurs one of every seven times couples use condoms. Not true. The curricula says 5 to 10 percent of women who have legal abortions will become sterile. Not true. Some curricula say life begins at conception, although viable life certainly does not, and Christians and scientists have different viewpoints about when life actually begins. One curriculum called a 43-day-old fetus a "thinking person" which certainly is not true.

Other curricula present stereotypes about males and females, including the stereotypes that girls are weak and need protection and that boys are sexually aggressive.[18] Yet these programs continue to be funded by the Bush administration at a cost of about $170 million per year, and proponents hope to increase the funding.

Studies have shown that these programs do not decrease teenage pregnancy or the risk of sexually transmitted diseases.[19] In fact, by themselves they don't seem to make much difference. If anything, they sometimes cause more problems than they solve, since many who take virginity pledges are less apt to use contraceptives if they do have sex, and are less apt to seek STD testing.

Glenn Stassen, who is a professor of Christian ethics at Fuller Theological Seminary and also a statistician, finds evidence that the number of abortions were lower during the Clinton administration than during George W. Bush's administration. This is the opposite of what would happen if this moral approach were working. When asked for an explanation, Stassen replied there seems to be a direct connection between economic hardship and abortion. Most who abort say they cannot afford the child. Since many of these women have no health coverage, no possibility of child care, and can't afford to give up their jobs to care for themselves while pregnant, or to care for their children, they feel abortion is their only alternative. The economic programs that have hurt the poor and middle class more under Bush are at least partially responsible for this choice.

There are no easy answers here. To stand clearly on one side or another demands we have to ignore some Biblical, moral, ethical, and/or spiritual responses to these issues. Where do we look for answers? We return to compassion, above all—for the woman confronting this most serious dilemma; for the fetus; and for our society, which must find a way through this problem. We do a disservice to everyone when we leave behind any of the people who are involved.

Chapter Five

Homosexuals:
Civil Rights? Civil Unions?

"The Lord said, 'who hath made man's mouth?
Or who maketh the dumb or deaf or the seeing or the blind?
Have not I the Lord?'"

Exodus 4:11

There are millions of homosexuals in the United States of America. Their presence is causing a lot of problems in our society, mainly because some Americans don't want them here. They don't want them near their children, or as their neighbors, or as their friends. They don't want them falling in love, having sex, adopting children, or living together. They don't want them discussing their dreams, desires, or relationships, asking for rights, or voting for legislators who will make their lives better. What are we to do about "those people"?

A Christian friend of mine told me a few years ago that children are hard-wired to need a mother and a father, so that traditional nuclear marriage is very important for raising children. I expect this is true in the United States, although many cultures raise their children through a community made up of mother, aunts, grandmothers, and sometimes the entire village.

If we had our wishes, many of us would agree that it would be a good idea for children to be raised with a loving mother and a loving father. But this is not realistic. Millions of children are raised in one-parent families, either because the mother isn't married, or because of divorce or death of the spouse. Many are raised by relatives, others by homosexual couples. Research has shown that a nontraditional family is no guarantee of failure. Nor is a traditional family a guarantee of wonderful children. We all know children raised in dysfunctional families, with an unloving father and mother. It is a fairy-tale expectation to think that we can find some ideal, correct family dynamic throughout our society. It is impossible to legislate that every child has to have a mother and a father and live in a loving nuclear family.

The definition of family has changed throughout our history. Many people see a family as a bond between or among people. This might be two married people without children (such as my husband and me), or married with children, or unmarried with children, or unmarried but living together, or a group of people living communally.

Similarly, the definition of marriage has changed and expanded. It used to be taken for granted that marriage meant children, and there was tremendous pressure put on a couple without children to fulfill their obligation and have babies. If they didn't have children, they were considered "selfish" or "different" and therefore "wrong." Some people believe that their own choices and the validity of their own marriages are called into question if individuals are all free to go their own way, to find their own love and bliss, whether through being a family with no children, or a same-sex family, or a commune. These people consider those choices dangerous, thinking that too much difference in our society could bring about chaos and a loss of stability. Although there already is plenty of chaos and instability in our society, most of it doesn't seem to come from people living their lives differently than the conventional model.

From various polls, it appears most Americans do not want a constitutional amendment describing what marriage is, although conservative Republicans are still trying to pass one. If they succeed, it would be the second time in our history that the Constitution was amended to legislate individual morality. The first time was the Eighteenth Amendment, which established Prohibition, and that was a failure.

Like abortion, same-sex marriage is a very divisive issue. Most Americans agree that long-term same-sex relationships should have rights that are equal, or near equal, to those of any married couple. Without these laws, same-sex couples can't rightfully make medical decisions for each other. Even if they've been together for decades, they're not allowed to visit each other in the hospital if one of their parents forbids it. If one is dying, the other is not allowed to hold the hand of the dying partner, because the hospitals don't consider them "family." Instead of bringing a family together at a time of tragedy, the hospital has the right to keep people apart.

Without legal protection, same-sex couples can't inherit from each other. Even if their wills are set up to give everything to the partner, the wills can be broken by a parent. These couples aren't eligible for each other's Social Security benefits, even if they've lived together for longer than most married couples.

Gay couples don't have the same rights to health care or shared pension plans that heterosexual couples have. Some school districts don't give the same opportunity to gay teachers that they give to straight teachers.

Many states and cities and corporations have recognized that the current laws are unfair and have incorporated same-sex benefits into their laws. Even religiously conservative Colorado Springs had same-sex benefits for people working for the city, until the new Republican mayor came in and immediately took them away. When one wealthy person volunteered to pay same-sex benefits to all long-term gay couples, the city refused. This has caused suffering for many people.

Homosexuality Is Legal

Sodomy, whether committed by a homosexual male or a heterosexual male, is legal in the United States. The last law against sodomy was overruled by the Supreme Court in 2003.[1] Whether a heterosexual or a homosexual, a man can legally have sex in a way that does not lead to the procreation of children. Since women cannot commit sodomy, whatever lesbians do has never been considered illegal in the United States.

Most sexual acts, whether between homosexuals or heterosexuals, are also legal in the United States, provided they're between consenting adults and usually provided they do not harm others. Democratic countries have generally not been in the habit of looking in the neighbors' bedroom windows to see what they're doing, and then reporting them. Most homosexuals are not promoting their lifestyle or their sexual practices— nor would it do much good. We don't "catch" homosexuality by being near them, and if we are hard-wired as heterosexuals, any sign they put up that says, "Become a homosexual!" won't be very effective.

Homosexuals don't spend all their time involved in homosexual activities. Their lives are about more than just sex. Besides their sexual practices, which they may, or may not, engage in more than heterosexuals, they also take care of children, work, do laundry, watch television, cook, and go to movies, art galleries, and the ballet. When heterosexual people think of homosexuals, they often think only about how much sex gay people are having and how they're doing it, rather than seeing the whole person.

Homosexuality as Identity

It is understandable that many people would have some trouble with the idea of homosexuality. There is deep-seated homophobia within many people. Particularly for heterosexual males, the thought of homosexual relationships is repellent. It seems unnatural to them, and, of course, it is unnatural for most of them. Some of this is based on fear—will a homosexual make a pass at them? Will they be raped by a gay man? There is also fear at the heart of racism and fear at the heart of sexism. Many fear people of another faith or another religion, which has led to anti-Semitic, anti-Islam, and anti-Christian (or anti–Conservative Christian or anti–Liberal Christian) feelings. This fear leads some people to want to forbid any activities they dislike, don't understand, or wouldn't do themselves.

I notice this fear far more in men than in women. I have talked to many heterosexual men who may be tolerant, and who may even be friends with homosexual men, but are emotionally repulsed by the thought of what gay men do. There is something deep-seated about this response, which goes far beyond any belief that Scripture says it's wrong. Some might say this is a natural revulsion to what is offensive to God, but I don't think so. It seems to simply be homophobia, and the reaction I hear from men is much the same as the reaction of some children who learn about sex for the first time. It's the "icky" factor, which contains both disgust and fear, and sometimes fascination.

I don't see this revulsion among women, even women who might believe that homosexuality is morally wrong. When I've talked to heterosexual women about lesbians, they often say, "Well, it's their business" or "I really don't care what women do in the bedroom" or "I guess they're just more attracted to women than men." Some women add, "Considering some of the men I've met, I can understand!" Even those who don't agree with the behavior seem to take it in stride. Some heterosexual men also are not at all repulsed by lesbian sex. In fact, they find it fascinating, and some find it even "chic" to think of women together.

Forbidding homosexuality is not a viable choice. It is estimated that between 3 percent and 10 percent of the population is homosexual.[2] That means millions of Americans, living in this democracy, and hoping for equal rights, have a sexual orientation or a lifestyle that millions of other Americans don't understand.

Although some Christians, such as Focus on the Family, have programs that try to convert homosexuals to a heterosexual lifestyle, there is no proof this works for most people. Those who are bisexual may have a better chance of making choices, but others are not capable of changing. It's simply who they are. One of my lesbian friends said, "Since our society promotes heterosexuality and vilifies homosexuality, if someone could have made us straight, we would be straight. We didn't choose to be homosexuals in a society that doesn't accept us."

Some years ago, I asked a gay friend to explain whether he had ever been attracted to a woman. He told me he believed that our sexual responses are on a continuum. There are some people who are on one end, such as he was. He said he is a "totally gay man." He had never been attracted to women, although he could be friends with them. Other people seem to be totally heterosexual (think James Bond!), always attracted to someone from the opposite sex, and never attracted to someone of the same sex. For neither of these groups is there any choice.

Others fall somewhere in between. They might be people who had homosexual feelings at times, perhaps during puberty, but chose not to pursue them and were happy heterosexuals as adults. Others married, and realized they were deeply unhappy because they were gay, and had not been willing to admit it. They were tired of living a lie, and found that only by choosing who they truly were could they be authentic people. Others were bisexual and found they could choose. At different times in their lives, they pursued relationships with the opposite sex. At other times, they chose someone from the same sex. For some, their time pursuing homosexual relationships filled them with a deep sense of guilt and estrangement. For others, it brought a sense of freedom and even stability if they fell in love. For some bisexuals, the choice of partners depended on their attraction. They found the spirit and personality of the person more compelling than the gender.

For many homosexuals, denying their attraction means denying their integrity and authenticity as human beings. Pretending to be someone they are not seems to them to be a spiritual offense. Some of them have told me that after much struggle, they came to believe that God made them that way. Just as some people are born blind or deaf, they were born as homosexuals.

We don't know why some people are homosexuals. The Lord says that we are not to question why we are made a certain way. In Exodus 4:11, the Lord says, "Who makes a person dumb or deaf, gives sight or makes blind? Is it not I, Yahweh?" In Isaiah, the Lord says, "Does the clay say to its potter, 'What are you doing? Your work has no hands!' . . . It is I who made the earth and I created human beings on it."[3] Romans says, "Something that was made, can it say to its maker: why did you make me this shape? A potter surely has the right over his clay to make out of the same lump either a pot for special use or one for ordinary use."[4]

Why are some people created as gay, and others as straight? Why do some report they have no attraction to the opposite sex, and never have? Why do some say they knew, from an early age, that they were different, and wondered why God had created them that way? Is it possible God made them this way for a reason? Or are they the rejects? If they're rejects, why is God making junk?

There are heterosexuals who accept homosexuals provided they're not practicing homosexuals. In this view, as many as 10 percent of the population should never allow themselves to be intimate, never love and commit to one other person, never experience the joys of sexuality, never accept their true identity, and never find the fulfillment others find with another human, just because they were born "different."

Scriptural Texts and Homosexuality

Many Christians are unclear what to think about this difficult subject. Others say the Bible is very clear about homosexuality and therefore they feel they must do something about it. There are Scriptural verses that seem to be against homosexuality, and there are some that seem to take no stand. There are still others that seem to support loving bonds, even between two people of the same sex.

What does Jesus have to say about homosexuality? Nothing. What does Jesus have to say about same-sex marriages? Nothing. What does Paul have to say about same-sex marriages? Nothing. There is no mention of homosexuality in the Ten Commandments. No prophet discusses it. It's not found in the Gospels, although it certainly existed in Biblical times. There is no mention anywhere in the Bible of committed homosexual relationships. There is no mention of lesbianism.

There are, however, verses referring to homosexual acts between men that can be found in both the Hebrew Scriptures and the New Testament.

The lack of verses leads both conservatives and liberals to interpret the Biblical stance about homosexual relationships in the light of other verses. More conservative Christians will interpret the stance of Jesus and Paul as being pro-marriage, since they mention the bonds between husband and wife, thereby implying they are for heterosexual marriage and against homosexual unions. To do this, these Christians have to overlook the fact that neither Jesus nor Paul was ever married.

Liberals look at other verses about love and marriage and see the Bible as affirming loving and committed relationships, even when unconventional.

During the course of writing this book, I have read innumerable interpretations of both sides of the issue. Personally, I am not convinced by either stance. The conservatives, such as Focus on the Family, have to interpret a number of verses out of context, or by reading into the Bible and saying that something is "Gospel Truth" when it isn't. Their interpretations don't look at the overall historical context of the time, nor do they involve much deep study about the origins of certain words used in the Bible.

More liberal interpreters are more apt to look at the specific words, and how they were used in Biblical times, and at the context of the times, but they still can find no proof that the Bible is in favor of homosexuals. They tend to make sweeping generalizations, although they are more apt to admit they are still struggling with the issues. What seems so clear to people of both sides always demands some interpretation.

Personally, I don't believe there are clear Biblical answers about this. I do believe it is worth struggling with, however, and that there are some spiritual answers conservative and moderate and liberal Christians can agree on.

What does the Bible say about homosexuality? The texts most often cited (which I will quote in full later) are Genesis 19, Leviticus 18 and 20, Romans 1, 1 Corinthians 6, and 1 Timothy 1:10. Out of the entire Bible, there are fewer than ten verses about this subject. Most of these are ambiguous, and some don't even mention homosexuality specifically, but talk in general about degrading sexual practices. Compare these to the dozens, or hundreds, of verses about money, about oppression, about how a king should rule, about incest, about hypocrisy, about quarreling. In fact, if you look up the word "homosexual" in a concordance, chances are you'll only find one verse—1 Corinthians 6:9. Because I was writing *Jesus Rode a Donkey*, I also checked to see how many references there are to donkeys—about 200. There has been an unbalanced amount of discussion about what people think is in the Bible, but isn't.

The Hebrew Scriptures

When Christians try to understand the meaning of certain Biblical texts, they take various approaches. I once asked a fundamentalist what she thought about homosexuality and she answered,

"I don't know. I have to ask my minister." Fundamentalists usually will turn to the authority of the Bible or the preacher to learn what a proper response should be. They will take the Bible literally, at face value. If there are contradictions, they try to square them up in some way, which sometimes works and sometimes doesn't. They generally will not study the context or the derivation of the word or put it into an overall Biblical theology.

Others, however, will study the text. They will do this by looking at the original meaning of the word and then looking at the context of the times. Although many think liberals tend to be too contextual in their analysis and conservatives tend to be too literal, every Christian picks and chooses verses to create an interpretation, particularly when the interpretation is ambiguous. None of us are perfect in our interpretation.

Focus on the Family begins its analysis of homosexuality by looking at Genesis 1 and 2, which define us as male and female, created in the image of God. We are asked to be fruitful and multiply. The organization's reasoning says that because we are made as male and female, we are asked to have sexual relations with each other and to have children to propagate the human race. Homosexuals don't procreate; therefore, homosexuals are not fulfilling the natural order and the command of creation.

Genesis 1 and 2 say nothing about other types of relationships that don't procreate but are recognized in the Bible—married without children, friendships, being single, being celibate—but yet we don't condemn these.

In a recent panel discussion about gay marriage between members of Focus on the Family and proponents of gay marriage, Focus on the Family spokesperson Glenn Stanton said marriage was the "biggest something" in God's plan, and that we are called to have sexual relationships between a man and a woman and called to be fruitful and multiply. He has five children. I can understand why he would be proud of following this command. However, I have no children, and neither do many of my friends. My ninety-year-old uncle, who married for the third time in 2004, is not expecting to have any with his beautiful eighty-something wife. If we all thought marriage was solely for procreation, it would deny the loving bonds many of us have with our spouses, whether we have children or not. If we take this argument to its logical conclusion, we can see that neither Jesus nor Paul were following God's commandment.

Most churches recognize that marriage is not just for procreation. The Catholic Church marries those who are infertile, and those who are past childbearing age. The Anglican Church, at the Ninth Lambeth Conference in 1958, passed a resolution that says "sexual intercourse is not by any means the only language of earthly love . . . it is a giving and receiving in the unity of two free spirits which is in itself good . . . Therefore it is utterly wrong to say that . . . such intercourse ought not be engaged in except with the willing intention of children."[5] If we interpret sexuality as being purely for procreation, it leads to the overpopulation that we now have, and which most Christians are doing little to "fix," either environmentally or socially.

Stanton also said "Adam wasn't complete without Eve."[6] Is this really how we experience our identity—only when we're in partnership are we complete? Of course, Adam and Eve needed each other to have children, but that doesn't say anything about our completion as human beings, in and of ourselves. Are we to believe that God did not make us complete in ourselves, that we cannot be complete human beings before God as widows and widowers, as nuns, priests, as single people? Although these Genesis verses are cited in discussions about homosexuality, they really say nothing about the issue.

The first reference to homosexuality occurs in the story of Lot found in Genesis 19. When angels came to Lot's town of Sodom, Lot welcomed them to his home. The men of the town gathered outside his home and asked him to give them the angels so they could "know" them, which is usually interpreted as having sexual relations with them. Lot didn't want to be inhospitable by throwing out the angels, so he offered his two daughters as a consolation prize. The Bible says nothing about whether his behavior toward his daughters was right or wrong, but the angels intervened, telling Lot that God was going to destroy Sodom and that he should take his family and escape. Lot and his daughters made it to a cave in the mountains, although the daughters' fiancés refused to leave. The daughters then made their father drunk, had sex with him, and got pregnant, presumably in order to preserve the family line. It is a strange justification for incest, but it's one more example of all the bad sex surrounding the story of Lot and his family.

If we look more closely at this passage, Lot doesn't mention their sexual behavior, but instead tells these men not to insult his guests. These men were seeking to violate the sanctuary of his roof.[7] Gray Temple writes that "Traditional Jewish interpretations of that chapter grasped the principle better than we do: the Sodomites were first and foremost inhospitable; they thought it good sport to humiliate foreign guests."[8]

Ezekiel 16:49–50 says that God destroyed Sodom (and Gomorrah) for their sins of arrogance, decadence, and complacency. ("Behold, this was the iniquity of the sister Sodom, pride, fullness of bread, and abundance of idleness was in her and in her daughters, neither did she strengthen the hand of the poor and needy.") The Book of Ecclesiasticus and the Book of Wisdom (both found in the Catholic Bible but not in the Protestant Bible) also mention pride as the sin of Sodom, because the Sodomites did not help the poor and the needy. Jesus implied that the sin of Sodom was inhospitality, which was why it was destroyed.[9]

The sins of Sodom were many. The story in Genesis 19 is not about any kind of normal sexual behavior; it is about gang rape. Whether performed by homosexuals or heterosexuals, this does not establish any kind of normative sexuality. Just as we wouldn't turn to these stories to tell us about heterosexual love, we have no reason to turn to them to understand homosexual love. Since other books of the Bible interpret this story and never mention homosexuality, the story seems to be about gang rape, incest, inhospitality, and degradation.

The strongest language about homosexuality comes from Leviticus 18 and 20, which are part of the section of Leviticus called the Holiness Code or Holiness Laws. The verses usually cited are from Leviticus 18:22, which says, "You shall not lie with a male as with a woman: it is an abomination," and from Leviticus 20, which says, "If a man lies with a male as with a woman, both of them have committed an abomination. They shall be put to death; their blood is upon them."

This seems to be very clear—homosexuality is wrong! In fact, it seems to say this is so wrong that all homosexuals should

be executed. If we look at other laws within this section of
Leviticus, we can see that people who commit other abomina-
tions also are to be put to death: children who curse their parents,[10] people who worship idols,[11] adulterers,[12] and those who
practice bestiality.[13]

In addition to these laws, there are a number of other laws
in Leviticus forbidding certain practices, such as the inbreeding
of cattle, sowing fields with two kinds of seed, wearing garments
made of two different materials, and harvesting fruit trees in under
five years. Round haircuts and tattoos are forbidden. Having sexual relations during a woman's menstrual cycle is forbidden.

One can take these verses at face value. Even then, we pick
and choose which verses we'll follow, because few of us believe
that adulterers should be put to death, partly because a number
of well-known Christians would now be dead. Few Christians
would suggest we kill our children if they curse us (although
some might want to!), and most of us wear garments made of
different fabrics.

So if we don't follow the letter of the law of most of these
codes, how can we interpret them? Theologians look carefully
at the historical context and the specific words to understand
why these laws were written and why these practices were an
abomination to God.

The Ancient Holiness Codes

The Holiness Codes were established when the Israelites entered
the land of Canaan, where Canaanites worshipped the god

Molech. God was establishing a new nation within a country where other laws and practices prevailed. Peter Gomes, a minister at The Memorial Church in Cambridge, Massachusetts, Plummer Professor of Christian Morals at Harvard College, and a gay Republican, analyzes these passages.

He says these rules were designed for "nation building; their setting is the entry into a promised but very foreign land. These are fundamental laws for the formation of a frontier community."[14] These laws were used for "cultural identity, protection, and procreation."[15] Any behavior that did not lead to populating the country was outlawed. Homosexual behavior did not lead to procreation. In a frontier community, it was imperative that there be many children born, to be raised up to create a new nation.

The word "abomination" is a very strong word. In Leviticus, abomination, or *toyevah*, has more to do with disgust and revulsion than with morality. It is against what the Gentiles do, and therefore is ritually impure, much like eating pork.[16]

Dr. Gary Rendberg, who holds the Endowed Chair in Jewish History at Rutgers University, and is an expert in the Bible and ancient Semitic languages, says, "There is no doubt in my mind that homosexuality is totally forbidden in these passages. However, these passages reflect the mores of 3,000 years ago. I do keep some of these laws. I still observe the Sabbath, I still keep kosher, but I don't stone my children if they curse me, and I don't own slaves. What always strikes me as a Jew looking at Christian opposition to homosexuality, [is] if Christians were so interested in upholding the laws of the Torah, why aren't Christians observing the dietary laws, and Sabbath on the seventh day? [There are] all sorts of ritual laws Christians won't observe, so why are they so concerned about this one? I don't think we should stone someone for collecting wood on the Sabbath. I don't believe that men should inherit and not women, unless there are no men in the family."[17]

We don't follow most of the other Holiness Codes set forth in Leviticus that tell us how to act. Although these Codes include prohibitions that we still follow—against rape, incest, adultery, necrophilia, and bestiality—they also prohibit celibacy, nudity, and birth control. Yet, we don't follow most of the Codes. Men trim their beards, even though Leviticus tells them not to. Women wear male clothing, such as jeans and slacks, even though they're told not to.[18] We ignore certain passages, deciding they no longer apply, and follow others. In ignoring certain passages, we don't dig deeper into why there are certain prohibitions. What was the context of the day that relates to mixing fibers? What kind of sexuality was prohibited, and why?

There are many interpretations of these Codes. There are some scholars who say homosexuality is against the established hierarchy between men and women because sexual relations between men reduce one of the males to a passive position. In the context of the times, it was important to keep the hierarchy intact.

Sexuality as Power

To better understand these passages, some scholars look at how sexual relationships functioned in earlier societies. Until 1869, the idea of homosexuality and heterosexuality did not exist as we think of it today. Sexuality was defined as power relationships, and what was clearly "wrong" was for someone to be used or manipulated by a stronger person.

Many sources emphasized that sex was about power and the natural hierarchy. For men to engage in homosexual practices meant one of the two men had to be in the weak, passive position. This was not "manly" and was an affront to male identity.

Sometimes the passive partner was a young boy who was often abused by an older man for his own sexual pleasure. This was a fairly common practice in Greece, Rome, and Canaan. The Israelites had laws against it for several reasons. First of all, there was an imbalance of power and lack of mutuality in these relationships. Second, the Jews were new to the land of Canaan. They were forming a cultural identity that was different from, and even in opposition to, the identity of Canaanites. Since homosexuality was more a common practice in Canaan, the Jews differentiated themselves from the Canaanites' sexual practices, as well as from their practices of idolatry, their dietary laws, and so on.

Other scholars look at how sexual identity is defined. "The human race used to divide itself into gender identities of 'strong' and 'weak,' not 'queer' and 'straight.'"[19] In the ancient cultures of Greece, Rome, Egypt, Sumer, Babylon, and throughout the eastern Mediterranean, there were no words for homosexuality, homosexual, heterosexuality, or heterosexual.[20] They had specific words for specific acts, but not general words for general concepts.[21] The crime was not homosexuality. It was always something else.[22]

Positive Verses about Same-Sex Orientation

Notice, in the Hebrew Scriptures, that nothing is said about lesbians. If one believes these verses are adamantly against homosexuals, it might be thought that lesbians are not mentioned because none existed during that time. But there clearly were lesbians at that time. They can be found in the erotic poetry of Sappho of the island of Lesbos as well as in various paintings. Some interpret these verses and believe lesbianism is implied by the prohibitions against male sexual behavior. But there is absolutely nothing in any of these verses suggesting this.

Those who believe that the Bible does not condemn same-sex relationships look to the story of David and Jonathan from 1 Samuel 18–20 and 2 Samuel 1. The Bible says Jonathan "loved him [David] like his very self."[23] "They made a covenant with each other."[24] "And Jonathan stripped himself of the robe that was upon him, and gave it to David, and his garments, even to his sword, and to his bow, and to his girdle."[25] David and Jonathan took great delight in each other and kissed each other.[26] David says to Jonathan, "Greatly beloved were you to me; your love to me was wonderful, passing the love of women."[27]

Any discussion and interpretation of these passage leads to huge debates and great fervor on either side. I was told by one scholar I consulted to leave this passage alone, because it will just bring about fire and brimstone. But if we are to struggle with other Hebrew Scriptures passages related to this subject, we definitely have to struggle with this one.

Focus on the Family sees this as a strong friendship, and says that revisionists try to interpret it as having a sexual component and that this is "morally wrong." However, there is nothing to revise here. There is only interpretation. What are we to make of one man recognizing that his love for another man surpasses his love for women? We don't know what this means in its Biblical context. We do know this is what a homosexual says to another homosexual. A Focus on the Family pamphlet says that these words can often be said between close friends, which may be true. But in the case of David and Jonathan, it's impossible to know what is meant. None of us have peered into the tent to see what David and Jonathan were doing to express their love for each other. We haven't followed them up to the hillside to see what they were doing. We can interpret, but it's impossible to know which interpretation is accurate.

Focus on the Family says there is no sexual meaning in the original Hebrew words for "being fond of" or "joy of the heart." Certainly the connotation of words needs to be taken into consideration when forming an interpretation. The organization sees the passage as being about deep friendship. Since the verses do not say David and Jonathan became one flesh, as in marriage, Focus on the Family comes to the conclusion that David and Jonathan didn't have a sexual relationship. But you can't create an interpretation through a negative. We can only interpret from what is here, and there is nothing said, one way or another, about what exactly transpired between them. We do know they kissed each other. Kisses are exchanged in friendship, and they are exchanged in sexual relationships. Nothing is said about what kind of kiss this was. We do know that the Bible makes no condemnation of the covenant they made between them, the kisses they exchanged, or the fact that they loved each other more than they loved someone of the opposite sex.

We do know that both Jonathan and David were married to women, and David had other sexual relationships with women besides with his wife. But we also know that his love for Jonathan surpassed these other relationships.

However we interpret these passages—as being about same-sex homosexual love, or about same-sex friendship that is greater than heterosexual love—we know that the Bible does not condemn this same-sex relationship. The Bible recognizes the strength of this loving bond between two people of the same sex.

The New Testament

What about the New Testament passages? As Christians, some would say we need to take them even more seriously. As with the Hebrew Scriptures, there are only a few passages mentioning homosexual acts.

In 1 Timothy there is a list of sins: "Those who kill their father or mother, or murderers, fornicators, sodomites, slave traders, liars, perjurers, whatever else is contrary to the sound teaching that conforms to the glorious Gospel."

Notice, nothing specifically here is said about homosexuals, and certainly nothing here is said about lesbians, although the word "sodomites" is thought to be referring to homosexuals (not recognizing that some heterosexuals also commit sodomy and lesbians are unable to commit sodomy). However, the Greek word for "sodomites" does not clearly refer to homosexuals. It's a rare term, and is thought to refer to a man who uses male prostitutes or a man who has sex with boys.[28]

The word in the original text for "male prostitutes" means "soft." As Catherine Griffith writes in an article on the Bible and same-sex relationships: "Biblical scholars say that the word in ancient texts referred to luxurious clothing, rich and delicate food, a gentle breeze, or was used to condemn immorality and faults associated with effeminacy, such as being weak, lazy, lustful, decadent, or cowardly. It had no relation to the sex of a man's preferred sexual partner, but more to a kind of soft decadence."[29]

In 1 Corinthians 6, Paul has a similar list: fornicators, idolaters, adulterers, male prostitutes (although nothing is said about female prostitutes), sodomites, thieves, the greedy, drunkards, revilers, robbers. In the King James version, the list includes "the effeminate, and abusers of themselves with mankind, and extortioners."[30]

For male prostitutes, Paul uses the word *malakoi* (from the original Greek) or *arsenokoitai*, which is translated as "sodomites." *Malakoi* means "soft, overripe, or squishy." It may not even refer to male sexual behavior at all, but to one who was "soft" on self-control.[31] The term *arsenokoitai* is only used twice in the New Testament and never in the Hebrew Scriptures, although the translation uses the same word as is used in Leviticus—sodomites. There is no clear translation of this word, although it was used later by Hippolytus to refer to a man who sleeps with boys. Author Robin Scroggs, in *The New Testament and Homosexuality*, suggests it might refer to "a young man who inveigles himself into the erotic affections of an elderly man in order to get included in his will and abscond with his estate."[32]

In Romans 1:18–32, Paul talks about sexual degradations and unnatural acts, saying "Their women exchanged natural intercourse *(chresis)* for unnatural *(para physin)* . . . and in the same way also the men, giving up natural *(physiken)* intercourse *(chresis)* with women, were consumed *(exekauthesan)* with passion *(orexis)* for one another. Men committed shameless acts with men and received in their own persons the due penalty for their error."[33]

In this chapter, Paul uses the word *chresis*, which is sometimes translated as "intercourse," though it actually is a term meaning "usage" that "referred primarily to food and sex."[34] It was not a term that implied relationship or mutuality; it was about exploiting another for one's own purposes. Paul, and many of us, oppose one person using another.

Notice, also, that there is nothing said about sexual behavior between two females.

Looking carefully at this passage, one can understand how it got misinterpreted, because we presume that women's "unnatural" acts means unnatural acts with each other. But a more careful reading of this passage shows that nothing is said about women with women; it only mentions women exchanging natural relations for those that are unnatural.

The focus is on the word "unnatural." According to Paul, "nature" has more to do with what is expected or accepted than what is morally wrong. What were women's unnatural acts? For a woman to be aggressive in sex was unnatural. For a woman to be flirtatious, or to mount the man, was unnatural.[35]

Homosexuality was not as natural among Jews as it was among Greeks and Romans. What was wrong, according to the Jewish code, was the domination of one sexual partner by another, in many cases men exploiting boys, or men put in a weaker position. The Jews objected to pedophilia, but the objects were never girls; they were upper-class boys subjected to the humiliation of someone in power using them.[36]

Sexuality was also unnatural if men were swept away by passion and lost their rationality. Their lust showed their weakness. Moderation was the best standard.

The word for "unnatural" is used in this section to discuss other issues that are not "natural," but not morally wrong. It's the same word used by Paul in 11:24 to clarify God's unnatural action when he "engrafted Gentiles onto the Jewish olive tree." According to 1 Corinthians 11:2–16 long hair for women and short hair for men are natural, so if a woman has short hair (like me), it is unnatural but (I hope) not morally wrong.

Unnatural sex might be unequal sex, since the cultural norm of the Christian era meant one partner was active and one passive, so anything but the missionary position would be considered unnatural. (For many years, some Christians believed that was true. Perhaps some still do!)

The more important thing about this chapter from Corinthians is the way Paul phrases his argument. Paul focuses on many ways we dishonor God—through passions out of control, by "injustice, rottenness, greed and malice . . . envy, murder, wrangling, treachery and spite," libeling, slandering, rudeness, arrogance, boastfulness; by being "enterprising in evil, rebellious to parents, without brains, honor, love, or pity." According to Paul, people guilty of any of these things deserve to die. Considering how many different sins are given, that means us too!

Then, just as Paul makes sure we're all included in his long list of sins, he adds one more—judgment. "It is yourself that you condemn when you judge others, since you behave in the same way as those you are condemning. . . . do you think you will escape God's condemnation?"[37]

Paul makes two important points with this argument. First, he lets readers know they should not judge, because they do the same thing. He's not concerned about prohibiting lustful homosexuality, which is just a symptom of a larger problem. Instead, he prohibits judgment. This same idea is repeated in many Bible verses—"Judge not," "Do not judge that you be not judged," "There is only one Lawgiver and one judge."[38] The "same ways" refers not to homosexuality, but rather to ingratitude to God and intemperate passions such as greed and lust.

Paul then finishes the letter to the Romans by admonishing his readers not to pass judgment on others, "but resolve instead never to put a stumbling block or hindrance in the way of another. I know and am persuaded through the Lord Jesus that nothing is unclean in itself; but it is unclean for anyone who thinks it unclean."

These verses from Romans are not a description of a healthy sexual relationship, but of sex that uses another person.

Paul saw the problem of homosexuality as being about lust, avarice, passions out of control. Most of us would agree. When we read about the bathhouses of San Francisco, which had a great deal to do with the AIDS epidemic, we can recognize that such behavior is wrong, and leads to great harm to individuals and society. When we read about, or take part in, any sexual behavior that uses another person, we know what sexual behavior that's degrading can do to the human spirit.

If we look carefully at all of these passages, we notice that of these references, most are not truly about homosexuality. Some that are used by various groups to show the anti-homosexuality of the Bible are actually about marriage, such as Genesis 1 and 2. Most of the other ones are in a list of degrading sexual behaviors, such as gang rape, that would be condemned whether it's done by heterosexuals or homosexuals. Probably most of us can agree there are degrading and abusive sexual acts—rape, incest, pedophilia, and sex trafficking, where women are sold into prostitution. Yet we don't condemn heterosexuality because some of it is degrading.

Other passages, such as the one in Romans, are actually an argument that ends up condemning the act of being judgmental. It seems that Leviticus 18 and 20 are the only two passages that seem fairly blatant in their condemnation, and even these need to be read in the context of the time. These passages do not clearly state whether all homosexual behavior is condemned, or only that which is degrading. To interpret these passages as condemning all homosexual behavior means we have to decide that these passages say something not clearly stated.

Notice also that none of these passages are about homosexual identity. The idea of homosexual identity was foreign to those in both the Hebrew Scriptures and the New Testament. Almost all of these verses refer to the "debauched pagan expression" of homosexuality.[39] If you know homosexuals in long-term loving relationships, you know from your experience that these lists of immoral behaviors are not referring to them. Reverend Gray Temple says in *Gay Unions*, "Those who insist that our gay sisters and brothers in the church are . . . impure or debased, or that they are uniquely prone to the actual sins that Paul just described, have simply not bothered to get to know their fellow Christians."[40]

A Consistent Christian Response to Homosexuality

Regardless of the interpretation of these various passages, there is one consistent response that comes from the churches—to love and respect the Other. We see this in the way Jesus related to women, to prostitutes, to tax collectors, to those who were different and on the fringes of society. Focus on the Family calls it a response of "compassionate love, gentle truth and authentic humility."[41] "Loving someone means . . . caring for them and extending the love of Christ."[42] For Focus on the Family, this means loving them whether or not they change and become heterosexuals. They add that it also means speaking the truth. And the truth varies among Christians and particular denominations.

With most churches, hate crimes are not acceptable Christian behavior. Humiliation and rejection are not acceptable responses to homosexuals.

Colorado Springs, the center of conservative Christianity, is also the number two city in Colorado for hate crimes. Many of these crimes are against homosexuals. Gays have often found this city to be inhospitable to them because there is so much anti-gay rhetoric from the churches. Regardless of Biblical interpretations, it would be good for Christians to make their love better known than their condemnation.

Other churches take various stances on homosexuality. The Evangelical Lutheran Church in America receives into membership all who profess faith in Christ, regardless of sexual orientation.[43] The American Presbyterian Church welcomes gays and lesbians as members, although as in the Lutheran Church, they cannot be elected to church office as an elder, a deacon, or a minister.[44]

Other churches, such as the United Church of Christ, the Metropolitan Church, and the Episcopal Church, do ordain gays. The Episcopal Church, amid great controversy, now has an openly gay bishop who is in a long-term gay relationship. The United Methodist Church had defrocked an openly gay lesbian minister, but changed its vote and restored her ministry credentials.[45]

Some churches perform gay marriages. The Metropolitan Community Churches have an explicit ministry to gays. The United Church of Christ and the Society of Friends decide, on an individual basis within each church, whether they will perform gay marriages.

Most, and perhaps all, Christian churches do ordain gay men and women, as long as the church does not know that they're gay. Notice the Catholic scandal about child abuse by priests. It almost always involves boys rather than girls. We are naive if we think churches do not have gay ministers and priests. From my own limited experience, I have known at least three women married to Protestant ministers who later learned their husbands were gay. The men hoped a marriage would, somehow, "cure" them, and then realized they were not living an authentic life and could no longer hide their sexual orientation. Divorce, and usually leaving the church, followed soon after.

From my years attending an interdenominational seminary, I knew several gay priests, some of them practicing homosexuals. My friends at the Catholic seminary down the road from my seminary told me this was not unusual. In fact, it is estimated that 10 to 50 percent of Catholic priests are gay. The Catholic Church is now trying to take the gays out of the priesthood, which means that gay priests have several alternatives—all of which raise ethical considerations. They can deny their homosexuality, thereby denying who they are; they can leave the priesthood, thereby denying their understanding of their calling to serve God through this ministry; or they can "out" each other, thereby betraying each other. The Catholic Church, which already lacks enough priests to serve all its parishes, will have to decide what to do when 10 to 50 percent of its priests, many of them kind, compassionate, and loving people who minister well to others, suddenly are no longer there.

If we try to make social policy based on a few verses, which are interpreted differently depending on the view of the Christian reading them, the research, the knowledge of the original Hebrew, and the knowledge of the historical context, we may, in the process, be doing great harm to millions of Americans. Many Christians say they truly love the homosexual. I have not yet figured out how to love people while condemning their lifestyle, judging their relationships, and being able to accept them only if they become different, and in the process, compromise their authenticity. Although many Christians say they love the sinner but not the sin, gays often attest to the fact that they don't feel loved, only condemned, regardless of whether the judgment comes with a hug or not.

A Spiritual Approach to Homosexuality

Sometimes, when the Biblical verses are not clear, a Christian might turn to other forms of spirituality rather than to Bible verses to look for answers.

Many Christians believe in ongoing revelation. They believe that the Holy Spirit continues to lead us. Discerning the work of the Spirit is, of course, not a sure-fire thing, but then interpreting a Bible passage is not a sure-fire thing either.

If a Christian slave owner were trying to discern a Christian response to slavery, he might begin by looking at the Bible and noticing that it seems to condone slavery. Owning another person seems to be part of an accepted social structure in both the Hebrew Scriptures and the New Testament. He might reflect on the meaning of that kind of control over another. He might pray about it. He might realize that it doesn't "feel" right. He might talk to slaves, or other slave owners. He might notice mistreatment of slaves by other slave owners and recognize this as immoral and uncaring. He might first decide that owning slaves is fine for him because he treats them well, but then decide his stance toward owning slaves is wrong. He frees them, and in retrospect, believes he made the right decision.

A spiritual approach to homosexuality might take the same course. One might begin by studying the Bible verses. The person might talk to a variety of homosexuals, asking questions, visiting a church where there are openly gay men and women, talking to ministers and priests. He might observe gay relationships. Or he might follow the example of Jesus, who dined with prostitutes and tax collectors and people considered "sinners" and let the Holy Spirit lead him to discern what he is to think and believe and feel about this situation. Of course, the dinner party won't be a success if one half of the table is judging the other half.

Christians might reflect on what it means to be an authentic human being, without denying flaws, but also without denying how one has been created. They might try to figure out how to treat someone who is "born that way."

They might then think about how they, who are in loving, intimate relationships, can ever deny intimacy to others. They might think about how they wouldn't deny loving partnerships to those who are blind, deaf, or disabled. Can they, in all good conscience, legislate that others are not allowed to ever have the joys of closeness and partnership?

They might meditate on the injustices the gay person encounters, sometimes daily, and on how they would feel if those same injustices happened to them.

They might, purposefully, seek out homosexuals and begin asking questions, to better understand their situation, and to better understand that these people are neighbors who cannot be ignored.

I have a number of gay friends, most of them in long-term relationships, some of them married, either through a church, or through a ceremony of commitment. I never sought them out. I didn't have to, since my normal course of living brought me in contact with a number of gays and lesbians. Our paths crossed, and in a number of cases friendships developed, perhaps because there was no judgment either way. I attended the marriage of one such friend, and talked to another both before, and after, he got married. The profound joy and love that I witness makes it impossible for me to condemn them, because my judgment would go against everything I've learned about spirituality. There is simply too much care and beauty around their relationships. I find the authenticity, wisdom, compassion, and kindness of several of these friends so profound that my spiritual life has been immeasurably enriched by knowing them.

A Democratic Party Approach to Homosexuality

The Bible is silent about homosexuality as identity and about committed homosexual relationships. We can't form national policy based on our own religious interpretations of the Bible. If a democracy is to protect its citizens, what rights do homosexuals have, and what does the Constitution say about equal rights?

The Declaration of Independence and the Constitution specifically state that we will not form national policy or behavior based on our own religion's interpretations of the Bible. There is a consistent movement, through two centuries of amendments to the Constitution, toward equality for all of our citizens. First the Constitution granted equality to propertied males; then to black men; then to women.

Gay marriage is not mentioned in either the Democratic or Republican platform. Democrats do, however, see this issue as a civil rights and states' rights issue. This doesn't mean they support gay marriages, although some of them do, just as some Republicans do. But Democrats are more apt to support civil unions in order to grant equal rights to homosexuals. John Kerry supported civil unions, and believes that people in long-term relationships should have the same rights as married people in a relationship. This means they should have the right to inherit from each other; the right to be at the partner's bedside in the hospital; the right to the same financial benefits that exist in committed heterosexual partnerships.

According to two different polling firms, the Democratic Peter D. Hart Research Associates and the Republican firm American Viewpoint, about 63 percent of Americans support the same rights and protections for homosexuals as for other Americans. According to another poll from the *Wall Street Journal* and NBC News, 53 percent of Americans would allow gay and lesbian couples to enter into legal agreements with each other that are not marriages but would give them the same legal and financial rights that married couples have. And about 50 percent of registered voters would support granting civil marriage licenses to gay and lesbian couples.[46]

Other polls come up with other numbers, ranging from about 45 percent against a marriage amendment to about 60 percent in favor of some sort of legal recognition for same-sex couples. One poll, from the Pew Forum, says that support for giving homosexuals the same rights as other Americans has grown even among evangelical Protestants, from 35 percent to 45 percent since 1992.[47]

Many Democrats favor civil rights for homosexuals because they recognize that the sexual identity of a homosexual is not something chosen, but rather an authentic part of the person's life.

The question of authentic identity is a complex one. During the debates, both John Kerry and George W. Bush were asked about same-sex marriage and whether they thought homosexuality was an intrinsic part of one's identity or a choice. Mr. Kerry spoke candidly, accurately, and with compassion about homosexuality. He said he believed that homosexuals, for the most part, are simply being true to their identity.

Mr. Bush said he didn't know whether it was a choice or not, but then affirmed his support for a constitutional marriage amendment. I found his answer very puzzling, because his vice president's daughter is a lesbian. If Mr. Bush were going to support a constitutional amendment adversely affecting millions of people's lives, why wouldn't he first talk to a few gay people, particularly Mary Cheney? I was amazed that there was no desire or effort on his part to find out anything about homosexual choices. He seemed to have no curiosity about the millions of people asking for equal rights under his government.

What about Marriage?

Republicans want a new constitutional amendment, one that defines what marriage is, to ensure that gays can't marry or enjoy the same rights that heterosexual couples have. Of course, a marriage amendment won't keep gays from marrying. Marriage is a sacred ritual that any church can perform, with or without the consent of the state. However, the marriage amendment would have negative consequences for homosexual relationships. Since limiting love and increasing distress does not seem to serve society, the amendment also could have negative consequences for society.

The Democrats emphasize that marriage is a states' rights issue. Each state has the right to define marriage, and it is the states that issue marriage licenses.

Most of the decisions in states that allow gay marriage are driven by the courts. When a gay couple confronts the court, believing that their constitutional rights are taken away because they don't have equal rights under the law, the courts respond, sometimes by allowing gay marriages. Sometimes the people respond by passing an amendment to the state constitution that defines marriage as being between a man and a woman. States have the right to respond either way. By the end of 2005, nineteen states had passed amendments recognizing marriage as being between a man and a woman and forbidding gay marriage. Connecticut and Vermont allow civil unions and give same-sex couples the same rights as straight couples. Massachusetts allows gay couples to marry. California and Hawaii are still struggling with this issue.

Other countries around the world allow gay marriages, including Belgium, Canada, Spain, and the Netherlands, and others allow civil unions, including Britain, Denmark, Finland, France Germany, Norway, Sweden, and Switzerland.

What might be the long-term effect of an amendment against gay marriages? Dr. Sean Cahill, co-author of *Family Policy: Issues Affecting Gay, Lesbian, Bisexual and Transgender Families*, describes some of these consequences. Among other things, the amendment would jeopardize the domestic partner health benefits that are offered in nearly a dozen states and in hundreds of cities, as well as by thousands of private employers. This would jeopardize the ability to get health care for thousands of citizens.[48]

The amendment also would jeopardize the same-sex families that are raising children. These people are our neighbors. There are same-sex households in 99 percent of all counties in the United States, and this crosses every ethnic, racial, and income group. Among these households, 34 percent of all lesbian couples and 22 percent of all male couples have at least one child under the age of eighteen. These children could be taken away from them, even though they are in loving homes, if equal rights are denied to same-sex marriages.

Some wonder what will happen to their state, or to their nation, if same-sex marriages are allowed. An argument always used by those against gay marriage is that it will, somehow, hurt the sanctity of their own marriages. We can look to Massachusetts to understand the effect that same-sex marriages have had upon a state's citizens. Massachusetts began allowing same-sex couples to marry on May 17, 2004. During the following year, more than 6,000 gay couples married, most of them having already lived together for a number of years in long-term relationships that had outlasted many heterosexual marriages. During that same year, there were almost 31,000 heterosexual marriages in the state. When the state began allowing same-sex marriage, public support was at 35 percent. A year later, when the people of the State of Massachusetts were asked whether they believed gay marriage had had a positive effect or no impact on their quality of life, 85 percent said that it was either better, or had no impact. Whether the same-sex couple living down the street was married, or not, had little impact on the respondents.[49]

What Might Our Response Be?

Every objection I've heard to homosexuals having equal rights seems to come from fear, including a fear of inappropriate behavior that would also be considered inappropriate for heterosexuals. Because there is no evidence that anyone can "make" someone become a homosexual, and because what my neighbors do in their bedroom is of little concern to me, whether they're homosexual or heterosexual, the tremendous focus on this issue seems to be masking something else.

C. S. Lewis puts this further into perspective: "I want to make it as clear as I possibly can that [sexuality] is not the center of Christian morality. . . . The sins of the flesh are bad, but they are the least bad of all sins. All the worst pleasures are purely spiritual; the pleasure of putting other people in the wrong, of bossing and patronizing and spoil sport and back-biting, the pleasures of power, of hatred."[50]

In Dante's *Inferno*, these sexual sins are in a higher circle of hell. What's at the bottom of hell? Deceit.

Some ask, "Why do same-sex couples want to be married? Why can't we just give them equal benefits and be done with this argument?"

Many homosexuals who form attachments, form long-term attachments. Many of these relationships last a lifetime, and are as loving and caring as any heterosexual relationship. Same-sex couples simply want the state to recognize their relationship and to give them all the rights of married people.

Many Christians agree, believing that wherever love and commitment reside, the union should be blessed. Some churches recognize the spirituality of this commitment, and have marriage ceremonies for same-sex couples. Although tradition has defined marriage as being between a man and a woman, some Christians recognize another viewpoint on marriage. The Rev. Gray Temple, an Episcopalian priest and author of *Gay Unions: In the Light of Scripture, Tradition, and Reason*, defines marriage as "a relationship between two persons consisting of human courage intersecting divine grace."[51] C. S. Lewis, in his classic book *Mere Christianity*, says, "The Christian conception of marriage is one: the other is the quite different question—how far Christians, if they are voters . . . ought to try to force their views of marriage on the rest of the community by embodying them in [their] laws. A great many people seem to think that if you are a Christian yourself you should try to make [it] difficult for everyone. I do not think that. At least I know I should be very angry if the Mohammedans tried to prevent the rest of us from drinking wine. My own view is that the Churches should frankly recognize that the majority of . . . people are not Christians and, therefore, cannot be expected to live Christian lives. There ought to be two distinct kinds of marriage: one governed by the State with rules enforced on all citizens, the other governed by the Church with rules enforced by her on her own members."[52]

His words raise important questions: Do democracy and equality demand that we recognize the rights of everyone? Or should our own personal morality influence decisions made for everyone else? With any new law, we should ask, Who does this law harm? And who does this law benefit? Forbidding equal rights to anyone because of sexual orientation is as wrong and undemocratic as forbidding rights to anyone because of race or gender or age. Of course, these things are done, but they are not just. Any law that forbids equal rights harms those who want to be part of our democratic society.

Some Christians say same-sex marriage harms society. I know, from my own experience, that the gay marriage of a neighbor or friend has no negative effect on my own marriage, nor do I see it as having any negative effect on others.

We need to put this issue into perspective. It deserves more research to learn what effect civil unions and gay marriages have on society. What are the consequences to society when we carry an attitude of hate that gives others permission to harm and kill? How do our political and religious decisions change when we ask homosexuals about their lives, about their concerns, about their spirituality? Where does the Holy Spirit lead us, on this issue of such concern to so many?

Chapter Six

War and Peace

"Blessed are the peacemakers;
they shall be recognized as children of God."

MATTHEW 5:9

How seriously are we to take these words of Jesus for a modern society? How seriously do we take the image of Jesus as the Prince of Peace? We talk about peace, we talk about "thou shalt not kill," but many Christians believe that this commandment is about murdering rather than killing in general, and that it's applicable to individuals, but not to society.

For 2,000 years, Christians have struggled with this question: To what extent can a Christian commit violence and take part in war? Their answers take a number of forms, all of which are recognized, at least through lip service, by the U.S. government.

For some Christians, the answer is an absolute. Under no circumstances should a Christian take part in any war. They look at the example of the life of the Prince of Peace: his refusal to become a militant Messiah in order to overcome the oppressive rule of the Romans, the many words of Paul and Jesus to leave all strifes aside, to love the neighbor—even when the neighbor is an enemy. Although the Hebrew Scriptures are filled with stories of wars, mayhem, murder, brutality, and the desire to have God smite the enemy, these attitudes are not found in the New Testament. There are no verses about war in the New Testament, except in the Book of Revelations, which deals with God's war, not ours.

This was the stance of all Christians beginning with Jesus and lasting at least 150 years. From approximately A.D. 150 until around A.D. 300 there were very few Christians in the military. Most refused military service. Some were executed for their stance, and they were considered martyrs for their faith.[1] In 314 the Church, under Emperor Constantine, opened the military service to Christians. In 325 Constantine presided over the Council of Nicea, and Christianity became the state religion.

In his book *God or Nations*, Dr. William Durland says, "Early Christianity eschewed military service, profit, competition, and power. . . . In an apostolic order of Saint Hippolytus of Rome in A.D. 217 it is written: The subordinate soldier may not kill. If he is ordered to, he may not carry out the order; nor may he take the military oath. If he does not agree, reject him [from church membership]."[2] Durland continues, "Numerous disciplines of the church taught categorically that one could not be a soldier and a Christian at the same time. A church order from Egypt reads, 'they shall not receive into the church one of the emperor's soldiers. If they have received him he shall refuse to kill if commanded to do so. If he does not refrain he shall be rejected.'"[3]

The Peace Churches—which include the Church of the Brethren, the Mennonites, the Quakers, and the United Church of Christ—believe war is not justified, and Christians from these denominations generally do not take part in war. Why? The Mennonite Church USA says "We believe that peace is the will of God. God created the world in peace, and God's peace is most fully revealed in Jesus Christ, who is our peace and the peace of the whole world. Led by the Holy Spirit, we follow Christ in the way of peace doing justice, bringing reconciliation, and practicing nonresistance, even in the face of violence and warfare. . . . This is our hope: The Biblical vision of a day when nations will no longer learn war,[4] a day when God will wipe away all tears and when death, mourning, crying and pain will be no more."[5]

The Church of the Brethren focuses on the costs of war: "Some 20 million children have been killed, wounded or displaced by war in the past 10 years alone. . . . Meanwhile the US government spends 100 times more on its military than it does on aiding the world's poor . . . since the beginning, Brethren have turned away from violence as a means of solving interpersonal or international problems. The basis for this conviction is firmly rooted in the New Testament, and more specifically in Jesus' teaching on loving our enemies and Paul's admonition that Christians seek to live peaceably with all and that they strive to overcome evil with good."

Quakers ask us all, when confronted with war and terrorism, to formulate "a carefully considered response that honors and affirms that of God in all humankind." It asks us to sow "the seeds of compassion and forgiveness even for those we may consider our fiercest enemies." And it asks for "effective engagement in and promotion of international forums that provide a voice for groups that are oppressed."[6]

Other churches also address this issue. The Baptist Faith and Message says, "In accordance with the spirit and teachings of Christ they should do all in their power to put an end to war. . . . Christian people throughout the world should pray for the reign of the Prince of Peace."

Christians have not had a good history of working toward peace. We go to war singing "Onward Christian Soldiers." We demonize the other side, so we can more easily kill the enemy. We easily go along with what our nation asks of us, whether or not the war is justified. Like the enemies we abhor, we too have killed hundreds of thousands, if not millions, of civilians with our guns and bombs. We may speak of peace, but we do not have a history of being peacemakers. We justify war because we feel we have no choice, but we have done little to create a world in which war is not necessary.

The Conscientious Objector

There are a number of Christians (and other spiritual people) who refuse to go to war. The United States government recognizes this stand and allows Christians, as well as others, to take a stand against war for religious reasons or for reasons of conscience. When the Constitution was being drafted, the Founding Fathers considered adding a clause to recognize the status of the conscientious objector (CO).[7] The clause never became part of the Constitution. However, CO status became legal in World

War I, for those who could identify themselves as members of one of the historic peace churches—the Amish, Jehovah's Witnesses, Mennonite, Church of the Brethren, and Quaker. After World War II any Christian, on a matter of conscience, could apply for CO status. During the Vietnam War, the requirement for CO status was broadened to include anyone's philosophical, moral, or religious beliefs. Conscientious-objector status is not selective—a CO has to be against all wars, not just against a specific war. Conscientious-objector status also is not politically expedient. An applicant cannot pick and choose which wars to fight.[8]

Requesting CO status is not an easy way out. The person requesting it has to go before the local draft board as well as talk with a chaplain and a psychologist to prove his or her sincerity. Applicants need to back up their beliefs with a clarification of their religious understanding of the issues.

Conscientious-objector status is not the same as avoiding military service. It is not the same as being a draft dodger. It also is not the same as having an educational deferment, as Bill Clinton did when he went to Oxford (which was legal and legitimate), nor is it the same as avoiding going to Vietnam by entering the National Guard and showing up only now and then (as George W. Bush did).

The right to not fight as a matter of Christian principle has not been easily won. Throughout history, some have gone to jail rather than be drafted. During the Vietnam War, some moved to Canada rather than go to jail. Others have entered the military in noncombatant roles, such as medics (who are often in more danger than are the soldiers). Others have done civil service at home.

A conscientious objector believes that the commandment "Thou shalt not kill" needs to be taken seriously and literally, and needs to be applied to societies and countries, as well as individuals. There are many reasons why COs cannot, in good religious conscience, take part in war.

Some believe if you love your neighbor, you obviously can't kill, since everyone is your neighbor. Others recognize the law of the military, which asks them to follow the orders of the person with higher rank and gives this officer absolute authority. They believe they owe absolute authority only to their conscience and to God. There are many stories of high-ranking commanders who have ordered or implied an order that is evil and unjust. Although the military rules give some leeway about this, soldiers could be dishonorably discharged, or even jailed, for refusing to follow an order.

Conscientious objectors see that all wars are about territory, greed, and power—all of which Jesus spoke against. They don't believe it is right to kill others over oil, or over boundaries.

The Holy War

Historically, most religions believed some wars were holy, fought for God and under God's command. Christians considered the Crusades a holy war, fought to regain the Holy City of Jerusalem. The Jewish holy war is called *herem*, and they too see their right to occupy the Holy Land. The Muslims' holy war is called *jihad*. They too believe they have a religious right to Jerusalem, and fight their wars to kill the infidels. "Jihad" means "striving," and usually implies the struggle within the individual to do the right thing. However, the word has been lifted by the violent extremists to describe their crusade against Christians and Jews.

Those who fight a holy war believe they are fighting to reclaim God's land and doing God's will. Muslims, Jews, and Christians all have fought holy wars. They all believe the area of Israel and Palestine is the Holy Land, and each group has a right to this area because of its history. Some Muslims and Jews believe the particular hill where the Temple of the Mount resides is the place on earth where the Light of God comes directly down to earth. Who is to have control over God's light and God's land?

In a holy war such as the present jihad, death is martyrdom. Followers of Islam who die in a holy war believe they will go directly to heaven, because they are fighting to advance the kingdom. Some think that, upon their direct entry into heaven, they will be met by seventy-two virgins, who will tend to them. They believe they are doing God's work—whether suicide bombing, or blowing up buildings, or fighting to the death. The Jews and Christians who respond in the same way, by fighting for what they believe is right (although they are less apt to do suicide bombing), believe they too are doing God's will.

Other Christians believe we are part of a grand crusade to spread democracy to other lands, and even to spread the Word of God to other countries. George W. Bush said the government of America was determined "to rid the world of the evil-doers."[9]

Since all of us are sinners and evil-doers, we may not have any people left by the time this goal is accomplished.

In describing the work that we have ahead of us, Mr. Bush himself called this a "crusade." This word made many shudder;

democratic foreign policy does not include taking over other countries, nor should we be thinking of our foreign policy as a crusade to convert others to either our religious or political value systems. Some Christians are frightened by any thinking that would push us into Armageddon, knowing how very volatile the Middle East is, and questioning whether the best way to deal with this area is through invasion.

While the warriors fight for what they believe is right, religious leaders the world over promote violence, either by encouraging it or through their silence.

Other Christians look at war as a necessary evil that must be fought in certain circumstances.

The Just War Tradition

Christians who believe war is acceptable only under very rare circumstances recognize that there are many reasons why we go to war. They determine whether a war is just or not, and only commit to a war that satisfies certain criteria.

Many Christians see war as a spectrum. On one end of the spectrum are those warriors who believe every war is just, and that they have the right to wage war under any circumstances. On the other end are those Christians who believe no war is just. The "Just War" tradition fits somewhere in the middle. The theory was first advanced by St. Augustine in the fourth century and then further developed by the Catholics.

The just war tradition leaves room in the middle for Christians who believe that, under certain circumstances, a war is just and necessary. It can act as a guide for Christian lawmakers to determine when it is right to wage war, and when it is not.

Catholic tradition believes war should always be avoided if at all possible and that as Christians, our doctrine should be "do no harm to our neighbors."[10] Since our neighbor is everyone else on earth, we are called to make decisions that don't harm anyone.

The just war theory first tries to restrict war by making it a last resort. Then it tries to reduce the horrors of a necessary war by setting limits and parameters to the damage done by the war, and creating ways to evaluate and think about war in order to reduce its horrors. It insists there be a very strong reason for overriding the presumption that exists in favor of peace and against war.

What is a just war? In order for a war to be just, it needs to fulfill the following criteria:

1. A war is permissible only when it confronts a real and certain danger. "The reason for war must be to redress rights actually violated or to defend against unjust demands backed by force."[11] The just war must not be pre-emptive or preventive. It is not a war of choice. According to this theory, we can't start a war because we think that someone, in the future, might start a war against us. However, according to this theory, a country can make a pre-emptive strike if there are troops at the border, or if a country is ready to attack. Some would consider the Six Day War of Israel in 1967 a just war because there were signs of imminent attack.

The Republican Party says "to forestall or prevent hostile acts by our adversaries, the United States must, if necessary, act preemptively."[12] The Republicans see the Iraq War as a pre-emptive war, even though there were no troops at our borders, no guns or missiles aimed at us, no direct threat at all. Although the government has used the word "pre-emptive" to describe the Iraq War, many historians and diplomats do not see the Iraq War as pre-emptive, but rather as a preventive war. There is a big difference between the two.[13] If you're about to be attacked, and you counterattack before that can happen, the war is pre-emptive. If you believe that a country might attack you some-time in the future, and you attack it first to keep that from happening, the war is preventive. Pre-emptive war has standing in international law, because you have a right to attack someone who is ready to attack you. Preventive war has no standing in international law. Many countries around the world, as well as citizens within the United States (including millions of Chris-tians), question the validity of the Iraq War, because it was a preventive war, and fear it is setting a very dangerous precedent for the future.

2. In order for a war to be considered a just war, it must be legally declared by a lawful government, not by private groups or individuals. A just war is nation against nation; it is not a group of people against a nation, or a group of people against a group of people. The ethnic cleansing of Bosnia and Serbia and the war against the civilian population of the Sudan is not just war; it's genocide. The 9/11 attacks, and attacks in Spain, London, Bali, and other places, are not part of a just war, because no nation sent the hijackers to attack these countries.

3. There must be a right intention. There must be a desire for a greater Good to prevail. Wars fought over territory, or over oil, or to keep up our standard of living, are not considered right intentions. The outcomes will not balance the deaths of hundreds of thousands, if not millions.

4. There must be a reasonable chance of winning.[14] A just war demands a reality check. If it will be nothing but a slaughter, with little chance of winning the peace, the war should not be declared.

5. Good must outweigh evil. "The means used in fighting the war must be proportionate to the end sought so the good which results must outweigh the evil which the war would do."[15] The damage to be inflicted and the costs of war must be proportionate to the good expected to result by taking up arms.

Soldiers must try to distinguish between armies and civilians and never kill civilians on purpose,[16] although it's difficult to keep the bombs away from the innocents in any war.

During World War II, millions were killed in the bombings of cities from both sides. The dropping of atomic bombs on the civilians in Hiroshima and Nagasaki still has ongoing medical consequences for those who lived through it. During the Vietnam War, there were several scandals over the killing of Vietnamese civilians. Although it's understood that there are often civilian deaths as collateral damage, the Vietnam War was one of the first modern wars in which American soldiers willingly killed civilians. Both Lieutenant William Calley and Captain Ernest Medina were tried for the massacre of civilians at My Lai (though only Calley, who claimed he was following Medina's orders, was convicted). Also during that war, the U.S. government dropped tons of the defoliant Agent Orange in Vietnam. Despite protests throughout the Vietnam War, including a long-term protest against DuPont, the company that made Agent Orange, the government continued to use the chemical. There have been continued long-term medical effects in those exposed to it.

6. The winner of the war must never require the utter humiliation of the loser. Many future wars have grown out of oppression that results from the terms of peace.[17]

7. The war must be the last resort after all other possible solutions have been tried and failed.[18] A war is never taken lightly, and the just war tradition recognizes that other avenues must be tried, and proven to fail, before moving to war.

Discerning what makes a just war is not easy. Every country that wages war believes it is doing it for the Good. During the Civil War, soldiers from both sides marched into battle with the Bible in hand, claiming that God was on their side.

In World War II, Germany, which considered itself a Christian nation, used the same justification for war that other countries have used, including the United States. The German leaders went to war to protect the fatherland against a perceived threat to their country. They believed they had to protect the interests of their country, as well as preserve the purity of the German race against the Jews, the mentally ill, the gypsies, and the homosexuals. By making their race ethnically pure, they were intent on creating a paradise on earth and bringing in the thousand-year reign of their version of the Second Coming.

The Catholic catechism recognizes it's possible for us to be wrong about our motivations for going to war: "Given techniques of propaganda and the ease with which nations and individuals either assume or delude themselves into believing that God or Right is clearly in their side, the test of compara-tive justice may be extremely difficult to apply."[19] We are to keep a good watch over our motives, and over the reasons given for why a particular war is necessary for the "good of the state."

Even if a war is considered "just," the consequences are always horrendous. Abraham Lincoln anguished over war, recognizing that "the evils of war even in the 'best wars' . . . breathed forth famine, swam in blood, and rode on fire; and long, long after, the orphans' cry and the widows' wail contin-ued to break the sad silence that ensued."[20] Garry Wills, in his book *Lincoln at Gettysburg*, says, "Lincoln had no illusions about war's 'nobility.' It is a cover for other crimes. And the longer it goes on, the more it outraces any rational purposes. Even noble yearnings serve savagery . . ."[21]

The American Un-Just Wars

The Founding Fathers, in an attempt to guard against the many dangers of war, added some other limits to the tendency to get into war. They wanted to make sure that the checks and balances of our government would keep any headstrong president from making executive choices without the agreement of a major-ity within the government. They said war must be declared by the Congress. Even so, this Constitutional law has usually been ignored and we continue to enter undeclared and ill-advised wars. The United States has taken part in about 175 wars throughout our history. Only five wars were declared by Congress—the War of 1812, the Mexican War of 1846, the Spanish-American War, World War I, and World War II. Wars not formally declared included the American Civil War, the Korean War, Vietnam War, Desert Storm, Grenada, Haiti, Somalia, Bosnia, operations in Afghanistan, and both Iraq wars.[22]

If we apply the just war theory to the Vietnam War, we can understand why many Americans, and so many Christians, protested that war. We had advisers in Vietnam starting under President Harry Truman (Democrat) in the 1950s. Dwight D. Eisenhower (Republican) continued to send more advisers. Our continued presence in Vietnam was carried on reluctantly by John F. Kennedy (Democrat), who sent over more advisers, although he hoped to get the country out of Vietnam during his second term. America's involvement escalated under Lyndon B. Johnson (Democrat) in 1968, when the conflict became a war, although it was never declared by Congress. The war brought down Johnson's presidency and continued dividing the country under Richard M. Nixon (Republican.) A peace agreement was finally signed on January 27, 1973.

Vietnam was America's longest war. It divided our nation between those in favor of the war and the protesters against it. Rather than listening to the millions of protesters, Mr. Nixon turned a deaf ear to them, intent on his course. He used his hatchet man, Vice President Spiro Agnew, to discredit the protesters, even though protesting has, historically, always been our right. I remember when Agnew said that those of us who were protesting the war were elitist pigs, and soon the country was divided between the government and the people who, eventually, decided this was an unwise war.

Nixon refused to listen to any of the pleas. Yet, the war violated at least six of the principles for the just war. There was no threat to our country. Our rights had not been violated. The war was never declared by Congress. The United States had virtually no chance of success in a guerilla war. We dropped millions of tons of bombs on Vietnam, destroyed much of the country, killed countless civilians, and our goal was unclear.

Although some considered the Persian Gulf War (1991) a just war, because the allies were repelling Iraq's invasion of Kuwait, there were others who did not consider it just. It wasn't a last resort. The destruction was not proportional. According to the United Nations, "the bombing reduced Iraq to near 'stone age' conditions in some places."[23]

The United Nations did not support us in the present Iraq War. The UN, along with other countries, does not believe the Iraq War fulfills the criteria of a just war.

Richard Clarke, in his book *Against All Enemies: Inside America's War on Terror*, said that immediately after 9/11, George W. Bush talked about going to war with Iraq, even though Iraq had nothing to do with 9/11 and was not a danger to us. Mr. Bush implied that Iraq was harboring terrorists and was responsible for 9/11, and even now, many Americans still believe this. But it isn't true.

Those who don't see the Iraq War as a just war do not see the proportionality of good versus evil to be weighed on the side of good. The damage does not seem proportional to the ends. Although the American government does not keep figures on how many Iraqis are killed (only on how many Americans and allies are killed), unofficial estimates place civilian deaths anywhere between 26,000 and 100,000. As of late 2005, more than 2,000 of the occupying force had been killed.

We have suffered the enmity of countries all over the world for our actions.

We say we went to war in the name of democracy. But if we truly want to establish democracy in another country, we have to realize that its ideas of democracy may not follow the principles of our own. We may not be happy with the country's self-will. Although we don't yet know how Iraq's democracy will play out over the years, the democracy being established in Iraq is not a true democracy because it does not protect the minority, and it is taking away some democratic laws that existed before the United States invaded. The democracy being established in Iraq gives power to the majority (the Shiites) without the protection of rights or adequate representation by the minority (the Sunnis). It seems the rights women had under Saddam Hussein are being diminished, and, in some cases, taken away from them, which may leave women with less democracy than they had under Hussein. Although some may think this was worth fighting and dying for, a government that takes away rights from more than half of its citizens is not a democracy, regardless of what we call it.

In order to have a democracy, there must be free debate, and free media that are willing to put the issues out to the people in order for them to decide. Public education that teaches critical thinking and examines issues and history is necessary for an informed public. If this isn't being addressed, there is no true democracy but only "spin" and coercion. As of the end of 2005, Iraq is not a country with a true democracy or with democratic institutions.

Christians who do not believe the Iraq War is just criticize it for a number of reasons. The Iraq War was planned before the attacks of 9/11, not after. In response to the failure in 1991 to go all the way into Iraq and get rid of Hussein, a small group of people decided Saddam Hussein had to go—including Colin Powell, Donald Rumsfeld, Richard Cheney, and Paul Wolfowitz. All of these ended up in the current Bush administration. Their desire to get rid of Hussein got nowhere under President Clinton. George W. Bush then planned to find a reason to get involved in Iraq. September 11 was "the New Pearl Harbor," which provided the catalyst needed to go into Iraq.

The war was justified by a lie. President Bush first told U.S. citizens there were weapons of mass destruction, which could reach us within forty-five minutes. Not true. He said this was an imminent danger even though there was no evidence of these weapons. If anything, there was some evidence that they did not exist. No one could find them. Going to war for something as vague as a possibility is not sufficient justification for war.

We were then told we had gone to war because Iraq was a terrorist state. But that wasn't true either. Al Qaeda was not in Iraq until we went into the country and caused so much anger that Al Qaeda saw virgin territory for its work. Most of the 9/11 terrorists were from Saudi Arabia, but we never discussed going to war with that country, which is the only one that had a close connection with the terrorists.

The war has fomented terrorism. We have given Al Qaeda an extra justification for its actions, since its members can now see themselves as freedom fighters trying to repel the invaders. Insurgents have become more powerful as they battle what some see as the occupying force, and others see as the Great Satan of the West.

We were then told we had gone to war to overthrow Saddam Hussein. But the United States has always recognized the sovereignty of other countries. We have never been in the business of overthrowing regimes because they're evil. If we were, we would have a great deal of work to do. How would we decide who to overthrow? Would we start with Amnesty International's list of the bad guys? If so, we'd start with Uzbekistan, which is number one on that list, and we would then have to continue on and depose leaders in more than 100 countries, ranging from Albania to Burundi to Rwanda to Syria and the Sudan. If we are in the business of warring only with despots, why is it the last three wars we have had were in oil-rich countries? Why are the other despots allowed to continue their tyranny?

By no means was this a last resort. The inspectors were in Iraq. Iraq was fairly quiet. The no-fly zone and sanctions against oil, against medical equipment, against metals, and against anything that could be used to make explosives or nuclear weapons were in place. We had been bombing Iraq every week during the Clinton administration. Iraq was not a danger to us. If anything, there was evidence Hussein was weakening, and any talk about his power was pure swagger. Even after weapons of mass destruction weren't found, many Republican leaders continued to say they were still there, despite the lack of evidence. When Colin Powell discovered he had been fooled, and given the wrong intelligence, he was furious. He had been persuaded that he had the truth, when really he had been forced to give false information to the United Nations and to Congress.

What was the real reason for the Iraq War and the Afghanistan War? Certainly it had to do with our need for oil, and our need for military bases in the Middle East. We wanted to bring democracy to the Mideast, believing that the "Road to Jerusalem went through Baghdad." We believed if we could change the government in Iraq into a democracy, the rest of the countries would follow, thereby removing the funding and support for the terrorists attacking Israel. However, the Carnegie Endowment says that we have a very low possibility of actually being able to promote democracy in Iraq.[24]

The pattern in Iraq is not new. The U.S. government has not had quite the sterling past that we would like to think it has. Historically, our country has not always done so well at choosing which despots to support, and which not to support. We supported the Shah of Iran, Ferdinand Marcos in the Philippines, Augusta Pinochet in Chile, Sukarno and then Suharto in Indonesia, and have gone back and forth about who to help and who not to help in Central and South America. It isn't only George W. Bush who is part of this pattern, but many administrations, both Republican and Democratic. Since Christians want a larger say in the government, it might be good for us to face our past, and try to rectify some of our not-quite-so-Christian foreign policy decisions.

The Laws of War

Once a nation has entered into war, there are laws governing behavior toward civilians and prisoners, as well as the behavior of its own soldiers. Many of these laws are part of the Geneva

Convention, which was signed in 1949. The Geneva Convention includes the following provisions to try to reduce the atrocities of war:

- The Geneva Convention forbids torture, mutilation, rape, slavery, arbitrary killing, genocide, and crimes against humanity, which include forced disappearance and deprivation of humanitarian aid.
- It forbids war crimes, including apartheid, biological experiments, hostage taking, attacks on cultural objects, and depriving people of the right to a fair trial.
- The Geneva Convention recognizes the difference between civilians and soldiers. For example, a civilian who shoots an enemy soldier may be liable for murder, but a soldier who shoots an enemy soldier and is captured may not be punished.
- Prisoners of war are to be treated humanely. Prisoners must not be subject to torture or medical or scientific experiments of any kind. They must also be protected against violence, intimidation, insults, and public curiosity. The public display of POWs is also prohibited.
- When questioned, it must be in the prisoner's native language. Prisoners of war must only give their names, ranks, birth dates, and serial numbers.
- Prisoners of war may not be punished for the acts they committed during the fighting unless the opposing side would have punished its own soldiers for those acts as well.

- There is to be no destruction of property unless justified by military necessity.
- Warring parties must not use or develop biological or chemical weapons.

When we went to war in Iraq, George W. Bush decided the United States would not follow the rules of the Geneva Convention. Instead, we would determine our own laws.

As a result, thousands of Iraqis have been detained, many in secret, in prisons in Iraq, Afghanistan, and Guantánamo Bay. Although the Supreme Court found this illegal, many prisoners still have not been released.[25]

Although we said we were there to bring democracy to Iraq, democratic principles are not followed. Prisoners are mistreated, and their Holy Book, the Koran, is disrespected. Prisoners are humiliated in a way that Muslims would find the most shameful: being naked together, having dog attacks them, having what seemed to be menstrual blood smeared on them,

Particularly troubling has been Mr. Bush's prisoner rendition policy. Rendition means if we want a prisoner to be interrogated, but we don't want to be the ones to torture him for information, we send him to a country that is happy to torture him for us. We can claim we're innocent of using torture as part of interrogation, but we are still coconspirators. We get around the values of democracy and Christianity by saying "it's not on our soil!" Prisoners have been sent to be interrogated in Uzbekistan, Syria, Afghanistan, and Jordan. In most cases, these prisoners had no useful information.

Whether the war is just or not, the Geneva Convention set down rules about how to treat prisoners and civilians in war. When Jesus said "love your enemy," and love your neighbor—even the person you hate—he was affirming that all people are God's children, and are to be respected. The Geneva Convention recognizes basic human dignity as part of human rights.

It's easy to justify inhumane treatment and torture by saying we need the information these prisoners have and that this information could save lives. But who gets caught up in the net? The innocent as well as the guilty. How good is information from prisoners who have been detained for two or three or four years? Not very good at all, according to most reports.

To Live by a Commitment to Peace

Many Christians have looked not at war, but at how to keep the peace. They ask how they can actually become peacemakers through their activities. They recognize that pacifism is not passive, but active.

Quaker founder George Fox struggled with how to react as a Christian to the issue of war. He recognized Christians' need to come to terms with this important topic, and that this may be a long spiritual process. When William Penn asked George Fox whether a Christian could continue to wear a sword, Fox replied, "Wear it as long as thou canst." If Christians can wear the sword or carry the gun with a clear conscience, then they may continue to do so. However, Fox believed that if Christians decide not to fight, then they have to work toward creating peace.

Fox said, "I lived in the virtue of that life and power that took away the occasion of all wars." Pacifist Christians recognize that almost all wars (if not all of them) begin because of unjust conditions. We sow the seeds of dissension long before they grow into conflict and war. If we can remove the conditions that cause war, peace has a chance.

We can look at almost all wars and see the occasion that gave rise to the war. Some of our past wars began because of unjust conditions. World War II, which most proponents of the just war theory believe was just, grew from the outcome of particularly severe punishments that were inflicted on Germany as part of the surrender after World War I. These reparations led to poverty, hunger, humiliation, and the political environment that became fertile ground for the rise of Nazism.

Sometimes wars have begun because our actions have allowed, and even encouraged, the occasion for war. We have given arms to various countries, which then use them against other countries, and eventually against us. We sold arms to Saddam Hussein to use against the Iranians. At that time, Hussein was our friend, and we were intent on helping him. Those same weapons have now been turned against us.

The same problem occurred in Afghanistan, when we supported and trained the Afghan soldiers against Russia, and gave them the weapons they could then turn against us.

We continue to act in ways that foment, rather than diminish, tensions. In 2005, George W. Bush sold arms to both India and Pakistan. Since these were two countries with a long history of tensions and conflicts, we have now armed both sides of a conflict, both of whom have nuclear weapons. We shouldn't be surprised if the India and Pakistan conflict begins to foment further, eventually erupting in war. We are adding fuel to the fire. Rather than working as peacemakers, we are creating the occasion for war.[26]

Giving to War Takes Away Money for Peace

War is one of the nation's most expensive undertakings. Once a war starts, more and more money is diverted into arms and taken away from other services. War is expensive. Combat pay is increased. New weapons have to be created and built and deployed. Tanks have to be built and fully armed and protected. Airplanes are shot down, and new ones are built. According to *Nation* magazine, the war in Iraq is expected to cost 1 trillion dollars. Imagine what that money could do if it were diverted to peacemaking and peacekeeping.

The Iraq War begun in 2003 was a war of choice. If we weren't ready, we could have waited. We didn't have enough troops to fight the war and create the peace, which led to deploying the National Guard and keeping soldiers in the Army long after their enlistment term ended. We went into war without sufficient protection for our troops in terms of body armor and protection for the tanks. Nor did we have enough money to be waging this war and still taking care of needed business at home. Although various people in the Bush administration have said we don't choose when to fight a war, they did choose. And the decisions were not good decisions. Plenty of rhetoric has told us that it's unpatriotic to question this war, and that we're not supporting our troops if we question it. But true support of our troops includes all the support they need to protect them—body armor, tanks that run, enough gasoline to run their machines, guns that shoot. Our troops are too important to put them in unnecessary danger.

According to a panel sponsored by the nonpartisan Council on Foreign Relations, "The costs, human, military and economic, are high and continue to mount." The council said the United States was ill prepared for the postwar needs, such as security, governance, and economic demands after the war. This undermined U.S. foreign policy and helped the insurgents. The report noted the billions of dollars of wasted resources in both Afghanistan and Iraq.[27]

Not only is money inadequate and wasted in military operations, but also in rebuilding operations. George W. Bush hired the Halliburton Company (where Vice President Dick Cheney had been CEO) along with its subsidiary company, KBR, to provide logistical support for the military and to rebuild the country, which is difficult to do in time of war. The company received a no-bid contract. There was no competition; no analysis of who would be best for the job. President Bush simply gave this most lucrative job to his vice president's former company. Halliburton's budget from May 2004 to May 2005 was $3.98 billion, and from May 2005 until May 2006 its new budget for rebuilding Iraq will be $4.97 billion, nearly a billion dollars more.

The company has already been accused of skimming off nearly $1 billion. The Defense Contract Audit Agency "has questioned more than $1 billion of Halliburton's bills for work in Iraq . . . which includes $152,000 for movie rentals and $1.5 million for tailoring and two multimillion dollar transportation bills that appear to overlap."[28] In spite of months of questioning about this overpayment, what is Halliburton's punishment for corruption? It continues to provide services with no consequences to the company and is given another no-bid contract, to help rebuild New Orleans.

The Government Accountability Office "found that the government could save $31 million—or 43 percent—on food services" by working through a subcontractor rather than with Halliburton."[29] Nevertheless, Halliburton continues to do the work.

We are also paying for the security protection of the highly paid Halliburton employees, which accounts for about 33 percent of each contract.[30] This has not always been successful. Since Halliburton entered the country, more than sixty-eight of its employees and subcontractors have died in Iraq, Afghanistan, and Kuwait as of August 2005.[31]

As a country, we have taken upon ourselves the responsibility of rebuilding Iraq, including building schools (I always wonder if we bombed the schools and are now rebuilding them, or simply decided to build schools as long as we were there). We are also trying to rebuild the bombed oil derricks and refineries; rebuilding electrical grids, water mains, and water purification installations; repairing roadways and airport radar; and building soccer stadiums. The list goes on and on.

Meanwhile, we don't have enough money in our country to deal with our own problems of schools that are falling apart, of insufficient power grids such as those that caused blackouts in 2004, of environmental problems and energy problems, of health care, education, social security, unemployment.

The Casualties of War

World War I killed 10 million people; World War II, 38 million. More than 100,000 were killed in a single day at Hiroshima. More than 56,000 Americans were killed in Vietnam, and there were reports that hundreds of thousands of Vietnamese, if not more than a million, were victims of that war. If we could neatly keep war away from civilians, we would have a better estimate of who has been killed in combat, and would be able to limit the casualties. But that's not possible in war.

In Iraq, more than 2,000 from the allied forces had been killed by 2005, with no clear number for the Iraqis. General Tommy Franks said "we don't do body counts," and the U.S. government's policy is to only count the deaths of the allied forces. In fact, the United States and the British try to limit the public's awareness of the dead, by not allowing the media to photograph the coffins returning home or cover military funerals. Conservative supporters of the war, such as bloggers found at blogsforbush.com, argue the military is taking the correct approach, that the "'liberal media' only want to report the 'bad news' of dead U.S. soldiers, but ignore the 'good news' about killed Iraqi insurgents." Of course, many people believe killing is not good news, no matter how it's masked.

The mental and physical costs of war are also high. In the Iraq War, more than 12,000 U.S. soldiers had been wounded by fall of 2005—young men and women who had lost eyes and limbs. Soldiers get sick from the use of chemical and biological warfare. Their lives and the lives of their families are often ruined, as they struggle for the rest of their lives with physical impairments and mental problems. One Vietnam veteran that my husband and I know told us he hasn't been able to sleep well since Vietnam. Another person we know ended up in jail, and told us that the mindset of war led to his illegal activities at home.

The harm of war does not come just from the deaths of hundreds of thousands of soldiers and civilians. Homes are destroyed. Cities are blasted. Businesses ruined. Children are unable to go out and play, because of the dangers from mines and bombs and shooting. The environment is compromised, sometimes ruined beyond any immediate repair.

How have we dealt with these problems? In many cases, we've ignored them. For some years after Vietnam, the government refused to recognize the consequences of Agent Orange. For many years after the Gulf War, no one wanted to recognize Gulf War Syndrome.

Economic prosperity is another casualty. The Congressional Budget Office estimates that the costs of deploying the troops in Iraq was $9 billion to $13 billion; the monthly cost of the war is about $8 to $9 billion; returning the forces to the United States will take about $7 billion, and the temporary occupation of Iraq costs about $1 billion to $4 billion per month.[32] This money could be spent on many of our needs at home.

There are many unfunded needs in social services. Schools at home are left to deteriorate. Environmental policies are not followed. According to George W. Bush, we can't afford to do anything about global warming because it would hurt business—but we can afford to spend billions each month on the war against Iraq. The prosperity of our country is compromised by this war. I have felt that my sense of safety and security and hope and vision are casualties. The constant presence on our evening news of roadside bombs, dead soldiers, kidnappings, and beheadings, plus the many searches at airports, the up and down of code orange, code yellow, code red, keeps my own fears at the forefront.

Peacekeeping in Place of War-Making

If we get rid of war, what do we put in its place? We know far more about peacemaking and peacekeeping than we did two or three decades ago. We have learned far more about conflict resolution, alternatives to violence, and other methods for averting war, as well as diminishing the aftereffects of war. In fact, if we applied the same amount of energy, and just a portion of the money, to peace as we do to war-making, to sports, and to entertainment, we could start to find ways to resolve problems without killing and destroying countries. World peace may not be around the corner, but we're never going to achieve it by going to war with every country that has oil or a despotic government. In fact, many studies of nonviolence have found that nonviolence is often just as effective, if not more so, than violence. Under those circumstances, which would we choose? There are many alternatives to war—many of which have been tried very rarely.

Historically, more than twenty countries have won independence through nonviolent means, or at least partially through nonviolence. The American Revolution began with a series of successful nonviolent protests. Before the American Revolution, the British tried to tax the colonists by introducing the Stamp Act, which taxed all printed paper, including legal papers, newspapers, cards, and pamphlets. When the ship carrying the stamps came into the Philadelphia Harbor in 1765, the city's church bells tolled all day long in protest, and the colonists' ships flew their flags at half-mast. Colonists refused to use the stamps, and by 1766, the Act was repealed.

The British then tried to pass the Townshend Acts, which imposed other unfair taxes on trade goods. Again, most of the colonists refused to buy anything that carried the tax. The names of any colonists who did buy the taxed goods were published on a list as a protest against their actions. The tax was repealed, except for the tax on tea.

In 1773, when a ship came into Boston Harbor carrying tea that would be taxed, colonists threw the tea into the harbor, refusing to accept the tax. Although the Boston Tea Party is not always considered nonviolent protest, since property was destroyed, it is considered a form of resistance that did not lead directly to war.

Other countries have practiced nonviolent protests with great success. Pontius Pilate once brought images of Caesar into Jerusalem, even though it was against Jewish law. The Jews begged him to remove the images, but he refused. In response, the Jews camped out around his house for five days and five nights.

Pilate then summoned the crowds to the stadium, surrounded the Jews with soldiers, and said that he would kill them unless they would accept these images of Caesar. As if of one mind, all the Jews fell to the ground, and proclaimed they were ready to be killed. When Pilate realized he could accomplish little with the deaths of thousands of Jews, he removed the images.[33]

Many countries achieved their independence, and peoples their freedom, through nonviolence. Examples include India in 1947 (in great part through the nonviolent work of Gandhi), Poland in 1989, the Velvet Revolution in Czechoslovakia in 1989, and South Africa in 1994, when black and white South Africans were allowed to vote together for the first time.

Although the U.S. government is not a full supporter of non-violence programs, there are a number of universities, colleges, and institutes that are studying how nonviolence can be used, and many are already using it in the world. The Center for International Development and Conflict Management at the University of Maryland studies how economic conditions cause conflict, and what methods can be used as a means to peace. The Center also offers conflict-resolution training and workshops and teaches negotiation strategies that can be used for resolving conflicts.

Many universities now have classes in conflict resolution and alternatives to violence. These include the study of how nonviolent approaches have worked throughout history and training in nonviolent methods. There are classes and studies of how to use language to lead to reconciliation, rather than upping the ante to create more violence. Peacemaking demands knowledge, experimentation, creativity, and understanding of the situation, the culture, the language, and the root problems. There is not a shortage of trained and knowledgeable people in peacemaking. There also are not quick solutions. But there are possibilities for resolving conflicts nonviolently, if the desire is there.

Peacemaking at the War College

The U.S. Army War College in Carlyle, Pennsylvania, has a Peacekeeping and Stability Institute that was created in 1993 by the Chief of Staff of the Army, General Gordon Sullivan. Sullivan recognized that the United States would be faced with peacekeeping in the future, but that there was no organization dealing with this.

I talked to Associate Professor William Flavin who teaches peace operations at the U.S. Army War College. Flavin had been a member of the Green Berets, and most recently helped in peace-building and peacekeeping in Bosnia-Kosovo.

Flavin said the Institute presents several classes on peace operations, rule of law, and international development. These courses provide the student with the opportunity to study the rule of law, peace-building, and transition planning.

Peace programs are designed to go on before a conflict, during, and post conflict. Flavin says, "Part of the idea is to expose everyone to each other so people can understand there are various ways of doing things. So we might have Jordanians and Israelis meet together. We've been trying to talk about a better conceptual model for peace-building. It's true, you might have to use security forces and military forces, but the over arching objective is peace building.

"The evaporation of the Cold War constraints with the fall of the USSR in 1989 and the success of several UN and UN-sanctioned operations encouraged member nations to support an ambitious agenda extending UN Peace Operations to several complex crises, including Cambodia, Haiti, Somalia and the Balkans. We found that sometimes, when separating people, no one understands each other, and the separation merely postpones the understanding and postpones solving the problem. So besides separating people, we had to have some mechanism in place, as in South Africa, to create justice.

"Initially, the Bush administration was not for this approach, because it thought the focus of the military should be combat, and the military shouldn't be doing these non-combat roles. But recently they shifted the focus as a result of the reality in the world, where military forces also have to do peacekeeping roles. However, that doesn't mean they have now provided the resources to be effective."

Bosnia was one of the countries where peacemaking and peacekeeping were very effective. "The European Union is now running Bosnia," says Flavin. "Originally, we thought we'd need about 600,000 troops on the ground in Bosnia and 100,000 in Sarejevo alone, based on a World War II analysis. But there are now only about 200 NATO forces left in Bosnia." I asked Flavin whether this would work in Iraq. He replied, "The principles of peacekeeping and peace-building are the same. There is no mystery about what should be done. But in Iraq, the process has been characterized by fits and starts. There have been at least three major phases in the process of building governance, each marked by a significant change in policy and implementation. The ad hoc and disjointed nature of these efforts exacerbated the challenge of establishing governance in Iraq. The process currently in place is the latest attempt to provide the legitimate governance.

"You have to take your time," he continued. "It's been over ten years in Bosnia, and we're still sorting it out. It is better to do this over a longer period of time, so you can gain consensus. You get people beginning to buy into things and eventually you have a working solution. If you try to force a solution there is no time to build consensus. The debate on the changing of the US Articles of Confederation began in September 1786 and our Constitution with the Bill of Rights was ratified in December 1791. Iraq was created in 1920 and has had what could be called their first truly free election just this past year. It is a challenge for them to create a constitution that will lead directly to legitimate governance in the space of a few months.

"The challenge is to convince the average citizen of Iraq, based on disjointed nature of the previous attempts, that the current attempt at governance is legitimate and valid so consensus can be built around the peace process. The governance decisions coupled with the decision to disband the entire Iraq Army and the de-Baath policy (who were supporters of Hussein) have established conditions that have exacerbated the instability and retarded the move toward stabilization."

Using Diplomacy

Another Christian approach, which has been used very little by the Bush administration, is the use of diplomacy.

Dr. Norman Graebner has been teaching American history and American diplomacy for more than fifty years, at the University of Illinois and then the University of Virginia. "My approach emphasizes diplomacy and emphasizes peace, not war," he says. "The problem occurs when people in power see America's role as to kick the world in the teeth. I see the purpose as to get along with other nations. Through diplomacy. Negotiation. With tolerance. With wisdom. When the secretary of state goes around and tells people off, it isn't diplomacy. That's not reaching a settlement on anything. You tell them off and walk away, make believe 'I was really tough there, I'm pushing democracy!' It looks good in the press, but it's not effective."

Dr. Graebner was one of the first teachers to teach democracy in Japan after World War II. He had to discover how to teach democracy to a country that had been ruled by an emperor. He says, "It's easy to talk about democracy, but how do you make a country democratic? Democracy is born from within, with the right leadership, the right education, the right security; you have to have a lot of things right. If a country doesn't have those things, it won't be democratic. If a country has what is right, it will have democracy no matter what the United States does or says."

Graebner is concerned about the way we become friends with a country (such as Iraq in the 1980s) and then enemies (with Iraq in the 1990s) without a consistent foreign policy. He quotes George Washington who said in his farewell address "The Nation which indulges toward another a habitual hatred or a habitual fondness is in some degree a slave. It is a slave to its animosity or to its affection, either of which is sufficient to lead it astray from its duty and its interest." Clearly we have been a slave to a number of countries over the centuries, moving from fondness to animosity in many of the countries where we are now fighting.

I asked him how American diplomacy is applied to such problems as war and conflicts. He answered, "The government has to think about the costs. You have to be clear about the goal, but you have to have the means to achieve that goal. You have to be willing to evaluate power carefully. Geography often determines who wins. We rarely win when we have a war on the other country's territory. In Iraq and Vietnam and Afghanistan we can't beat them because there are too many [people] and geography gives them the advantage. In these situations, you have to use too much of your power to try to achieve the objective. We learned that in the American Revolution. Britain couldn't defeat us. You cannot fight Americans on equal terms in America. In World War II, Germany learned they couldn't defeat all of Europe on the other country's land. About eighty-eight percent of the Germans killed in World War II were killed on the Eastern Front."

There are rules for diplomacy. "In diplomacy, there is always a quid pro quo. When dealing with someone, you always have to have something to give in exchange. Diplomacy is not demanding, it's dealing. There is always a payoff; if not, there is no diplomacy. Otherwise, all you do is demand and you become the bully. Moralism puts an end to diplomacy.

Dr. Graebner sees many problems with the war in Iraq, many of which could have been resolved with diplomacy. "There was a refusal to discuss or debate. Everyone was supposed to buy the party line. There was intimidation, calling those who didn't go along as unpatriotic. There wasn't majority rule. The major countries in the world weren't with us. All the experts were against the war. In democracy, you have to listen to the majority and there has to be free debate. There is an assumption that wisdom is generated by free debate and the best ideas come to the surface. In the case of the war in Iraq, too many wise voices were ignored."

Graebner says in order to work in the world, we have to have good relationships with other countries, for two reasons: "First of all, you may need the support of other nations if you get into trouble, and secondly, because these other nations might be right. If we believe in majority rule, when the majority of other nations are against us, they may be right. In this case, they were proven to be right."

A Christian Choice

Whom do we choose—Barabbas, who was a Zealot and advocated the violent overthrow of the foreign government, or Jesus? Are we willing to love our enemies, to not seek revenge, to not pay back evil with evil, to try to live at peace with everyone?[34] Becoming peacemakers may be a process. We may not learn it all at once. It is a radical and difficult challenge. The struggle for peace calls for discussion, listening, wisdom, and restraint. It is a Christian process that seeks methods for creating, establishing, and maintaining peace.

Although both Republicans and Democrats have voted over and over again for war, there is a strong and emerging Christian voice that questions whether war is the best approach to resolve conflicts. To reach for peace, many Christians recognize we have to replace old ways of thinking with new visions. We have to overcome fear with hope.

There is a prayer written by a Palestinian Christian that challenges the ease with which we create enemies and divide people: "Pray not for the Arab or Jew, for Palestinian or Israeli, but pray rather for ourselves, that we might not divide them in our prayers, but keep them both together in our hearts."[35]

Chapter Seven

Confronting Terrorism and Fear

"'For I know what plans I have for you,'
Yahweh declares, 'plans for peace, not for disaster,
to give you a future and a hope.'"

JEREMIAH 29:11

J esus told us to "fear not." He brought us a message of hope,
not fear. Is this a reasonable message, considering there are
threats all around us—to us as individuals, to our cities, to our
nation, threats to our security and safety?

We live in frightening times. Our country is still reeling
from the attacks of 9/11 and terrified of another attack. We
know our nuclear plants and our ports are not adequately protected. We go through careful and invasive searches every time
we fly, knowing that someone could take a shoe bomb, or a scis-
sors, or a pocket knife on board, and bring down another plane.
We hear, almost daily, that Iran and North Korea are working
to build nuclear bombs that they may use against us, or against
their neighbors.

The terrorists seem to continually grow in numbers and gain more power. We hear that Al Qaeda is active in Iraq, and seemingly almost everywhere else in the world. We hear that the Taliban is active again in Afghanistan.

We worry about our retirement and the perils of all the safety nets being removed if Social Security doesn't get fixed quickly. We see the stock market going up and down, and we wonder if we'll lose all our savings. We read about corruption in corporations, and wonder how many other businesses will fail, and how it will affect our jobs, our money, our services, our lives.

We wonder if Armageddon is around the corner, with the problems in the Middle East, with the rise of China's power, with war and rumors of war, with famine and earthquakes,[1] insurrections, persecutions, calamity, and plagues,[2] hurricanes, fires, global warming—all threats of great disasters.

In the 2004 Republican Platform, there are thirty-nine pages discussing the problems we need to fear. There's a page about Cuba, and the threat to us from their government. There are pages about Pakistan and Palestine and Israel, although there is only a very brief mention of Osama bin Laden, who we understood to be the main threat in 2001, but who seems to be missing from our radar screen these days. It is clear we have a great deal to be afraid of, and it is imperative that we have a government that can stand up to the horrors in our world. In fact, a number of polls said many people voted for George W. Bush because they didn't want to change presidents during a war. They thought he could best protect our country.

But a state of constant fear can be just as dangerous as being in the midst of terror. The Bible repeats, innumerable times and in many different ways, that we are not to fear and instead are to put an emphasis on trust and hope. We are to do what is right and not give way to fear.[3] We are told that there is no fear in love,[4] that fear has to do with punishment.[5] We are to fear no evil,[6] or the terror of the night.[7] We are not to fear bad news,[8] or fear mortal men,[9] or the sword.[10] Who or what are we to fear? Only God,[11] for those who fear him lack nothing.[12] In the midst of fear and trembling, we are to know that perfect love casts out fear.[13]

Why does the Bible kept telling us not to fear? Certainly there was as much to fear in Biblical times as there is now. Enemies attacked. Women were raped. Children were massacred. Innocent men were executed by a government that oppressed its citizens daily.

Fear is a good controller of any citizens. In an oppressive government, it's the daily threat of fear that keeps the citizens from protesting, from demanding rights, from having an uprising to change their government. Even in a democratic government, fear can control and keep us in a state of panic, so we're unable to get on with our lives.

If we give in to fear, we give over our power to others who, we hope, will make everything right. We blindly trust when we fear. We don't question the scenario described to us. We believe what the government tells us, even allowing the government to take away our rights in the name of national security.

During a time of fear, we mistrust our neighbors, not knowing whose side they're on, or whether their opinions will endanger us further. It becomes very important for us to know who's right—about opinions, attitudes, and actions—because it seems to be a matter of life or death. We saw fear work during the Red Scare of the 1940s and 1950s, when we feared the Communists would take over our country, or the countries of our allies, or drop a nuclear bomb on us. We practiced hiding under our desks at school, in case the siren went off and the nuclear bomb was on its way.

When people, or governments, can engender enough fear, people seem able to get away with anything. The fear of communism led to Senator Joe McCarthy's witch hunt for anyone who had, at one time or another, been in the Communist Party or who knew someone who was in the Communist Party. The fear was used to build up the military-industrial complex and to overprotect ourselves, to the extent that within a few decades, we had enough bombs to kill everyone in the world many times over.[14]

On both a national and personal level, the fear was insidious, changing the lives of many. People were falsely accused. Careers were ruined. It is not truthful, wise, or decent to build up false fears.

Many of us experienced the same kind of fear during the attacks of 9/11, particularly in those immediate hours after the attacks, when planes were still in the air and nobody knew how many had been hijacked. I was visiting Colorado Springs at that time, and knew this city would certainly be a target, because NORAD, Peterson Air Force Base, Fort Carson, and the Air Force Academy all are within twenty minutes of where I was staying. I grabbed my keys, got into my rental car, and drove back to Los Angeles. At times, when driving through the beautiful and isolated country of western Colorado, I thought: "If I only stay right here, without a house in sight, maybe I'll be safe." It was, indeed, a false hope.

The Consequences of Helplessness

Whether or not it's true, we feel the world is out of control, and we fear there is little we can do about it. The effects of constant fear not only give our power away to anyone who promises to keep us safe, but have caused many children and young people throughout the world to act out this fear through escaping to drugs and alcohol or sex, or at the extreme, becoming suicide bombers because they feel they live in a hopeless world where only threats, hatred, and us-against-them seems to rule.

The Founding Fathers were particularly concerned about how fear could affect our country. They were concerned about the creation of a democratic government because democracy can easily turn to tyranny, particularly in fearful times. James Madison was concerned about periods of insecurity, because at those times the power of the president becomes greater. Checks and balances lose their place. Reasonable discourse gets lost in the angry and fearful rhetoric.

When George W. Bush told Congress, and the American people, that Iraq had weapons of mass destruction that could be turned on us, and reach us within forty-five minutes, he raised the fear level within all of us. What were we to do about it? We gave him what he asked for—the power to declare war against Iraq, whenever he wanted. Congress said yes, and the few who voted against these expanded powers were considered soft on terrorism. At that point in history, President Bush had more power than any king or ruler in any country. He had absolute power to make any decision that he wanted about this war. It didn't matter whether he was right or wrong. It didn't matter whether there was proof about his accusations. It didn't matter whether some in Congress wanted more information or wanted more reasonable debate to prevail. This was expanded power, beyond what the Founding Fathers wanted. It was exactly the power that the Founding Fathers most feared.

Fear Breeds on Secrecy

A fearful response leads to lost freedoms. Shortly after 9/11, Congress passed the Patriot Act. This act allowed the government to snoop into which books we were checking out of the library, what we were reading on the Internet, which documents we had downloaded, all with a cloak of secrecy. We had no rights to a lawyer, no rights to due process. We could be held in total secrecy in prison, without anyone knowing where we were. We could be deported if we were under suspicion, even if we were innocent. Ben Franklin said, "Those who would trade liberty for security deserve neither." Many American people were willing to accept the tradeoff.

In fearful times, information is not as accessible. Information is guarded and protected, partly in the interests of national security, and partly because government officials tell us they know best.

As a result, we don't know whether secret policies are effective. Has the Patriot Act truly stopped other terrorist acts? We don't know. There is total secrecy around how the Patriot Act is applied, whether it's effective, how many terrorist acts it has prevented.

There is secrecy around the prisons at Guantánamo Bay and the prisons used for detainees in Afghanistan, Uzbekistan, Jordan, and Iraq. Has the information we gained from the prisoners stopped a terrorist attack or helped us uncover other terrorists? We don't know. The information is guarded, and we have no way of assessing whether this method works, or to what extent it works.

In times of fear, reason and evaluation are usually not part of the process. We feel there's no time to take a deep breath, get advice from others, think, reason, evaluate, and stop ourselves from reacting in knee-jerk fashion. In times of fear, we are in great danger of retaliating, of allowing our vengeful nature to take precedence, of telling ourselves we have to do something fast. We lose our ability to think clearly.

The result is that fear bolsters power. We turn to our leaders to give us security, to take care of us, to not let anything harm us. We want to trust them. We want to see a show of strength, a command of the situation. When they say they're handling it, we would just as soon not know what is happening, but we believe that whatever is being done must be the right thing. We often prefer to deal with fear by putting our heads in the sand, forgetting our fannies are still in firing range.

Look at almost any tyrant and see how that person rose to power. Usually it was a time of great threat and of great despair. Before World War II, when Germany's economy was in ruin, Adolf Hitler rose up to help form a new national identity. Hitler brought the country together again, stoked up the fear of the "others" out there who meant to humiliate Germans, and created a strong defense system that could handle that threat. The country banded together.

Out of fear, we lose our cool. We are in a state of constant panic, and have no idea what to do about it. We sometimes respond by finding safety in groups. We identify with a particular group or a particular party that believes its approach is right, and demonizes anyone standing against it. There is too much at stake to be kind or welcoming to the Other. We form communities, but they often are communities that bond together out of hate and fear and lash out and attack the enemy. It is the bonding that comes from a defensive posture, ever watchful of what is "out there," rather than from a community that works together to create an effective solution.

Fight or Flight

We respond to fear in different ways. Generally we respond with some form of fight or flight.

Like many animals, some of us run the other way as fast as we can when we see a threat. If we can't run, we find other forms of fleeing. We might deny the threat to make it less real. We might say "It won't happen here" or "We have good leaders. They know what they're doing" or "It's not as bad as it seems" or "Everything will be all right."

Denial is dangerous because it can easily get us into trouble. We tune out the reality of the situation and are not prepared when the danger is upon us. Though counterterrorism expert

Richard Clarke recognized the potential threat of a terrorist attack in the United States, George W. Bush didn't take the time to see him and listen to him. This was denial—thinking that it can't happen here.

Those who don't flee out of fear often turn to fight. They become full of bravado and bluster, and let the enemy know they won't back down, they won't give up their territory, they won't be a wimp or a wuss.

This stance raises the stakes of the fight. If one person starts the battle by holding one rock, the other has to have two. If one has 100 bombs, the other has to outdo him with 200. We arm ourselves to the teeth, and let the other know that we're going to get him, which leads to the other side, out of necessity, arming itself. We demand an "eye for an eye," but soon all we have are two blind soldiers.

The fighting stance adds fuel to the fire and more danger to everyone. When Bush said "Bring it on!" toward the start of the Iraq War, his stance served to continually up the ante. We refuse to back down, because this seems like defeat. We keep doing more and more. We throw more money at the war, then more money at security forces to guard our soldiers, our civilians, and the citizens of the country we're occupying. When that doesn't work, we add more troops. The other side then recruits more ground troops, who bomb everyone they can find, at every checkpoint and around every corner. We add more planes and bomb the enemy back. They keep up the pressure. Everyone digs in their heels and refuses to budge. Who really wins? No one. Winning only after a country is in ruins and hundreds of thousands of people are dead or wounded is not really winning.

The fighting stance has nowhere to go except out of control. There is no evaluation, because that would mean someone would need to back down, regroup, rethink. There is no wiggle room for us to take another approach, to try another tactic, to see if we can negotiate or reach some agreement.

To keep the hatred at a high pitch, we have to objectify the enemy, making them less than human. We demonize the enemy, calling the leader of the country "Another Hitler, another Stalin, the Great Satan, the evil empire, the axis of evil." Once we do that, there is no room for discussion or debate.

The Hebrew Scriptures are filled with stories of battles and wars and the desire to defeat the enemy. The Psalmists ask God to come and heap burning hot coals on the enemy, or to protect them against the wrath of the enemy by delivering the enemy to Hell (in one form or another).

The Gospels and Epistles have none of these stories, even though Rome was the occupying power and was a cruel and ruthless nation. What did Jesus do? He told the Truth. He forgave. He healed some of the Romans when they asked, and let his Light shine to change hearts and minds.

What are we to do? Is there an alternative to fighting or fleeing?

Recognizing Our Vulnerability

Americans are constantly being told we are the richest and most powerful nation in the world. As a result, we can easily believe we are invulnerable, that nothing can touch us, that we're strong enough to fight back against anything. But we're not.

The Bible continually harps on us to recognize we're helpless and dependent creatures. It uses a number of metaphors to describe who we are, and many of them are metaphors of the helpless—that we are the lost sheep who are in need of a shepherd,[15] that we are to be like little children,[16] that we might be the person who has fallen among thieves, in need of a Good Samaritan to help us.[17] Sometimes God compares himself to the poor and vulnerable and small. He is like the widow who searches for a lost coin.[18] He is like a hen that gathers her little chicks together against the threat.[19] Ultimately, He is the Son who was an itinerant preacher, with little money, who was beaten and killed by the religious authorities and the authorities of Rome. "Gentle Jesus meek and mild" shows a part of Jesus that truly is vulnerable and helpless and even seemingly defenseless.

It's as if God is saying to us, "You are helpless. No matter how much you do, that's just how it is! Get used to it!"

Learning to accept our vulnerability allows us to put our trust in God. We learn we can't do it by ourselves. We are in need of a Savior.

Although we may pay lip service to this idea, we don't like the feeling. Part of our defensive posture comes from a belief that somehow, if we're strong enough, and have a big enough army, and spend enough money on defense, we need never believe our human condition is one of vulnerability. If we started with an understanding of our vulnerability, our responses might be quite different from the immediate knee-jerk response we usually have when threatened by the Other.

Dealing with the Terrible Neighbor

We gain strength knowing that God is on our side. Not our side as Americans, or because we think that we're right and therefore God is on our side and not on the other person's, but knowing that God is within us, guiding us through loving responses rather than hateful ones. And God is also on everyone else's side, in one way or another.

When we change our perspective of others from the enemies to the neighbors, the relationship between us begins to change. In a sense, we are much the same as the neighbors. Usually, they have concerns similar to ours. They too want justice, freedom from oppression, and the freedom to live good lives. How they and we go about achieving these things may be drastically different, or they may be much more similar than we think.

The Bible has a great understanding about the enemy, some of it contrary to how we think the world actually works. We believe we best deal with enemies by keeping them in their place, never letting an ounce of love or understanding or compassion come between us and them. They are, and must remain, totally evil.

Of course, our enemies are not letting any love or understanding come from their side either. But that's the point Jesus made. He said if you love people who love you, it isn't anything extraordinary; everyone does that.[20] Christians are asked to go another step: to love their enemy.[21] Loving enemies seems to be impossible unless we decide to try it. It's a radical message, yet that's what we're commanded to do—to treat everyone as the neighbor, and to love them. How are we able to do this impossible task? By the work of the Holy Spirit.

We can start loving our enemies by recognizing we have no choice in the matter.

If there's a mad dog in the neighborhood, we can't ignore it. If there are threatening neighbors, we have no choice. We have to deal with them. We move from denial of the problem to looking clearly at the reality of the situation. As Christians, the immediate response of "Bad people, let's get rid of them!" may be the last response, but we should guard against it being the first. It's not unusual to get rid of one neighbor, only to have someone worse come in instead. The problem hasn't really gone away. It's just gone to another neighborhood.

We first must recognize the danger to be addressed. What is the threat? Where is it coming from? How bad is it? There is no denying there are true threats, of terrorism, war, killings, and various forms of mayhem. This isn't just a threat to us in the United States; it's a threat to the world. It can kill hundreds, thousands, or millions. The threat will stop at nothing. It affects us all. We can't ignore it, deny it, or pretend it won't happen to us. We still must protect our property, and our citizens.

We can begin working with the threat by working to dissipate the danger, not add fuel to the fire. We don't appease the terrorists, but we need to clearly understand the threat and let wise heads prevail. We can't get sidetracked about it. Responding with fear and trembling, and giving power away to the government, is not the answer.

Unfortunately, that's the first response we had to the war on terror—we got sidetracked. We got trigger-happy. We changed our focus. We looked the other way. After 9/11, we were of one mind with much of the rest of the world—we had to face the terrorists and we had to do it together because it affects all our neighborhoods. We recognized that there were terrorists in many countries, and if we shared information, worked together, established a common goal, maybe we could effectively diminish, or even remove, the threat.

But we didn't do that. Instead, we started shooting at the wrong targets. We got confused about who was doing what to whom. The terrorists came from Saudi Arabia, and we decided to shoot at Afghanistan. That might have worked—if the problem had been defined as the oppressive rule of the Taliban. But that wasn't the problem; the problem was terrorists. Not only did we not stop the terrorists, we weren't even truly successful with Afghanistan. The Taliban is now coming back. The elections were corrupt. We spent a lot of money, bombed many places, and killed a number of people—but we didn't solve the problem.

We then went into Iraq, a country that had nothing to do with 9/11. We spent a lot of money, bombed a lot of places, killed a lot of people—but we haven't solved the problem. In fact, we've made it worse. Now Al Qaeda is in Iraq. Before, it wasn't.

If we can't define the problem, we can't solve it. Many say, "It's the Muslims!" No, that's not a clear definition of the problem. It's a particular group of Muslims. Just as I wouldn't want to be put into the same category as some Christians, most

Muslims wouldn't want to be put into the category of the terrorist Muslims.

The Koran calls on Muslims to be peacemakers and not to hate. "Be upright for Allah, bearers of witness with justice, and let not hatred of a people incite you not to act equitably."[22] There are plenty of verses within the Koran about justice and mercy, which, like many verses in our Bible, are being misinterpreted to justify hate and war and killing of the innocent.

Know Your Neighbor

Unfortunately, we know very little about the enemy we're fighting, nor do we seem to want to know, since that means recognizing their motivations. It's like having a neighbor down the street who spends a lot of time in his basement, exhibiting some occasional strange behavior, and there's no Neighborhood Watch to keep an eye on him. We need to know our enemy, and also know our neighbor!

This is not a war against a country. Terrorists live and work in more than sixty nations, on every continent. Bombing one country after another is not going to solve the problem. Deposing one bad leader after another will not solve the problem. We need to start asking, What's really happening here? What's beneath the surface of these events?

Nobody does evil acts just because they woke up that morning and decided to do evil acts. After 9/11, one of my graduate-school teachers asked the question, "Why do they hate us so?" Some would answer, "Because they're evil" or "Because they hate Christians and Jews" or "Because they have no respect for human life" or "Because they are jealous of capitalism." These are made-up, superficial reasons. They tell us virtually nothing about the real reason. We have to go deeper than this to solve this problem. Why do they hate Christians and Jews? Why would they be jealous of capitalism? Since they say they're doing it for God, then in their own eyes they aren't evil, any more than we consider ourselves evil for going to war in Iraq.

Most of us know virtually nothing about the Middle Eastern culture and about the Muslim religion. We know very little about jihad, or what it means to fight a holy war, or why they're fighting it, or why they're fighting it now.

Have you noticed no one is asking about the real reasons? We are so eager to get rid of our enemies, and kill them, and wipe them off the face of the earth, that we have not been realistic about the fact that we can't do that—there are too many of them. Nor have we been realistic about knowing who they are and why they do what they do.

Unlike many Europeans, who do more traveling to other countries, many Americans have very little experience with cultures abroad. Since 1988 I've worked in about twenty-five different countries, although never for more than three weeks. I know my knowledge of cultures is not as deep as that of someone who has lived abroad for months or years. Even from my limited experience, I discovered, through the unwitting faux pas I have occasionally committed, that people and cultures and religions are not the same. I can't deal with problems in Italy the same way I would in Germany. The way I ask questions in Japan needs to be different from the way I might ask a question or make a statement in Norway. Cultures are not all alike—not in their motivation, behavior, or goals. If we assume that everyone thinks the same way that we do—about democracy, about civil rights, about what's best for a country's citizens, about religion—we provide the first spark in the powder keg of misunderstanding.

I've wondered why the White House doesn't seem to be talking to Muslim leaders who could give us some understanding into a people, and a culture, we know virtually nothing about. Yes, we've been friends with some Westernized Muslims, such as Ahmed Abdel Hadi Chalabi, who fed us some lies and tried to manipulate the situation to his advantage. But what about the others? Where are the Muslim diplomats, who could give us insight? Where are the Muslim scholars and theologians, who could give us more insights into the culture and the religion? Where are the commissions that are analyzing the problem by helping us understand the culture? I have come to the conclusion we don't have a sufficient idea of what we're doing, and are basically shooting in the dark. How can we create effective policy if we don't know the neighbor?

To understand Muslim culture, we also need to recognize that our culture is not a perfect culture with such high values that every right-thinking person from another country wants to be Americanized.

There are those Muslims who truly hate the values of the West. We presume our values are the best values, but a number of other cultures find us far too materialistic—with far too much focus on making money and having money. They see us as dogmatic and self-righteous. They see our families and communities as fragmented, and only have to read the papers to know that even our Christian religious groups can barely talk to each other. We export our values throughout the world, beaming them into people's television sets every night. But there are many cultures that feel oppressed by our constant presence.

If we believe America is perfect, it will be impossible for us to listen to and comprehend any other position. If we're open to hearing the other side, we gain knowledge that can be helpful in fighting terrorism, and turning the enemy into at least a neighbor, if not a friend.

Where do we find out about Muslim motivations? From Muslims. After the bombing in London, and after the arrests in the city of Leeds, several Muslim youth were shocked, although not completely surprised, that their friend, Shehzad Tanweer, was one of the suicide bombers. They explained how they understood his motivation: "He was sick of it all, all the injustice . . . why, for example, don't they ever take a moment of silence for all the Iraqi kids who die?"

Another friend of the suicide bomber called it a "double standard." "I don't approve of what he did, but I understand it. You get driven to something like this, it doesn't just happen." Many of his friends shared the same sense of outrage, of siege, of otherness, the sense that Muslims were "helpless before the whims of greater powers." In each case, none of the youth condoned the behavior, but they understood the anger.

This is what the fighting stance does. It pushes those who feel defeated over the edge, and they come back with some underhanded tactic, doing what they can do to win. Terrorism is the cheapest form of warfare—no army, little equipment, lots of attention, lots of bang for very little money. They bomb the subways and trains in Madrid and London, they blow up the buildings in New York and Washington, they blow up planes, trains, and automobiles and resorts and nightclubs. We have been warned, from the story of David and Goliath,[23] that the little guy can stand up to the big guy, and sometimes the little guys win, or at least they can keep us on edge for a long period of time. And the little guys don't go away.

The government seems to have little understanding of the situation, and little desire to understand it. Republicans have accused the Democrats of being soft on security, and accused them of "wanting to start a support group to talk about it!" This is demonizing the Democrats, since they never said such a thing, nor have they ever done such a thing—although a bit of support and talking to each other might help. This response is part of an overall stance by some Republican extremists who demonize other Christians, Democrats, Iraqis, Middle Easterners, Muslims, and anyone who doesn't agree with them.

This is not about being "soft." It is, however, taking into consideration the possibility that understanding might help us better deal with this problem. We have a dilemma to confront, which is religious, political, ethical, and psychological. How are we to deal with terrorists, without demonizing them, being naive about them, and without making matters worse?

Who Are These People?

There are a number of different types of terrorists. There are those who aren't Muslim, but are capable of doing the same kind of ruthless killings. The Oklahoma City bombing was not done by Muslims, nor were the many bombings done by the Basques who wanted their independence from Spain, or the Irish Republican Army who wanted British rule out of their lives, or the many killings in South Africa before apartheid was ended.

Some Muslims are new to terrorism—alienated youth who are looking for a cause, who feel wronged, who see little being done to address their problems. These are the ones that seem to be behind the London bombings.

They are also the ones being recruited by hard-core terrorists who use these young people's sense of injustice and outrage and inequalities—which do exist—to stoke up their religious fervor and desire for revenge.

Dining with Sinners

Suppose we look at the example of Jesus. What did Jesus do when dealing with sinful people? In many instances, he began by asking questions, by accepting and respecting the Other, by peering into the heart of the Other. He saw their true situation, whether seeing how the poor were in bondage or how the rich were in bondage. He saw their hurt, their pain, their misery, their oppression. He saw their hypocrisy, their vengeful spirit, their judgmentalism. He didn't excuse the sin but he dealt with the person. He understood.

He looked into the real meaning of the event. In many instances, people told him their interpretation of an event. He spoke to the blind man, who said the reason he was blind was probably because of his own or his parents' sins. Jesus said that wasn't true, and explained the real reason—it was so God could do his work.[24] He was told not to pick corn on the Sabbath, and was told the reason—because the Scriptures say so. He replied, "No, the Sabbath was made for man, not man for the Sabbath."[25]

Jesus peered deeply into the meaning of the event, without accepting what it looked like on the surface. He didn't accept the first knee-jerk interpretation. Nor did he accept the interpretation that always put the worst light on the action. Things weren't always what they seemed.

Jesus also went a step further, by becoming involved with others. Instead of removing himself from sinners and outcasts, he ate with them. He dined with prostitutes and tax collectors, with fishermen and with women. He was willing to relate closely with others, even the outcasts. He was willing to continue the dialogue.

Can we get anywhere if we refuse to talk with, and dine with, sinners? Without some kind of discussion, there is no possible way that we can understand motivation, reasoning, or what the problem is. Nor can we start to develop bonds of trust and understanding if we refuse to be in the same room as our enemies. We cut off communication with whomever we consider our enemies—such as North Korea and Iran—and we even alienate ourselves from our friends, if they don't agree with us. We boycott French champagne because that country won't join us in our war. We decide we even want to change the name of "French fries," even though the French are only exercising their democratic right not to agree with us. How small-minded we have become!

I don't expect us to sit down and have a nice conversation with terrorists. But we can talk with leaders of the countries. We can talk with those who understand the countries and culture. Rather than dismissing them, we can relate to them.

We might feel that the Other is impossible to love, understand, or care about. We might feel we must put our Christian values aside, and decide this problem is simply too great and our loving religion simply not practical. But if Christianity isn't practical in the worst of circumstances, it's no better than any religion that serves us well when things are going well, but isn't workable when life is difficult.

Last Act Ethics

The Quaker author Dr. William Durland uses a term called "last act ethics." It means we tend to make a judgment on someone's last action, rather than going to the root cause. If someone sets a bomb, we then create all of our ethical responses based on the bombing, not on what has gone before. We don't want to deal with the whole action, but only with the most dramatic part of the action.[26] Durland says, "Last Act Ethics . . . means that we tend to hold the person who commits the last sinful act in a chain of sinful acts . . . responsible for the entire progression of wrong-doing."[27] Since the action that is most apparent is clearly wrong, we make a judgment about it and feel good about ourselves. We know evil when we see it, and set ourselves up to be able to call it correctly. Of course, the other side is doing the same thing. They see our evil, call it as they see it, and then respond. Then we do it back—they shoot, we shoot back. They bomb, we bomb back. They're evil. We are simply getting rid of the evil.

Jesus saw cause and effect another way. Rather than looking at the end result, he saw that there are chains of events that lead to sin, and that the last person may not be the one who most deserves punishment. When Jesus saw the adulterous woman who, we are told, was caught in the act,[28] Jesus knew that her sin was not her sole responsibility. He must have noticed the man was not around to be punished, even though adultery can't be done alone. She was not punished, but was told to sin no more.

The Bible tells us "what you sow you shall reap."[29] True, to some extent. But Jesus broke the chain that said everything in life is based on cause and effect. He brought grace into the equation. Grace does not depend on what we deserve, but is a gift.[30] Durland calls grace "an immense gift that God gives us to change the state of things before our very eyes and to revolutionize history. Grace breaks the chain of everlasting cause and effect and is, in a sense, an in-breaking of God into history. It means God is everlastingly kind, even to those who do bad acts."[31]

We are all estranged from God, because of our "fallen" nature. If we have been given grace, by getting not our just deserts but good deserts instead, then we are asked to also treat others with the grace that we have been given. Rather than being measly, we are asked to be generous. Rather than being judgmental, we are asked to forgive others as we have been forgiven.

Jesus told us that before we judge others, we need to look at ourselves. This is good advice for us as individuals and as a country. We don't have a very introspective government. It is busy blaming others but not looking at the log in its own eye. We can begin by looking at those elements of our own behavior that set up the occasion of wars, and that set up unjust situations. We are not wholly innocent here. Although some people seem to be against soul-searching and think we're soft if we look at ourselves, Jesus made it very clear that this is exactly what we're supposed to do. We are to look at our own behavior and take the log out of our own eye before peering at the speck in the other person's eye, and make repentance if necessary. By looking at ourselves, we might also get a better understanding of the Other. We might learn a little humility. If we and the Other are so much alike in our evil, perhaps we might also be somewhat alike in our goodness.

We Don't Do It Alone

The United States sometimes seems to have a cowboy mentality. I live in the West, and I love much about the cowboy culture, but there is a part of this culture, often seen in the old Westerns, that believes in the rugged individualism of the Lone Ranger, forgetting that even the Lone Ranger didn't work alone. Americans have a history of being self-sufficient and self-reliant. We believe reliance on others shows our weakness.

Rather than recommending rugged individualism, the Bible emphasizes community, the bonds of working together, the importance of banding together and helping each other. The early Christian Church became powerful because of the strength of the community. Its members supported each other, guided each other, and were eventually able to destroy the oppression of Rome.

After 9/11, we banded together into a world community, creating a coalition against terror. Colin Powell sought support from all over the world, including from organizations such as NATO, the United Nations, the European Union, and the Organization of the Islamic Conference for the fight against terrorism. In spite of the grief I shared with our nation, I also experienced a sense of power and hope, feeling we had become "one world" and it was possible to resolve this problem—together.

But we didn't follow the policy of coalition-building. Instead, we returned to the individualism that says we'll do it alone. Rather than listening to the wisdom of others, we vilified them if we didn't agree with them, and chose not to talk to them.

From the Three Rs to the Four Rs

It is possible to overcome our fear and to deal with terrorism in an effective and Christian way. We can move from the evils of revenge, retribution, and retaliation to the good of repentance, reconciliation, rehabilitation, and restitution.

It is natural for us to want revenge when we've been wronged. We easily turn to retaliation—do unto them as they have done unto us. We only need to look at the history of the world to realize this has not been totally effective. The Biblical standard asks us, in most instances, to take the opposite actions.

My career consultant, Judith Claire, taught me a process to use whenever I had wronged another, or been wronged. She said, "First think about your part in it. If you wronged someone else, why did you do it? Did you do something to cause this response?" We are not to think about our actions in order to justify them, but in order to understand them so we don't do them again. Then, we are to repent and make amends. I have a great respect for people who apologize, although it is sometimes looked at as "eating crow" or being weak. But apologies are the first step to reconciliation.

After we apologize, we try to make it right, in whatever way possible. We reconcile with the other by asking for forgiveness, and asking what we can do to reconcile. This might include restitution—doing something to make up for past wrongs; repairing the damage; giving a gift to try to bring us back into a loving relationship.

Judith recommends, "Ask yourself what was your part in this process. Was there an old grievance that didn't get resolved? Had something been simmering for some time that you ignored? Even if their response to you was out of proportion to what you had done, still, look at your own part in it first." If we have been attacked and the degree of the attack against us seems greater than the proportion of the wrong we have done, we still need to look at our part in it. Most terrorism comes from grievances in the past about what we have done, or others have done, to create an unbalance or an injustice. Sometimes the lashing out from terrorists is not specific—it seems as if the rage will lash out at anyone. Sometimes it is very specific—what you did to me, I'll do back to you at a similar target.

Beyond "Tit for Tat"

There is another way of responding, which is not tit for tat. We usually believe in tit for tat; doing the same to enemies that they did to us. Of course, a case can be made that we've overdone our part of the equation. Nineteen hijackers killed more than 3,000 innocent people on 9/11. We have now killed far more than that in Iraq and in Afghanistan, even though neither country was behind those attacks. Tit for tat usually gets out of hand.

There is another approach, called tit-for-two-tat, which has been developed by game theorists who look at how to win against aggression.[32] Robert Axelrod discusses this theory in his book *The Evolution of Cooperation*. Instead of aggressively responding in kind, we respond to defuse the situation. This doesn't mean we don't respond, but we give them an opportunity to "take it back" or to change their behavior. Coalition-building is an example of not responding in kind, but rather responding with a nonaggressive though potentially effective stance. If that doesn't work, rather than upping the stakes by responding with more force, we diminish our response, always coming in with a less aggressive stance or an equal stance. The 1986 bombing raid against Libya, during Ronald Reagan's presidency, and the 1993 attack on Iraq's intelligence headquarters during Clinton's, showed that, as Bill Clinton writes, "American power could deter states that were directly involved in terrorist acts against us; neither nation attempted another one."[33]

There are other possible responses. We might also respond not with hate, but with love and compassion in a way that gains the goodwill of most of the people. Though we recognize that there will always be evil in the world, we can help diminish its power.

What would have happened if we had truly helped the Afghans rebuild their country rather than diverting our attention to Iraq? What would have happened if we had truly tried to help the Iraqis living under an oppressive rule, rather than feeding that rule with guns and with our friendship for more than a decade, and then delivering sanctions against the country that took its worst toll on the innocent? What would happen if we spent our money rebuilding countries and bringing justice, rather than continuing an endless cycle of bombing, propping up leaders countries don't want, and interfering with their internal policies?

If we are self-righteous, we can't even start to have any level of understanding. If we can't reflect and look at ourselves, we can't remove the one problem we do have some control over. If we can't listen, we can't discover the truth. If we keep putting new wine into old wineskins, we just keep repeating the same ineffective approach, over and over again.

Casting Out Fear with Hope

The alternative to fear is hope. Not unrealistic hope, or Pollyanna hope, or denial of the reality, but a vision. The Bible is filled with verses about the necessity, and the greatness, of hope over fear. We can practice hope, live hope, respond with hope. Hope sees potential. Hope changes our stance. Rather than becoming immobile out of fear, we become actively creative out of hope.

Quakers like myself believe there is "that of God" in everyone, and when we relate to another person, we look for the glimmer of God. We have found, throughout our history, that this belief has enabled us to relate to others who are considered the no-hope-people, those who have been written off as "impossible," "not worth it," and "less than human."

In the early days of our country, when other settlers were warring with the Indians, and were being attacked and killed, their houses burned down and their children kidnapped, the Quakers were on friendly terms with the Indians. The Indians baby-sat the Quakers' children when the parents had to be away from home. The Indians had an agreement among themselves—not to attack a Quaker home or to shoot a Quaker.

Why this difference? The Quakers always treated the Indians fairly. They paid for the land they wanted, rather than just taking it. They signed treaties with the Indians, which are some of the few treaties in our history that were never broken. They never locked their doors, so the Indians knew they were welcome in their homes. They respected their ways. Likewise, when other missionary groups have been kicked out by repressive governments, Quakers have often been allowed to remain.

Responding to fear through hope and respect and trust is not often a natural response. It is a learned response. But Quakers have proven that it is possible to treat the enemy humanely, not by colluding with the enemy, but by listening, reflecting, and trying to set policies in place that have a better chance of remedy and reconciliation than do more labeling, more anger, more hatred, more shooting, more war, more deaths, and another cycle of anger, hatred, war, and death.

Hope trusts and believes that when we work together, something larger than each one of us gets created. If we only surround ourselves with like-minded people, it's easy for us to become unyielding in our "right-ness" and the enemy's "wrongness." We do what's been done before. We think someone else can fix everything for us. We begin to look for others who agree with us, so that our combined, powerful voices can drown out other answers. We become blinded to the possibilities that others can bring.

Hope is different. Hope believes in alternatives. It respects others, encourages everyone to think creatively, listen, brainstorm. It believes in God's impossibilities.

Working Together

Bill Clinton ran for president as the "man from Hope" (both the town in Arkansas and the idea), and he emphasized the possibilities. John Edwards, in his speech at the 2004 Democratic convention, said "Hope is on the way!" What is the hope that the Democrats speak about, versus the fear that is so prevalent with the Republicans?

The Democrats see there is hope if we work together by rebuilding our alliances so that we are, once more, working together. We are divided at home and in the world, most of it of our own doing. The Democratic Platform clarifies what the party sees as part of the reason for this problem: "The Bush Administration has walked away from more than a hundred years of American leadership in the world to embrace a new—and dangerously ineffective—disregard for the world."

When we try to be the big kid on the block, we have no support when something goes wrong. Why should anyone come to our aid, when we haven't come to theirs? Why should others come to help us, when they warned us not to go into danger in the first place? We keep thinking others will join us in our efforts, and are surprised when they don't. Considering how we've treated our allies since 2003, it's not surprising that they have no desire to join with us in our foolhardy endeavors.

It's human nature to rejoice in seeing the bully on the block get taken down a few pegs, and find he's not quite as popular as he thought. Sometimes, we have to work against our human nature.

The Democratic Platform defines the problem: The Republicans "rush to force before exhausting diplomacy. They bully rather than persuade. They act alone when they could assemble a team. They hope for the best when they should prepare for the worst. Time and again, this Administration confuses leadership with going it alone and engagement with a compromise of principle."

The Democrats put the emphasis on an America "that listens and leads." They recognize the importance of listening, of respect for the other. "We believe in an America that people around the world admire, because they know we cherish not just our freedom, but theirs. Not just our democracy, but their hope for it. Not just our peace and security, but the world's."

Any kind of victory against this threat needs to be a multi-pronged approach, since the threat has many tentacles, reaching out to us in many different ways. Democrats suggest a variety of approaches, some of which continue Bill Clinton's approach to stopping the threat. Mr. Clinton's strategy was to capture and punish terrorists through international cooperation, "interrupting the flow of money and communications to terrorist organizations, cutting off access to weapons of mass destruction, and isolating and imposing sanctions on nations that support terrorism."[34] President Clinton's administration also stopped several terrorist attacks that could have been as costly as 9/11. There is the reality that there will probably be other attacks. But we can stop some, perhaps many of them.

According to the party's platform, what would the Democrats do differently than the Republicans? The Democrats would cut off terrorist funds, including the financing that comes from Saudi Arabia: "We will put an end to the Bush Administration's kid-glove approach to the supply and laundering of terrorist money." The Democrats would also prevent Afghanistan from continuing as a terrorist haven. Two years ago, George W. Bush promised that the United States would help rebuild Afghanistan. Instead, the administration has turned its back on that country, not carrying through with its promises, and has allowed it to, once again, become a haven for terrorists as well as a center for the opium trade.

The Democrats would help nations struggling with the terrorists in their own countries—countries such as Somalia, the

Philippines, Indonesia, Morocco, and Turkey. They need "international help to close down terrorist havens."

At the core of this conflict is a struggle of ideas: "democracy and tolerance against those who would use any means and attack any target to impose their narrow views." The Democrats would help educational efforts, and work with the voices of freedom in the Arab and Muslim world. They would support human rights groups and labor unions, which are dedicated to building a democratic culture from the grassroots level.

Changing the Reaction

Any response to fear includes the reflective and the active. We reflect on our own fear and try, very hard, not to give in to it. Trappist monk Thomas Merton said "The root of war is fear." Fear of the Other, and fear of each other.[35] Fear can lead us into dangerous directions that engender more danger. Out of fear, we abuse prisoners, bomb civilians, threaten and bully others, and take a defensive stance, ready to fight and shoot at any moment. In turn, the enemy fears us, and does the same to us. All of these fearful reactions do nothing to make the world safer. They raise the threat level, putting the whole world on edge.

We need to accept our fears, and to take time to feel our fears. Americans aren't used to being victims. We're not used to being attacked, and being vulnerable. But if we allow ourselves to experience being victims, to grieve, to feel the pain, we have the potential to empathize with the millions of others around the world who have been victims of oppressive rule and unjust attacks. We move from being the most powerful nation to recognizing we are also a vulnerable nation—like every other nation in the world. We stop believing we are safe, or that we can be safe if we only have the right leaders in power, or if we only have enough weapons. We begin to learn what God has been trying to teach us, through the many wars in the Hebrew Scriptures, through the prophets, through Jesus and Paul: the human condition is not one of safety; it is not one of trusting in our own strength; it is not one of being so righteous that we're untouchable by danger.

We live in a dangerous world. We live in a flawed world. There is plenty of sin on all sides. And we are always in danger of responding to any threat out of our worst side, not our best. When an injustice has been done to us, we need to make sure we don't become like one of "them," and become part of the vengeful cycle of hatred. James Wallis, author of *God's Politics*, says, "We should respond out of our deepest values, not the terrorists'."[36] We need to learn not to bypass the wisdom that comes from fear, but to surrender to trust, be willing to bring love and compassion into our responses, and to believe in the leading of the Holy Spirit, who teaches us to abide in hope.

Chapter Eight

Secrets, Lies, and Deceptions

"You will not spread false rumours. You will not lend
support to the wicked by giving untrue evidence. . . .
you will not pervert the course of justice."

EXODUS 23:1–2

It seems to be the nature of politics that there are lies, deceptions, and "spin." Politicians do it to win elections. The media do it because hyperbole makes good news. We believe the deceptions because we can't believe that the nice guy from our party could possibly lie, although we can easily believe it about the other guy from the other side. Depending on which side we're on, it always seems the other side gets away with everything, and even the littlest flaw from our side is made into a glaring sin, capable of erasing any good that has ever been done.

Reagan was sometimes called the Teflon President, because no matter what he did, whether illegal or simply unwise, nothing seemed to stick to him. In some views, the Iran-Contra scandal was not only illegal, but possibly even treasonous. Nothing much seemed to come of it, though, once Reagan said he didn't remember what had happened.

There are always plenty of lies in politics, on both sides. But lies need to be addressed—on whichever side they happen. The media have not been helpful and honest about this. They have not always asked the hard questions or explored, fully, the deceptions. And the cost of these deceptions has been enormous.

A continuing theme in the Gospels and Epistles is the need to call each other to account. We are to speak the truth. Our "yes" is to be a "yes," our "no" a "no."[1] No lying. No covering up. No trying to get away with anything or put the blame somewhere else. We are to bear witness.

In the 1985 film *Witness*, a young Amish boy is a witness to a murder. An honest detective, John Book, learns the murderers come from his own corrupt police department. When he realizes that his own life, and the life of the boy, are in danger, he escapes to the Amish farm where the boy lives. At the end of the film, the three policemen who were conspirators in the murder come to the Amish farm, try to kill John Book, and threaten the family. As the violence escalates, the boy rings the supper bell to summon all the neighboring Amish to come to stop the violence. They stop it not by fighting back, or by saying anything, but simply by being there. In the light of day, their silent witness makes it impossible for the dishonesty and violence to continue.

When this film first came out, I discussed it with my Mennonite friend, Rachel. She said "to witness" is to bring the truth into the light of day, which is why it was important that the last scenes take place during the daylight, not at night. It is easy for us to obscure the truth in the darkness; is easy for us to decide not to see the truth or face the truth. The bright light of day, and the bright Light of Christ, make it possible for us to see truth and to recognize lies.

As I watched the film again, I also realized the director had to show, in many ways, that the little boy was a good witness. He noticed. He observed. And then he told the truth. We also are called to be witnesses to the truth—whenever, wherever, and however we may find it.

Politics and the Truth

Unfortunately, truth is something not often valued in politics. The end is often seen as justifying the means—even if there are lies along the way. Winning is valued at any cost, including the cost of a lie. The perception of being truthful and right is valued, even if the perception is wrong.

Republican Christians have an ethical dilemma they have not addressed. They have to decide whether to side with a president who sometimes may be, or is, wrong, or to side with truth. Too often, they have sided with the falsehood, the spin, the perception.

Republicans and Democrats alike get caught up in their lies and deceptions. Sometimes they get away with it, and sometimes they don't. It is particularly difficult to respect those who are supposed to abide by the truth when they call themselves Christian, and then, together with other conspirators, hide, obfuscate, and deny their lies.

We don't have to look far to see the many lies in government, or their consequences. Richard Nixon lied about Watergate and brought down his whole government, with forty government officials and members of Nixon's re-election committee convicted on felony charges. Lyndon B. Johnson ran on a peace ticket in 1964 at the same time he was planning on increasing the American troops going into Vietnam. Ronald Reagan either lied about or managed to have plausible deniability of knowledge of the trading of guns for hostages during the Iran-Contra affair. George Herbert Walker Bush promised "no new taxes" during his election campaign, and as soon as he got into office, he raised taxes. Bill Clinton lied about his affairs, including his affair with Monica Lewinsky, and was impeached for it, although not found guilty.

We never like to think our leaders lie. And some probably don't. But we've learned to distrust politicians since, it seems, the very process of getting elected demands spin, fudging, exaggeration, and deception. If they're part of our own party, we try to justify it, saying "Our lie wasn't as big as the other party's lie!" or "It wasn't quite like it seemed!"

Some explain away the lie, saying our leaders can't tell the truth because of "national security," and we simply must trust them. Lying, and not sharing important classified information because of national security, are two different things. Any president has the right not to tell truly secret information to the public, although how much needs to be secret from the Congress is another story.

Protecting national security is not the same as withholding information. There was no reason to withhold all the information necessary about John Bolton before appointing him as ambassador to the United Nations. There was no reason to withhold information about John Roberts or Samuel Alito, who may be Supreme Court Justices for the next twenty or thirty or forty years. There is no reason to withhold information when Congress needs the information to get at the truth.

We prioritize our lies. We vote according to what we consider the worst kind of lie and who we consider the worst liar. A friend of mine told me she considered Bill Clinton's sexual escapades in the Oval Office the worst lie and the worst behavior she had seen from any president. She could never vote for someone who had immoral sexual behavior, but she would vote for someone who lied in other areas, with more severe consequences. She is a dyed-in-the-wool Republican. Since this is her priority, I understand why the Republicans get her vote, because there is no denying the sexual infidelity of a few of the Democrat presidents, including John F. Kennedy as well as Mr. Clinton.

What's the problem with lies? Why is it so important, as a statement of Christian values and as a statement of our commitment to truth, justice, and freedom, that our leaders tell the truth?

Truth Matters

The eighth commandment is clear about lying: "Thou shalt not bear false witness."

As individuals and as a nation in a free society, we are called to make effective choices and good policies. Our Constitution and the history of our government show us an ideal way to reach the truth: through free and open debate and discussion that lead us to decide how best to accomplish a goal.

When a president carefully selects who will be in the audience for his speeches, making sure those who disagree with him are not allowed in the room, he has stopped the open debate necessary in a democracy.

When a president decides what information the Congress can see to help it reach a reasonable and informed decision about confirming justices, or bills, or policies, he is stopping the ongoing discussion that can lead to a wise decision about very important matters.

We get at the truth by consulting experts, forming commissions, looking at evidence, discussing the best policies to better our country, debating the pros and cons.

We cannot have good and effective policy without basing it on truth. We have far too many important issues to decide: We need to decide if, or when, we're to go to war. We need to choose the best energy policy, one that will most effectively take away our dependence on foreign oil in order to satisfy our country's very large energy needs. We have to decide what to do about the problems of poverty, discrimination, and health care. We need to determine which laws best keep our lawmakers honest.

C. S. Lewis said that he believes in democracy not because people are perfect, but because they are not. He realized that "Mankind is so fallen that no man can be trusted with unchecked power over his fellows."[2] As a result, he recognized that we need the protection of checks and balances to keep us honest.

It's imperative that we hold our government to a high standard of truth-telling in order for our society to function. During the Clinton years, millions and millions of dollars were spent on trying to find out whether the Clintons were telling the truth about their Whitewater real estate deal. They were. Millions more were spent on an impeachment hearing, to decide whether President Clinton should be kicked out of office for telling a lie about his relationship with Monica Lewinsky. Although by no means condoning his behavior or his lying about it, the Senate decided his personal misbehavior, and the lies he told about it, were not enough to convict him.

The George W. Bush administration has also lied, although it has not been held as accountable. There has been a Republican Congress throughout Bush's administration, which has made it impossible to get sufficient votes to investigate Mr. Bush's actions. There have been investigations—such as the 9/11 Commission and the prison abuse investigation—but most have been investigations of events, not of the top-level Republicans in office.

There are not sufficient votes in Congress to call President Bush to account. When Bill Clinton was president, the Republican majority in Congress spearheaded the investigation.

Jesus never let up on calling anyone to account. Nor did the prophets. As Christians, we have to hold ourselves to a higher standard, not a lesser standard. We have to believe truth matters.

Lies come in many forms. There are the big and small deceptions, the half-truths and the full lies, the little white lies. There is the refusal to tell the truth; the obfuscations, clouding over, covering up; the fudging of facts. There is blindness to what is really going on, and a lack of integrity in not calling a lie a lie.

The Lies

There have been a number of costly lies in the Bush administration. Some of these lies have led to policies we would not have followed if we had known the truth. These lies have led to dire consequences for our country.

The most glaring one, for many of us, is the information that Iraq "possesses and produces chemical and biological weapons. It is seeking nuclear weapons . . . the Iraq dictator must not be permitted to threaten America and the world with horrible poisons, and diseases, and gases, and atomic weapons. . . . The danger is already significant and it only grows worse with time. If we know that Saddam Hussein has dangerous weapons today—and we do—does it make any sense for the world to wait to confront him as he grows even stronger and develops even more dangerous weapons?"[3] This lie was supported with other lies. Colin Powell showed the United Nations some photographs that he was told showed evidence of weapons of mass destruction (WMDs). They had been taken some years before and were actually photos of empty trailers that may once have held some weapons. The photos were so dated that even if the trailers once had weapons, the evidence would have been irrelevant.

There also was some rather unsound intelligence given by Iraqis who had a stake in telling us incorrect information. We believed them, even though a number of people in government warned Mr. Bush about their lack of credibility and even though their information was contradicted by the findings of United Nations weapons inspector Hans Blix, who could not find any evidence of WMDs. George W. Bush and other Republican leaders continually said they were there—"Trust us!" And many did trust Mr. Bush, believing if he said it, it must be true. But it wasn't. How many WMDs did anyone actually find in Iraq? Zero.

Deceptions and Denials

There also were deceptions. "Deception" could be defined as implying something that isn't true, without actually telling a lie. It was implied that the Iraqis were responsible for 9/11. Therefore, the Iraqis had to be punished and stopped. In a speech Mr. Bush gave in June 2005, after it was clear from all investigations that Iraq had nothing to do with 9/11, George W. Bush continued to pair 9/11 and Iraq to justify the Iraq War, even though the two had no relationship to each other.[4]

President Bush also implied Iraq had helped train these terrorists. In a speech in 2002 he said, "And we know Iraq is continuing to finance terror, and gives assistance to groups that use terrorism to undermine Middle East peace. . . . We know that Iraq and Al Qaeda have had high level contacts that go back a decade." Yet, there was no evidence that Al Qaeda was training in Iraq, or being subsidized by that country in any way. If we attacked every country that had some Al Qaeda members there, we'd have more than sixty countries to invade. And others would have good reason to invade our country, because there are terrorists here as well.

George W. Bush implied that Afghanistan was behind 9/11. It wasn't. True, it had the training camps where the terrorists had trained. True, the country had provided a good haven for Osama bin Laden, following the Muslim code of giving sanctuary to those who asked. True, they had done nothing to stop the training. But the terrorists were not part of the Taliban, or part of the Afghan government, nor were they from Afghanistan. Although the Afghan government was repressive, it was not behind the 9/11 attack.

Each of these deceptions helped justify the Iraq War to the American people. Congress voted overwhelmingly in October 2002 to allow George W. Bush to attack Iraq, at whatever time he deemed appropriate. Congress gave Mr. Bush a blank check, and many Americans, including most in Congress, trusted him. But the truth was, he was wrong about most of what he said. Yet at no time has he admitted he was wrong, nor has he changed policies to reflect the new facts we have learned. A number of legislators have said that in retrospect, they would not have voted for the war if they had known the truth.

There is another kind of lie—denial. It comes from either the naiveté of the government, or from a government that hopes for the naiveté of the American citizens. It's the denial of facts and history that happens in almost every war. We're told it will be an easy war, and easily winnable. We're usually told the enemy wants us to come into their country and liberate them. We were told the Iraqis would welcome us with open arms, throw down their weapons, and there would be much rejoicing. Not true. Although some might wonder how we would know these things weren't true, others say we should know this because it has happened in almost every war, including the American Civil War, World War I, World War II, and Vietnam.

There is a rosy optimism from George W. Bush that ignores the reality of the situation and the reality of history. We are told about his own hopes as if they're the truth. It's not really the truth—it's simply his hope.

The spin only looks at one part of the story. We follow this story believing it's realistic, but it's not. We want our government to have the information and to tell us the truth, not to sell us the hope. Although many presidents do this, it's very costly for the country to be naive or to be in a state of denial.

Broken Promises

Many times politicians make big promises to get elected, and then soon after break their promises. Instead of telling the American people they can't promise something if they don't know for sure they can deliver it, they tell us what we want to hear. Promises are not to be taken lightly. If we say we're going to do something, it's a matter of integrity that we carry out our commitments. If we don't believe we can fulfill our vow, we shouldn't be making it in the first place. The Bible takes promises very seriously, and sees them as a solemn oath. We are called to do likewise.

Mr. Bush has claimed to be a fiscal conservative, yet he is the biggest spender in the history of our country. This administration began with a surplus and has created the biggest deficit in history. Although George W. Bush made a campaign promise to cut the deficit in half over five years, this is not realistic. This is supposed to be a conservative administration, but it clearly is very liberal when it comes to spending for the programs it favors.

Mr. Bush says he wants to reduce the deficit, but he has not vetoed a single piece of legislation while in office, even though many of the bills coming through Congress are filled with "pork." It is not unusual for Congress to pass bills that include too much fat. Many politicians do this. Congress is set up in a way that allows members to pad the bills for their own districts, and sneak in unnecessary spending. They're able to do so because there is no line-item veto. Given the size of our budget and a promise to cut the deficit, we would expect our president to start vetoing any bill that contains too much fat. But George W. Bush doesn't.

The Republican Party claims it is for states' rights and less government interference, but it is the Republicans who have been most intrusive in individual affairs—from the Terri Schiavo case, to various gag orders about abortion, to wanting to legislate personal relationships so they conform to the Republicans' moral code. Yet, they don't intrude in the affairs of corporations and big businesses.

The Republicans claim they care about the environment, but their actions say differently. They claim to protect veterans, but veterans' benefits have been cut.

They claim to care about the poor and middle class, but their tax policies have helped the super-rich, not the super-poor.

George W. Bush said he would be a uniter, not a divider, yet he has done little to unite us. He has not listened to Americans. He says he doesn't care about the polls, even though polls let him know what we think about, what we care about. He does nothing to seek anything close to consensus. We are, as a country, more divided than ever—over the war, over how we define our values, over the economy, over one group fighting another group.

Overselling the Truth

There's a saying about politicians: "If his lips are moving, there is probably some fudging of the truth." Whereas most presidents fudge the truth, George W. Bush makes blatant assertions, many of which cannot be proved or are later proven wrong.

In this sense, he is almost the opposite of Bill Clinton. Mr. Clinton was one of the best fudgers, constantly qualifying what he said. He knew just how to qualify everything so we thought he was telling the truth, though he was fudging it to make us believe something that was not exactly true. When he said he had tried marijuana, he fudged by saying he didn't inhale; therefore it didn't count. He said he hadn't had sexual relations with Monica, but his definition of sexual relations did not include oral sex.

President Bush is not a "fudger," but more like a salesman who believes, absolutely, in his product. Whatever he says, he says it as if it is the absolute truth, even when it clearly is not. Whereas Bill Clinton always left himself lots of wiggle room, which led to his own brand of lies, George W. Bush is the opposite. He is overconfident with his bald assertions, leaving no room for qualifying his statements.

He oversold his No Child Left Behind as a salvation for the educational system, but there have been few results. The law focuses on testing, not really fixing the educational system. Many states are refusing to participate because of the cost and insufficient federal funding and insufficient proof of its effectiveness.

He oversold the Iraq War, without admitting that the intelligence raised many doubts about his actions. Many people told him this would be tougher than we thought it would be, and that we knew nothing for sure about the weapons.

He oversold his willingness to cut spending, and he oversold his environmental programs, his educational programs, and his military programs.

Like a used-car salesman, Mr. Bush believes everything will be just fine, if he says it will be. He has an air of confidence that citizens respond to in opposite ways. Some love the fact he knows who he is and what he wants and what he believes, and is never swayed. They trust him—almost absolutely. In the view of many Republicans, there is no room for another point of view, not even an informed, wise, thoughtful point of view that has agreement from millions. They like the fact that in Mr. Bush's view, there are never two sides to an issue. There's only his side. In school, he was a cheerleader, and he knows how to get the cheering section going. He rarely expresses doubts, even about complex issues.

But others are very nervous about this confidence. They know complex issues are not black-and-white, and that people who think they are, are usually wrong. Cheerleading can be a good thing. But if we're cheering for the losing team, we may want to tone down our enthusiasm.

Labeling, Name-Calling, and Mud-Slinging

We also bear false witness by labeling others untruthfully to make sure the truth stays hidden. Since the year 2000, Democrats have constantly been told we're "un-American" and "unpatriotic" for questioning various policies of the government. As Christians, we're told we're "un-Christian" to question certain Republicans. As American citizens, we're told we are "unsupportive of our troops" if we question this war.

Why is labeling deceptive?

First of all, none of us fits neatly into categories. Even to call any of us "conservative" or "liberal" does not really clarify our stances on issues. Many people are conservative on some issues, liberal on others. As pointed out in other chapters of this book, sometimes the person called "liberal" is the one who actually wants to "conserve" values and look deeply at the root of Scripture, becoming more fundamentalist and conservative than those who carry those labels.

Second, labeling is an obstacle to honest debate. Bullying and tyrannizing those who don't agree with us gets us nowhere.

Ideas are dismissed because they come from the "other party." We hear more pontificating than communication. There is more libeling than listening.

Name-calling is an excuse for not dealing respectfully with another person. It puts the label of "rejected" on that person, and allows the name-caller to turn his back on him or her and decide the other person's opinion doesn't matter. It's un-Christian, because it rejects a person Beloved of God. It is undemocratic, because it's classist to believe that one person is far better than another.

Name-calling is not the same as critiquing another person's recommendation of how to resolve a problem. In the latter case we are asked to put the emphasis on the idea, not to demean the person.

Hypocrisy and Double Standards

Hypocrites can be defined as people who have a double standard—a lower one for themselves, and a higher one for other people. They see the speck in the other person's eye, but not the big log in their own. Jesus' main problem with the religious authorities of his day was their judgment and hypocrisy. In fact, as Christians, we need to be extremely careful about our self-righteousness and becoming judgmental. Jesus did not take kindly to hypocrisy.[5]

Self-righteousness, hypocrisy, and judgment come from pride, considered the greatest of the Seven Deadly Sins. Those who are prideful set themselves up as gods. They believe they have all the answers, and become self-righteous. They stop listening to others, because they don't believe anyone else has any Truth to share. Instead of brokenness, we have confidence in our own perfection and think we have all the answers.

Hypocrisy confuses us. Whenever anyone proclaims his or her Christianity too loudly, we need to be suspect. Many of the spokespeople for the Republican Party believe Christian values lie on their side. This is a dangerous stance for anyone, or any party, to take. It is tempting to believe that God is only on their side, but it is wrong. And many Republicans have fallen for it, rather than attesting to the Truth.

The standard we hold for one group of people has to be the same standard for others.

If we believe that it's wrong for Saddam Hussein to condone torture, then we must also hold ourselves to the same standard, and recognize that our torture of prisoners is also wrong.

If we believe that Democratic members of Congress have to be held to a high ethical standard, then we have to also believe that Republicans such as those under investigation—Tom DeLay, Bill Frist, I. Lewis (Scooter) Libby, and Karl Rove—have to be held to the same high ethical standard.

If we believe that Terry Schiavo deserved to keep her feeding tube, then we have to hold the same standard for others in a coma who need a feeding tube to keep them alive. And we have to be willing to fund these patients, rather than follow the example of Tom DeLay who wanted to take away the funding for health care, and feeding tubes, for the poor.

If we believe in democracy for our own country, then we must respect the decisions of other democratic countries who don't agree with us—countries such as France, Germany, and Spain.

If the Republicans want the right of freedom of speech and freedom of religion for themselves, they must be willing to give these same rights to the Democrats.

Hiding the Truth

In order to make good policies, legislators need to know the truth, the whole truth, and nothing but the truth about a person or an event. Many times, George W. Bush has tried to make sure the truth is not shared. Whether being asked for information about John Bolton, or about John Roberts, or about his own military record, Mr. Bush has chosen not to share information.

The Quakers believe that when we have trouble finding a workable solution to a problem, we usually need more information. We might read more, research more, talk more about the problem. We might brainstorm alternatives. We try to move deeper and deeper into the problem and find out more information so we have everything necessary to make an informed decision. Quakers believe that the Spirit moves us to unity. Since all Quaker decisions are made by consensus, rather than majority rule, we have to put our egos aside and stop digging in our heels, because we cannot make anything happen without agreement among ourselves. We know that the best way to make a good decision is to get all the information out in the open.

George W. Bush might be refusing to reveal the truth for a number of reasons.

He might be hiding something, knowing he won't get his way if it's known. In that case, he's putting his pride ahead of the best interests of our country.

He might believe the information he's asked to provide is not important, but that is not for him to decide.

He might think the information will endanger national security—an excuse many presidents have used. Although it's true that the citizens should not always have the information, it still can be provided to those members of the government who have security clearance for classified information.

President Bush also might refuse to reveal the truth because he wants to control the information. That is a misuse of power. It is not serving the truth, and it is not the best way to run a democratic country.

The Hidden Subtext

The word "subtext" is used in drama to identify the hidden motivations that lie beneath the text of what we say. Sometimes these are unconscious, even to ourselves. Other times, we understand them, but don't want to tell anyone else.

When the wife asks her sulking husband, "What's wrong?" and he answers "Nothing!" he is implying a subtext. Obviously something is wrong. His text (the actual words) imply nothing is wrong. But the subtext—the message underneath the words—

tells us something is very wrong. We just don't know what it is, and we can't deal with it because either the husband doesn't understand the problem, or refuses to express it. Subtext keeps the truth hidden. Some people go to therapy for years, trying to find out the unconscious truths that govern their lives.

Good writers spend years learning how to imply subtext in great drama. We want to see it in drama. We don't want to see it in real life. Many lies in government are motivated by hidden agendas that usually are known to the government but not shared with the citizens. Sometimes, they're not even known by government officials.

There's a real problem with subtext in government. We never know, for sure, the real motivation for an action. We get a funny feeling that something is motivating an action but we're not being told what it is. The reason for our war in Iraq keeps changing—from the dangerous WMDs to stopping Al Qaeda, to promoting democracy. When one reason is proven wrong, another pops up.

So why are we at war in Iraq? Many of us don't know, really. There is undoubtedly some subtext here, but it's difficult to know exactly what it is.

Some say the subtext is our need for oil. Iraq is an oil-rich country. We are fast using up our oil and we're dependent on Mideast oil. If they're our enemy, forbidding their oil to us, we have a real problem. Our country needs oil, and plenty of it, to maintain our standard of living. We don't like to be denied our SUVs, our trucks, our gas guzzlers. We look for an excuse to get their oil, and 9/11 became the excuse.

Some say the reason was the unfinished business of the first Gulf War. From 1991 on, many of the people involved with the first Gulf War (Cheney, Rumsfeld, Wolfowitz, etc.) wanted to finish it off. The terrorist attack of 9/11 was a good excuse. Bush Sr. felt that going into Iraq would have ended up in a quagmire, and he had no strategy for winning the peace. As a result, he stopped at the border. President Bush had his father's business to complete.

Others say we had no base in the Middle East, and it was imperative we have a strong presence there. With the War in Iraq and Afghanistan, we have now accomplished the objective of troops and bases in this important area.

Some say we're there to stabilize the Middle East, although it is less stable now than it was in 2000.

Some say it's to bring democracy to the Middle East, although we have never been in the business of forcing our type of government on other countries and democracy usually takes years to build, and needs to come from within, rather than be imposed from without.

Some have advanced the theory that our presence in the Middle East is justified by a belief that Armageddon will take place there, and that we have to be there, either to fight the good battle, or to hurry the Second Coming. Christians, particularly some conservative and fundamentalist Christians, see signs the Second Coming is near. There are Muslims to convert. There are Christians to join together in battle.

It is difficult to know how seriously to take this theology, or how seriously to suspect this theology could be driving some of our political decisions. And it's frightening if, in some way, political policies are being driven by thinking we can hurry the Second Coming, or driven by the desire to proselytize the unChristian.

Bearing Witness to the Truth

Secrets and lies—all with consequences. The consequences, so far, are an American economy in trouble, more than 2,000 Americans and allies killed, an estimated 25,000 to 100,000 Iraqis killed, billions of dollars spent, our country deeply in debt, the stock market going down, gas prices going up, and a country divided.

By no means am I saying that Democrats never lie and Republicans do. Anyone, with a little research, can make up a list of all the lies and half-truths and obfuscations of the Democrats, or the Green Party, or the Libertarians, or the Independents. There are plenty of lies around, and politicians seem to be good at making the lies sound truthful. But we don't get closer to the truth by saying "The other guy does it too!"

Everyone—Republican or Democrat—needs to be called to account for any false witness. To pretend that the Republicans are the party of Truth, and the Democrats are a bunch of liars, has been raised to the level of ridiculousness by some of the Vicious Extremists. We are not good witnesses if we don't identify hypocrisy, deception, secrets, and lies when we see them. We are not good Christians if we don't witness to the bearing of false witness.

Chapter Nine

Crossing the Political Divide

"You should all agree among yourselves and be sympathetic;
love the brothers, have compassion and be self-effacing.
Never repay one wrong with another,
or one abusive word with another,
instead, repay with a blessing."

1 Peter 3:8–9

We say we want Christian values in our government, but we won't get them by fighting with each other, and wasting all of our energy on the fight, not the solution. If Roman Christians and Greek Christians and Egyptian Christians could get along in the early years of the Christian era (although with a great deal of scolding from Paul as well as others), certainly we can begin to try to create a better nation, and a better world, together.

Jesus and Paul saw that our judgment of each other, our pride, and our self-righteousness were major obstacles to advancing the Kingdom. A number of times, Paul explained that diversity is good. We all have different gifts. It is through these different gifts that we build up the Kingdom—not by trying to be alike.[1]

Begin with Empathy and Compassion

In the 1980s, my husband and I were part of a workshop sponsored by the National Conference of Christians and Jews (NCCJ). The NCCJ was founded in the late 1920s by a Catholic priest, a Jewish rabbi, and a Protestant minister to help people understand where their prejudices came from and how to overcome them. In the 1990s, the organization changed its name to the National Conference for Community and Justice because it had expanded to helping other religions, races, and groups be understood and included in a diverse America. The founders of the organization recognized that the first step in breaking stereotypes was simply bringing people together and having them begin talking to each other. Our group was made up of about twelve participants—about one-third Jewish, one-third Catholic, and one-third Protestant.

One of the Jewish women recounted how difficult Christmas was for her. She felt that Christianity was blaring at her, constantly, with little respect for her own religion. I had never looked at Christmas through the eyes of another religion, so this was a revelation to me. She cried as she talked about her hurt over my favorite season. I felt as if I had stepped across a religious divide into her viewpoint, and understood something about what she must be feeling.

Crossing the divide begins with empathy and compassion. We have to walk around in the other person's shoes for a bit. We have to be willing to admit that the other has a valid point of view. We have to care enough to be willing to accept, sympathize, and empathize with another person.

The workshop had a profound effect on me, because I learned that I could cross over. I wanted to do the same workshop with Christians and Muslims, since I knew little about Islam and had nothing but stereotypes to guide me. I wondered what I'd learn talking to Buddhists or Hindus. It never occurred to me, at that time, that Christianity would become so split that I would see the need for people of different denominations and different political parties to talk to each other and to break the stereotypes they have of each other.

Give Our Viewpoint

I used to be intimidated when I talked to conservatives, because I felt they would judge my theology as not being conservative enough. I would become very quiet. Or I would tell them only those parts of my perceptions that I was sure they would agree with. As a result, I cowered before my brothers and sisters in Christ. In retrospect, I was keeping us from having an honest conversation because I was refusing to be truly present in the conversation. I wasn't trusting their kindness and acceptance. I was presuming that all conservatives were judgmental, which wasn't true. Perhaps more important, I was distrusting my own spirituality, even though I had spent at least as much time attending church as they had, at least as much time reading the Bible as they had, at least as much time studying theology as they had, at least as much time as a Christian as they had. I decided it was time to speak the truth, with everyone.

This meant, over time, to speak the truth about political and social issues that mattered to me. It meant listening, discussing, being vulnerable by clarifying areas where I was struggling, and trying to work together to find good and workable solutions.

I discovered that most conservatives aren't quite as closed and intolerant as I had thought. In fact, I have had many rich and wonderful and compassionate conversations with my conservative friends about homosexuality, abortion, and politics.

In the same way, I talked to liberals whose lives were very much directed by their Christian faith and who had very penetrating, well-thought-out insights into the Bible and into how to practice their spirituality. I found that many liberals pray daily, have devotional time every day, and love the Limitless God.

With all Christians, I found we had many, many areas of agreement, if we could get past the rhetoric and the stereotyping, which were serving no one, especially not God.

Stop the Rhetoric!

Rhetoric is one of the biggest barriers to our effectiveness. It has done no good to have the Republicans accuse the Democrats of being un-Christian, or vice versa. There are, however, some differences between the rhetoric of the two parties. The Republicans have tended to call Democrats un-Christian as a group. The Democrats have tended to attack Republican policies as un-Christian. Has either attack done anything to help our country resolve problems or reach goals? No, not at all.

Some of these attacks are coming from the extremists, who always seem to be in the forefront of the news. Senator Bill Frist and Representative Tom DeLay have been particularly vocal with constant attacks on Democrats as un-Christian. On our side, Howard Dean's rhetoric went up a few notches, until other Democrats asked him to tone it down and not add to the divisiveness. I give the Democrats a great deal of credit for wanting to diminish the rhetoric, and for being willing to make their wishes known to their party chairman. I wish the Republicans would tell a few of their members to tone it down as well.

We can't be effective until we get past the strife and see the larger picture. In many passages, the Bible sees dissension and strife as one of the biggest problems between Christians. Over and over again, the Bible tells us to love one another. Clearly the early Christians were much like our Congress and the many spokespersons for both the Republican and Democratic parties, judging and blaming and creating anything but a loving community. It is easy for us to want to be right, rather than to want to be effective. It is easy for us to overidentify with a party, because it gives us a strong sense of belonging and helps us, clearly, know who we are. But there is only one identity we need—as followers of Christ.

Look at the makeup of the Congress. It's made up almost entirely of Christians. Christians say they want Christian legislators, but they already have them. Christians say they want a Christian government, but they already have exactly what they've asked for. It's time to start working together and to put God above party.

If we truly want a Christian nation, how are we to work toward it? How do we define what it means to have a Christian government and a society that expresses values? How do we guard our Christian values as well as our democratic values?

If we always think that we have the moral high ground ourselves, and if we always demonize the other side, all we've done is to bring pride into the discussion. It's time to let the Holy Spirit work.

Quakers believe that we find Unity by first listening to each other. When Hillary Clinton ran for senator, she had a "listening campaign." Many had no idea what to think of a candidate who focused on listening, not talking. They had never heard of such a thing. But she wanted to know what the voters thought; what they cared about. And she won with a good solid majority.

Without really listening, we presume what the other person wants and needs and means simply by their words. When we listen deeply to our neighbors, we hear the struggles and the striving for answers and the false starts and the figuring it out that are part of the process of intuiting what the Spirit is telling us.

Find the Right Models for Discussion

There are some good models for how issues can be discussed, and sometimes even resolved.

Throughout our country's history, there have been town meetings to bring communities together to discuss issues. These can be healthy, provided that the meetings are open to every viewpoint, and aren't just filled with people who will only say what we want to hear. Many of our last few presidential candidates have held town meetings. Bill Clinton was particularly good at handling a crowd, listening, and responding with empathy. George W. Bush has tended to stack these meetings with people who follow his viewpoint. Unlike Mr. Clinton, Mr. Bush has not been known as a good listener. Whereas some see his absolute confidence in his viewpoint as a virtue, others see it as close-mindedness that has led to many tragic decisions. If town meetings truly could be a time for airing opinions and sharing ideas, even with those who disagree with us, our government might become more responsive to its citizens.

In the politically and religiously divided city of Colorado Springs, there has been some movement toward dialogue through panel discussions, and through looking for ways to bring together people who often have diametrically opposed viewpoints. In March 2005, the Vanguard Church in Colorado Springs brought together conservatives and liberals to discuss the issue of homosexuality and gay marriage. The sanctuary was packed, as was a large adjoining room that had been set up with video monitors to try to accommodate the larger-than-expected crowd. Clearly there was a desire for dialogue. When I saw the notice about the discussion, I was astounded that this kind of interchange was happening in my city. I knew nothing about Vanguard Church and assumed that it was, perhaps, a very liberal Methodist or Presbyterian Church. It wasn't. It was Southern Baptist.

Although the conservative Christians were only represented by Focus on the Family members, the more liberal members of the panel included a Quaker, a minister from the United Church of Christ, and a member of the Pikes Peak Gay and Lesbian Community Center.

For this meeting, there were ground rules. The communication was to be civil and respectful. No one was to applaud for their side and boo the other side. No one was to make radical statements. The panel had been invited by Rev. Kelly Williams, the minister of Vanguard Church. Kelly is a graduate of Liberty University (Jerry Falwell's university), and he attended the nondenominational Dallas Theological Seminary, which was started by a Presbyterian minister. Another of my stereotypes kicked in—certainly Rev. Williams must be very conservative and was doing this to give Focus on the Family an airing. Wrong again. Kelly put a halt to all my stereotypes.

I was very impressed by his ability to bring together groups that usually are divided, and to create an atmosphere for one of the most civil, respectful, and effective dialogues I have heard. I asked if I could interview him for this chapter. I asked how many Democrats were in his Southern Baptist church, knowing that Baptists usually are Republicans. Although he said he had never asked his congregation, he estimates that they have a fairly good balance. One weekend, he asked how many people believed we should have gone to war. Half said yes; half said no.

Kelly's goal is to create dialogue and bring unity. "I'd like to do other panels," he said. "I'd like to do one to deal with major world religions and another to discuss emotional and psychological problems that so many of our young people face. I see our church as a holistic symbol in the community that shows that people can come together. We believe that everything is tied back to spirituality. It may not seem to be spiritual at first, but everything is interrelated to everything, so as we learn to function physically, emotionally, relationally, that enables us to connect more deeply with God. Anything that divides a relationship hinders your ability to love God, and to love humanity. Our goal is not to change people. Our goal is to love people, and that is a huge difference. Many churches have come to the conclusion that it's our job to change people. I would argue that the first two commandments of Jesus are the ones that should guide us—to love the God who made us, and to love the people that God created."

This panel led me to wonder if we could overcome some of our Christian divisions if churches would give more space for dialogue between groups.

Look For, and Affirm, Agreement

There is more agreement than we might expect. "For the Health of the Nation: An Evangelical Call to Civic Responsibility" is a very reasonable, civil document that crosses denominational lines. Although liberal Christians and conservative Christians will disagree on certain issues in the document, they probably could agree on 90 percent of the ideas discussed. (Chapter 2 discusses this document in some detail.)

I don't expect that we will be able to talk to the vicious extremists that exist in every religion and every form of Christianity. But it's not imperative that we do. If Christians in communities started talking to each other, and did not give over the public space to the extremists as our representatives, we could reach agreement in many areas of public policy. When we band together in areas of agreement, our numbers and our effectiveness ripples outward, so that the power of the public voice of Christianity no longer comes from the extremists, but from a place of reason and civility.

When the voice of democracy doesn't come from the extremists, but from a more central and reasonable position, we have a more civil society that runs the way it was meant to run—with checks and balances, and without secrecy and power out of control.

It would seem that it would be impossible for diverse groups to reach consensus on any issue, particularly when there seems to be so little that we can agree on. But consensus, or near-consensus, is possible. The Quakers have been practicing it for more than 300 years and have been effective in using it for such social policies as eradicating slavery, reforming prisons, bringing about equal rights for the disenfranchised people in our country, and setting up programs to work for peace.

Many United Nations policies, particularly the position papers created from the organization's international conferences, are created through consensus. When I attended the 1995 U.N. Women's Conference in Beijing, China, I was surprised that it was possible to create a document through consensus that represented the views of women from many different cultural, ethnic, and religious backgrounds, as well as gays and straights, religious and not religious. There was much that we could agree on.

When there is consensus, or near-consensus, on issues, there is no one to sabotage the solution. Energy is not wasted on bickering. All work together, and the power of many voices creates effective legislation.

Certainly we cannot expect complete consensus in our government with the myriad opinions on most issues. But there may be places where consensus or near-consensus can be reached. We would do better as a nation if we looked for more than majority rule. Consider the number of hours spent when George W. Bush kept trying to get his nominee for United Nations ambassador confirmed, when even his own party had doubts about the man. There were months of haggling over this nomination, even though, in the past, ambassadors had been fairly easily confirmed. Of course, a president has the right to try to sell his nominees and his programs, but consider the alternative of trying to work together, of trying to reach more of a consensus about who, and what, would serve the common good, especially for a position that needs the backing of Congress. When decisions are made with a margin of only one or two votes, clearly the Congress is not in sufficient agreement.

Create Partnerships

There are those in Congress who are crossing the political divide. Senator Hillary Clinton has been particularly effective at this.

She has cosponsored a number of bills with Republicans. Some of these partnerships are surprising and unlikely. Senator Clinton partnered with former House Speaker Newt Gingrich to help pass a bill to increase electronic record-keeping in the health care industry. This will help make the health care system more efficient and reduce medical errors and sloppy records. They have also talked about working together on other health care issues as well as national security issues to help improve our military readiness.

In fact, Gingrich, who once led the fight for impeaching Bill Clinton, has good things to say about Hillary Clinton: She's "very practical . . . very smart and very hard working . . . I have been very struck working with her."[2] He said that he had been impressed by the job she was doing as senator, and that she had what it took to be the Democratic nominee for president.

Although some Republicans have been upset by what they see as too cozy a relationship, I see it as a very positive sign that it is possible for people to work together.

Other senators are also working together on bills that will make the government more effective, as well as helping citizens. Bipartisan bills to expand the accountability and openness of government have been introduced by Senators John Cornyn (R-Texas) and Patrick Leahy (D-Vermont). George W. Bush and Ted Kennedy worked together to structure the "No Child Left Behind" bill, although Kennedy has said that it was underfunded.

Bipartisan bills to combat human trafficking and slavery have been introduced by Republican Senators John Cornyn and Lindsey Graham and Democratic Senators Patrick Leahy, Charles Schumer, and Hillary Clinton.

There are other hopeful signs of bipartisanship in Congress and between Congress and the presidency. When Supreme Court Justice Sandra Day O'Connor retired in summer 2005, as the partisan bickering about replacing her began to get out of hand, President Bush called together the leaders of both parties to talk, which was, at least, a beginning.

In June 2005, representatives of more than forty religious denominations gathered at the National Cathedral in Washington for a Convocation on Hunger. The group was made up of members of evangelical churches and mainstream Christian churches, as well as Jews, Buddhists, Muslims, and Sikhs.

Jim Wallis, an evangelical liberal and author of the best-selling book *God's Politics*, has worked with Senator Rick Santorum as well as with Democrats on antipoverty proposals. Broad-based Christian groups have also backed efforts to combat AIDS, and have backed peacemaking groups sent to the Sudan.

Look for True Christian Dialogue

Quakers use the metaphor of the Light to emphasize the many Scriptural verses about turning toward the Light of Christ. The Light overcomes the darkness. We talk about seeking the Light, running toward the Light, trying to live in the Light. We can cross the political divide between Christians if we look for the

Light and affirm wherever it is shining and whoever is carrying the Light. If we see Truth, then let us affirm it, whether it comes from conservatives or liberals, Republicans or Democrats. If we see partial truths, then let us affirm those as well. Even a sliver of Light can begin to pierce the darkness.

If we learn to discern the log in our own eye, and are willing to admit that we might be wrong, certainly that ability can lead us also to discerning where Truth and Light reside.

What Are We to Do as Christians?

There seem to be some consistent issues where the ideals of the Democratic Party and the ideals of Christianity come together. We are to:

- Help the poor, the needy, the widows and the orphans, the disadvantaged, those who are on the bottom rung of the ladder. Stand by them, and with them.
- Care for the oppressed, and be an advocate for those who have nowhere to turn.
- Be good and responsible stewards of this Garden, which we've been asked to care for; be visionaries in our policy in order to better care for the earth.
- Be inclusive and caring for others; love our enemies, and love our neighbor as ourselves.
- Be peacemakers by forming coalitions, by being good friends with our allies, by practicing diplomacy. Be strong and wise on issues of national defense, but also

be creative in our methods. In the best of all worlds, we would beat our swords into plowshares, and study war no more.

- Judge rightly; be open to wisdom from wherever it may come; hope in the future; and always, continue to love our neighbor against all odds.

As Christians, we need to stop being intimidated by those who speak the loudest, with the nastiest rhetoric and the most strident use of their authority. We have given these people far too much power. Do most Christians really believe that the religious extremists in Congress best express the concept of a loving Christ? Do the extremists think that when they talk about hate and revenge they are representing the God that most of us worship? When Christians say they want a Christian nation, run by Christians, does that mean we really want the hate and divisiveness that many Christians have created in our country?

At this point in our history, the us-against-them attitudes are coming from the Christians far more than from the non-Christians. And what non-Christian will see a loving Christ in any of this?

We can let the non-Christians know that this is not a true expression of our faith. There is more at stake here than which party wins. If we are evangelical Christians, in any sense of the word, then what we need to show the world is light, not darkness, and love, not hate. The world looks at us, we who call ourselves Christians, to see what our religion is all about, just as the world looks at the hate and revenge of the extremist Muslims, and forms opinions about the entire religion by the actions of those who cause the greatest damage.

Conservative Republican Christians could do much to cross the political divide by asking their leaders to tone down the rhetoric and reach across the chasm that seems to separate us. That might mean asking their powerhouse spokespersons, such as James Dobson, Tony Perkins, Jerry Falwell, and Pat Robertson, to show a little more love in their statements. It might mean asking members of Congress to show more respect for their fellow Christians.

I would ask the same of the Democrats—that they censor each other when necessary, reach across the divide to try to form partnerships, and not assume that there is no common ground.

I would ask my Republican and Democratic friends to not look for the bad in each other, applauding when they find it, but to affirm that which is good, valuable, helpful, and effective—wherever it may come from.

I would ask the media to stop buying into this divisiveness because they think it makes good news. They are not serving the truth if they show only one side of the issue. I am not suggesting that they stop airing the views of conservative Christians. But they need to recognize, publicly, that there are hundreds of other Christians who can balance the views of all the conservative and fundamentalist commentators.

Perhaps we need to rethink our overall goal. Is it to win elections? To be the party that is always right? To denounce the others, and let the country know how wrong those people are? Or is it to create policy with values that promote the Good? I expect we can agree on at least some of this policy.

Of non-Christians, I would ask that you not judge us by the loudest and most dramatic of our members. Forgive us for the way we have treated you. Read the Gospels to find out who this person named Jesus truly was. And know that at least some of us recognize that your highest values, and our highest values, are not just Christian values, but universal values that can bring us together as we try to create a just and compassionate society.

All of us must seek light and love and truth. When we see it, we must look to it, run to it, and serve it.

Christian Values and Christian Viewpoints

Why is it so difficult to define Christians and Christian values? Because "Christian values" covers many different concepts. We understand our Christianity through how we understand the Bible; through its interpretation according to various church doctrines; through church history and tradition; through our own spiritual experiences; and through the theologies that we construct. When we define "Christian," we are talking about a broad range of viewpoints. The following gives some brief definitions of terms often used about Christians.

Most contemporary *Fundamentalist Christians* believe that the Bible is the literal Word of God, the inerrant truth.

Conservative Christians also see the Bible as the Word of God, but tend to take reason and study into account as well, sometimes interpreting Biblical passages according to the context of the times and interpreting words according to their original Hebrew, Greek, or Aramaic meanings. Conservatives want to conserve the tradition. They tend to want to keep the status quo, because they believe that this is where Truth resides.

Evangelical Christians constitute a larger theological umbrella that can include fundamentalists and conservatives, and also some liberals. They believe that our work on earth is to spread the Gospel of Christ to all nations. They heed the Great Commission to "Go ye therefore, and teach all nations, baptizing them in the name of the Father, and of the Son, and of the Holy Ghost: teaching them to observe all things whatsoever I have commanded you" (Matthew 28:19–20). They call us to belief in Jesus Christ as one's personal Savior, believing that God has a plan for each individual life, and that we need to be born again and commit our lives to Christ. At their best, they dedicate their work and their lives to Christ, and try to live in accordance with his Will, as expressed through Scripture and the guidance they experience in prayer.

Mainstream Christians are usually thought of as belonging to churches such as Presbyterian, Lutheran, Methodist, and Episcopal, although these denominations contain both liberals and conservatives. Catholicism also has its groups of conservatives and liberals within the church. Many mainstream Christians also take the Bible very seriously, and many see it as the Word of God, but they also focus on theological study and practical theology. A sermon in a fundamentalist church might be more like a Bible study, while a sermon in a mainstream Christian church will often focus on overarching theologies and how to apply our Christianity to our contemporary life.

Liberal Christians see Christ as standing against the established order of his day, both religiously and politically. They see that He brought in a new law—the Law of Love—which they believe they're called to apply to our modern society. They believe that if we follow the two Great Commandments—to love God and to love our neighbor—this will lead us into right thinking and right action. Liberal Christians may, or may not, take the Bible as the inspired Word of God, but they are more apt to believe in continuing revelation, and to believe that the True Word of God is not the Bible, but Christ Jesus, who continues to reveal Himself to us, and continues to move us, touch us, and transform us.

Liberal Christians are often found among Methodists, Lutherans, United Church of Christ, some Presbyterians, Quakers, some Episcopalians, and some Catholics, as well as among some social service groups that focus on helping the poor, such as the Salvation Army, shelters for homeless or battered women, and many charities that focus on bettering conditions for the oppressed.

Progressive Christianity, a relatively new term, refers to Christians who work toward a more just and compassionate world and engage in a theological and practical struggle against racism, sexism, homophobia, and other human oppressions. Progressive Christians are grounded in the Bible, but because of certain contradictions, they do not believe that it is infallible. They recognize that there is truth in other traditions as well, and they strive to overcome dogmatism and all the "isms"—sexism, racism, ageism, and classism.

Christian Mystics put the focus on the Holy Spirit dwelling within. They believe that the authentic life is the Spirit-filled life, and we can nurture the Holy Guide within us through prayer and meditation. Some mystics are contemplatives, with ecstatic experiences of the living Christ. Many of these, as well as mystical religions like the Quakers, combine their mystical devotions with social action, believing that the work of the Spirit naturally leads us to manifesting the work of the Spirit within the world.

Theologies and Interpretations

Within with these broad categories of Christians and their viewpoints, people use many different theologies and methods to help interpret the Bible and form their Christian values. Various schools of Christian theology include:

- Creation theology (discussed in Chapter 3).
- Liberation theology (discussed in Chapter 2), which also includes feminist theology and womanist theology (referring to black feminist theology), as well as liberation theologies that refer specifically to Hispanics, Asians, or any oppressed group.
- Process theology, systematic theology, and others.

Christians also turn to *church tradition* to form their Christian values. From the time of the early Christian Church, Christians have struggled with the formation of Christian doctrine. Is there a Trinity, or is God a Unity? Is there a priesthood of all believers, or should our faith be interpreted by the clergy? Is the Pope infallible, or not? Should women be ordained? Historically,

Christians formed councils to debate the issues, came together in conferences to change their statements of faith, and created dogmas to express their own particular Christian stance.

Church history, combined with church tradition, interprets religion by not only looking at the Bible, but also at ways Christianity has been thought about, and lived, by the Church Fathers and Mothers, by the saints, and by theologians. Some churches take their history and tradition more seriously than do others. The Catholic Church relies heavily on church tradition, sometimes more so than on the authority of the Scriptures. Other churches respect their traditions, but don't follow them if they seem outdated.

Sometimes Christian values are thought of as *Christian morals*. We might define morals as right action and right behavior. We seek to find the best way to live out our values and express them in our daily lives. Sometimes we discover that issues rarely are black-and-white. What is the best moral stance toward war? Which stance manifests the most Good—to be for or against abortion? We struggle as Christians within a democratic society about how to apply our Christian beliefs and put them into action.

In *Christian ethics*, we try to think critically about our human choices, and whether they lead to moral behavior. Whereas we might follow moral rules to decide what is the best behavior, ethics often asks that we struggle with complex issues that are not black-and-white but demand that we reflect on the lesser of two evils, or try to determine what to do in areas that have rarely been discussed. Bioethics deals with the best ethical response to new scientific achievements, such as the ability to clone, to use stem cells to heal, or to keep people alive artificially.

Ethicists generally believe that there are stages of ethical development. As we grow ethically and spiritually, we learn to think of the greater good, rather than our own selfish desires. We learn to recognize that the ends do not justify the means. Christians believe that there is a higher law than the law of the nation, and that ethical behavior demands that we confront immoral and unjust laws, even if it means going to prison or death. In our history, many have confronted discriminatory laws against blacks and women, which sometimes led to imprisonment and death. Some have confronted capital punishment laws where sometimes the innocent are executed. Others have confronted what they believe are unjust wars, even though it meant imprisonment or exile.

Many Christians turn to *spirituality* rather than organized religion to discover a code of political behavior. Spiritual and Spirit-filled Christians focus not just on reading the Bible, but on daily prayer and meditation and listening, not just talking, to God. They ask, What would Love do in this situation? Where is the Spirit leading me? Might the Spirit lead me in a new direction, or cause me to question something from the past?

There is sometimes a very fine line between listening to the Holy Spirit and listening to our intuition. Spirituality tries to help us understand when they're the same, and when they may be different.

Any of these approaches can guide us in formulating our Christian value system, which then leads us to create specific policies that best express what we believe will make us a righteous nation.

Even if we could be perfect in our Bible reading and listening to the Spirit, Christians are still flawed sinners, capable of making mistakes, capable of misinterpreting, capable of expressing all the Seven Deadly Sins. Christians often are blind to the fact that their sins, rather than the Love of Christ, are guiding their decisions. Christian values still demand interpretation and balancing these many aspects.

Study Guide

This study guide is intended to provide an opportunity for you to reflect on your faith as it relates to politics, either by yourself or in a group. You might pick and choose certain chapters, depending on what is currently in the news, or of particular interest to your group. You may want more than one session on each issue. I doubt if you can cover the "War and Peace" chapter in an hour or two. In some of the questions below, I mention other resources that you might want to pursue; you also may want to study some of the books mentioned in the chapter endnotes, which follow this Study Guide.

It is my hope that Democrats and Republicans can study these issues together, examine issues in the light of Scripture, and perhaps even be moved to action. You may be led, as a group, to write a letter to the editor of your local newspaper, or respond in some other ways. I would recommend that you look for consensus if you are doing this as a group.

The study guide can be used by Christian or secular groups. The questions under **(A)** are more general non-religious questions. The **(B)** questions are designed to lead to reflection and discussion and, hopefully, help deepen one's spiritual response.

Those who aren't Christian may want to study some of these issues from the viewpoint of their own spiritual tradition and possibly refer to that tradition's own religious and spiritual writings.

Chapter 1:
How Would Jesus Vote?

1. **(A)** Look at the various definitions of "conservative" and "liberal." In what ways do you see yourself as conservative? In what ways are you a liberal? What are the dangers of both points of view when taken to the extreme?

    (B) Read Matthew 7:1–2, 1 Corinthians 5:12–13, Luke 12:14, and John 12:47. Why do you think Jesus and Paul so often asked the early Christians to "Judge not, that you be not judged"? What are the problems and consequences that result from a judgmental attitude?

2. **(A)** If you're a Republican, what are the policies within your own party that you feel are ill-advised or problematical? What policies or people within the Democratic Party do you most admire? If you're a Democrat, what policies in your own party bother you? What Republican policies and people do you admire? Why? (If you can't find any, you

may be demonizing the other side and need a more open mind. Think harder!)

(B) Look at the values that are implied in Jesus' actions in 1 Corinthians 7, John 8, Matthew 5 and 18. How did Jesus change the law? Why did he change it?

Chapter 2:
The Poor, the Needy, Widows, and Orphans

1. **(A)** Which values that help the poor and disadvantaged would you like to see exhibited in your country? Which of these values need help from the state? What can best be done by individuals or groups?

   (B) What is your church's stand on caring for the poor and needy? Print out a copy of your church's doctrine (most are found on the Internet) and discuss its stand. Do you agree, or disagree, with most, or all, aspects of the doctrine? Who does your church help in their priority of needs? Church members? The community? People from other religions or other cultures? How well does your church do?

2. **(A)** Why are there poor people? To what extent is it their own fault? What social and political structures contribute to poverty? Have you ever been poor? How much interaction have you personally had with the poor? Were any stereotypes broken as a result of being close to poverty or to those who are poor?

(B) Read the Bible verses on caring for the poor that are mentioned in the beginning of this chapter. Why do you think God cares so much for the poor? To what extent do you have problems with the poor? Are you afraid of them? Feel burdened by them? Feel vulnerable because they might want what you have and steal from you? Why does God call them "blessed"?

3. **(A)** What government programs do you know about, or wish to see, that would create a more compassionate society?

   (B) Print out a copy of the "Call to Civil Responsibility" from the National Evangelical Association (on the Web at *www.nae.net/images/civic_responsibility.pdf*). Read the sections that have to do with the caring of the poor and needy. Notice that no legislation is mentioned. What government programs do you know about, or wish to see, that would address these issues? What church or charity programs could help? Keep in mind that the poor and needy may not be Christians. How would that change your understanding of your responsibility?

Chapter 3:
Beautiful Savior, King of Creation

1. **(A)** What in nature do you love? The sea? The forests? The mountains? The birds and animals? How do they nourish you? To what extent do they enrich your life? How often do you spend time allowing nature to have an effect on your life?

(B) Read Genesis 1. Why did God call the creation "Good"? What's good about it? How does this Goodness impact your own personal life? To what extent do you appreciate and love God's creation? To what extent do you find God present in creation?

2. (A) Create a short paragraph about your philosophy on nature. What are some bills or policies you would like to see the government support to better preserve the earth?

(B) Read your church's doctrine on the environment. If your church doesn't have one, read the Quaker doctrine, or Church of the Brethren doctrine. You can find some of these at: *www.webofcreation.org* and at *www.brethren .org/ac/ac_statements/91Creation.htm#11*.

Do you see a relationship between your religion and the environment? What more could you, charities, and the government do to protect this legacy?

Chapter 4:
The Ethical Dilemma of Abortion

1. (A) What are your views about abortion? How have you arrived at these views? Have there been experiences, readings, discussions, and so on, that have led you to your personal philosophy?

(B) Whether you're pro-choice or pro-life, which Bible verses or theology support your viewpoint? Which verses or theology can you think of to support the opposite view? Why do you think this is such a difficult ethical problem?

2. **(A)** What can be done to stop unwanted pregnancies? Are you aware of programs (whether from government, charities, the church, etc.) that are effective? Are there other possibilities that you can think of?

   (B) What is a Christian's responsibility to help unwanted children? What are you willing to do? What is your church willing to do?

3. **(A)** Read the Democrats for Life policy statement found at *www.democratsforlife.org*.
   Compare this to the Republican stance about abstinence. Do you find elements in both are helpful? Or unhelpful?

   (B) Compare the theological statements from *www.consistentlife.com* and the Focus on the Family document found at *www.focusonyourchild.com/hottopics/a00001286.cfm*. To what extent do you find these arguments compelling? Are their loopholes?

Chapter 5:
Homosexuals: Civil Rights? Civil Unions?

1. **(A)** If you're heterosexual, what is your experience with homosexuals? Do you have gay friends, associates, or

acquaintances? How much have you learned about homosexuality from them? How much from the media?

In what ways have you experienced differences between yourself and homosexuals? If your group includes homosexuals, discuss how they experience differences between themselves and heterosexuals. Move beyond defining people purely in terms of their sexuality.

If you have not known homosexuals as friends or neighbors, or as members of your congregation, your group might ask someone to come to talk about their lives. You can contact a local Gay and Lesbian Alliance, or a Metropolitan Community Church, whose ministry is centered on gays and lesbians.

(B) How do you feel about gay marriages? C. S. Lewis says that maybe marriage should be a sacred ceremony, not a civil union, so that churches decide who they'll marry, and everyone else can marry through a judge. Is this a good idea? What about gays who aren't religious but still want to be married? What about heterosexuals who want some kind of religious ceremony, even though they are only nominally religious? Do you think society will be harmed, or not, by gay marriages?

2. **(A)** Consider some of the equal rights that homosexuals want, such as no discrimination in jobs or housing, and being able to adopt as a single person, in much the same way that a heterosexual single person is able to adopt. Then, consider some of the benefits that gay couples in long-term

relationships want—hospital visiting rights, the right to inherit, the right to the other person's Social Security benefits upon their death, the right to have and raise children, and so on. Which of these rights do you think are fair? Which are not? Why?

(B) Read Genesis 19, Leviticus 18 and 20, 1 Timothy, Romans 1, 1 Corinthians 6, 1 Timothy 1–10. Discuss the interpretations of these verses (as found within Chapter 5). You may also want to read Focus on the Family's comments, which can be found at *www.family.org/married/topics/a0025114.cfm*.

What are the problems in interpreting these passages? Where are they clear and not clear?

What other degrading sexual behavior might you add to these lists? How does sex use people? How does it harm people? Why does the Bible value sex in a loving relationship, but speak so harshly about these other forms of sex?

3. **(A)** If you're a heterosexual, put yourself in the place of a homosexual in American society. What problems would you face? How would you feel about yourself? How would you internalize social and political attitudes? If you're gay, put yourself in the place of a heterosexual. Why do you think they have a problem with homosexuals?

(B) What do you think should be done about homosexuals in American society? What would you consider just? Fair? Caring? Loving? Christian?

Chapter 6:
War and Peace

1. **(A)** Are you a pacifist, or have you known pacifists? On what philosophy or theology do pacifists base their stand? What do you see as the pluses and minuses of that philosophy?

   (B) Why do you think the early Christians were told not to take part in war? What changed? Why did it change? What would happen if Christians continued to take this nonviolent stand?

2. **(A)** Discuss the Just War theory in relation to several wars. Did the wars fulfill all the criteria? Are the criteria realistic and practical, or useless and impractical?

   (B) What is the occasion for war? What can we do, as Christians, to take away the problems that lead to war? What can individuals, churches, and a government that is led by Christian principles do to help take away the occasion for war?

Chapter 7:
Confronting Terrorism and Fear

1. **(A)** What problems in our country cause you to fear? Discuss the ways that fear begins and is maintained.

(B) What were the fearful situations in the Hebrew Scriptures that the Israelites encountered? Were they resolved? If so, how? What were the situations in Jesus' time, and shortly after, that caused fear? How did the early Christians deal with them? Were these methods effective?

2. (A) Brainstorm actions and policies that our nation could take to confront the problems of terrorism. Is it possible to be as wise as serpents but as innocent as doves when confronting these?

    (B) If you are in a situation of conflict and fear, in what ways do you draw on your faith and your relationship with God? How has your response changed the dynamic of the situation? Has it been effective? What can you take from this situation that would be helpful for our international relationships?

Chapter 8:
Secrets, Lies, and Deceptions

1. (A) What is the difference between a secret and a lie? What are valid secrets? When are secrets not valid but used to cover up? List some of the secrets and cover-ups that you've observed in our American history.

    (B) When Jesus said "The Truth will make you free" (John 8:32), what did he mean? How is truth freeing?

2. **(A)** Why do politicians feel the need to lie? Is a lie ever justified?

   (B) In the 1960s, Joseph Fletcher wrote a book called *Situation Ethics*, in which he argues that Jesus followed situation ethics when he picked corn on the Sabbath, let the adulterous woman go rather than have her stoned, and healed on the Sabbath, among other examples. As a Christian, to what extent are we to hold to a single standard of truth, and to what extent do we need to recognize the moral and ethical complexities of certain situations? Is there a governing principle that we can follow, such as "do no harm" or "whatever the Bible says" or "never lie" or . . . ???

Chapter 9:
Crossing the Political Divide

1. **(A)** How difficult is it for you to cross the political divide? How difficult is it to talk to someone from the other party? Why do you think this problem is so prevalent?

   (B) Some people of one party hate those from the other party. What are the qualities that you could admire in those from the other party if you could put your conflict, or even hatred, aside? If you can't find any good qualities, read or ask others; you may have objectified the Other, which rejects that person as the Beloved of God.

2. **(A)** Where do you see places of agreement between the two parties? On what issues, if they could be seen in a broad perspective, might we find agreement? Consider the issues mentioned in this book—ranging from ecology and health care to the national debt, war, terrorism, homosexuality, abortion, and so on.

(B) What could you do to help create less divisiveness and more unity among Christians? What could your church, or any religious or charitable group you belong to, do? Might you create discussion groups? Or a reading list? A prayer group? Would the example of Kelly Williams work in your group? Are there other models you could use?

Notes

Chapter 1:
How Would Jesus Vote?

1. One only has to read the newspapers or go to a bookstore to see the number of books that attack the other side. For instance, in his book *Let Freedom Ring: Winning the War of Liberty over Liberalism*, conservative television commentator Sean Hannity says that if the Left takes power, civilization is at stake. In his book *Deliver Us from Evil*, he lists "evil" people, parties, and groups, including Bill and Hillary Clinton, Jimmy Carter, the Democratic Party, John Kerry, Al Gore, Edward M. Kennedy, John Edwards, Joseph Lieberman, Richard Gephardt, Howard Dean, Wesley Clark, and the United Nations. He blames Bill Clinton for the September 11 attacks.
2. This is found in a number of articles, including "Democrats Sensitive to Alleged 'Assault on People of Faith'" by Susan Jones, CNSNews.com (Morning Editor, April 19, 2005).

Also "Bill Frist's Christian Jihad," from watchdog.com, April 16, 2005.

3. Colbert I. King, "Hijacking Christianity," *Washington Post*, April 23, 2005. Also Leo Sandon, "Who Are These People of Faith," *Tallahassee Democrat*, April 30, 2005.

4. C. S. Lewis, "Democratic Education," in *Present Concerns*, ed. Walter Hooper (San Diego: Harcourt Brace Jovanovich, 1986), p. 36. Originally published in "Notes on the Way" in *Time and Tide*, April 29, 1944.

5. In spite of many of Bush's actions to the contrary, Sean Hannity says in his book *Deliver Us from Evil* that Bush is the "personification of moral clarity" (p. 9).

6. I have heard this a number of times, including in a prayer said at a Conference on Human Trafficking in Los Angeles in spring 2005.

7. Twenty-two percent of Evangelicals voted for Kerry, 78 percent for Bush. More Latino Protestants (63 percent) voted for Bush, and more black Protestants (83 percent) voted for Kerry. About 77 percent of people of other faiths and 73 percent of Jews voted for Kerry. Pew Research, "Beyond Red vs. Blue," the 2005 Political Typology.

8. Galatians 5: 22–23.

9. Quoted from Juan Mateos in *God and Nations*, by William Durland (Baltimore: Fortkamp Publishing Company, 1989), pp. 53–55.

10. Deuteronomy 6:5, Mark 12:30.

11. Mary Dyer was one of the many Quakers who continually spoke out for religious freedom in Massachusetts, eventually being put to death for her beliefs. Her advocacy of

religious freedom eventually led to religious freedom being included in our Constitution. Other sources about Quaker persecutions include "The Quakers: Hostile Bonnets and Gowns: Governor Endicott's Threat," *The Colonial Gazette*, 1998, 1999, 2000 (*www.mayflowerfamilies.com/enquirer/quakers.htm*, retrieved October 12, 2005); and "Quaker History," from Wikipedia, found at *http://en.wikipedia.org/wiki/Quaker_history*, retrieved October 12, 2005.

12. Max Savelle, "Roger Williams, a Minority of One," in *The American Story: The Age of Exploration to the Age of the Atom* (Great Neck, NY: Channel Press, 1956), pp. 52–53.

13. Herbert J. Storing, *What the Anti-Federalists Were For: The Political Thought of the Opponents of the Constitution* (Chicago: University of Chicago Press, 1981), p. 47.

14. Bob Moser, "The Crusaders: Christian Evangelicals Are Plotting to Remake America in Their Own Image," *Rolling Stone*, April 7, 2005. Also Stanley Kurtz, "Dominionist Domination," *National Review*, July 24, 2005.

15. Ibid.

16. "Christian Dominionists Stand against Liberalism" From Web-Ministry, *www.web-ministry.com/linaer/php?postID=8632*. January 26, 2005. Retrieved June 2005.

17. Peter Wallsten, "The Nation: 2 Evangelicals Want to Strip Courts' Funds; Taped at a Private Conference, the Leaders Outline Ways to Punish Jurists They Oppose" [Home Edition] *Los Angeles Times*, April 22, 2005.

18. Chris Hedges, "Soldiers of Christ II: Feeling the Hate with the National Religious Broadcasters," p. 6. Article posted on Harpers.org on May 30, 2005.

19. "Religious Affiliation of U.S. Congress: 109th U.S. Congress (2005–2006). From Web page *www.adherents.com/adh_congress.html*, retrieved on July 15, 2005.

20. C. S. Lewis, "Equality," from *Present Concern: Essays by C. S. Lewis* in *The Quotable Lewis*, ed. Walter Hooper (San Diego: Harcourt Brace Jovanovich, 1986), p. 17.

21. Notes on the State of Virginia, Thomas Jefferson, 1781.

22. Psalms 9:8, 140:12; 2 Thessalonians 1:6; Hebrews 2:2.

23. Among other verses are Matthew 6:24, 25:15–30; Luke 3:14, 16; John 2:14–17; 1 Timothy 6:10; Hebrews 13:5.

24. Matthew 25:15–30, Luke 15.

25. "Biggest Deficit in History? Yes and No," FactCheck.org, February 27, 2004. *www.factcheck.org/article148.html*.

26. Terence Samuel, "$7,782,816,546,352 in Debt," from *The American Prospect*. Reported on CBSNews.com, Washington, August 12, 2005.

27. Ibid.

28. John 4.

29. Luke 10.

30. Luke 8:1–3.

31. Luke 10:29–37.

32. Matthew 21:31.

33. Luke 23: 43.

34. 1 Corinthians 7.

35. John 8.

36. Matthew 18:22.

37. Matthew. 5:21–26.

38. Matthew 5:43–44; Luke 6:27, 10:27; Romans 12:20.

39. Matthew 5:42.

40. Matthew 12:10, Luke 6:7.

Chapter 2:
The Poor, the Needy, Widows, and Orphans

1. Isaiah 61:2.
2. Isaiah 10:1–2, Ezekiel 22, Micah 2.
3. Psalm 72, Proverbs 29.
4. Psalm 49:13.
5. Amos 2.
6. Psalms 9–10, 34; Job 5; Psalms 107, 132; Jeremiah 2; Isaiah 25.
7. Gustavo Gutiérrez, *A Theology of Liberation: History, Politics, and Salvation*, rev. ed., trans. and ed. by Sister Caridad Inda and John Eagleson (Maryknoll, NY: Orbis Books, 1971, 1998), p. 165.
8. William Durland, *God or Nations: Radical Theology for the Religious Peace Movement* (Baltimore: Fortkamp Publishing Company, 1989), pp. 41–42.
9. Leviticus 19; Deuteronomy 24; Ruth; Deuteronomy 14, 26; Leviticus 25, 14; Exodus 23.
10. Karl Barth, *Church Dogmatics IV, 3, The Doctrine of Reconciliation*, 2nd ed., trans. G. W. Bromiley, T & T Clark Ltd, Edinburgh, Scotland, 1958, p. 891.
11. Jeremiah. 2:7.
12. Jeremiah 2:34.
13. Jeremiah 5:27–30.
14. Jeremiah 7:5–6.
15. Jeremiah 22:16–17.

16. Matthew 6:33.

17. Matthew 4:17, Mark 1:15.

18. National Association of Evangelicals, "For the Health of the Nation: An Evangelical Call to Civic Responsibility." Paper presented and approved at the National Association of Evangelical Conference, Spring 2005.

19. Gutiérrez, A Theology of Liberation, 9.

20. Ibid., 23.

21. Ibid., 35.

22. Ibid., 40.

23. David Cay Johnston, "Richest Are Leaving Even the Rich Far Behind: Tax Laws Help to Widen Gap at Very Top," New York Times, June 5, 2005. Based on material collected from the Heritage Foundation, the Cato Institute, and Citizens for Tax Justice, as well as data from economists, the Federal Reserve's Consumer Finance Survey, the Tax Policy Center, the Urban Institute, the Brookings Institution, the IRS, and the President's 2006 budget.

24. Ted Turner, "Super-rich Don't Need Another Break," USA Today, March 12, 2001.

25. Robert Pear, "Under New Medicare Prescription Drug Plan, Food Stamps May Be Reduced," New York Times/ AOL News, May 8, 2005.

26. Andrew Taylor, "House Reverses Cut in Public Broadcasting Funds," Associated Press/AOL News, June 24, 2005.

27. Greg Winter, "College Aid Rules Change, and Families Pay More," New York Times, June 6, 2005.

28. Statement of Joseph A. Violante, National Legislative Director of the Disabled American Veterans before the Committee on Veterans' Affairs, United States House of Representatives, February 16, 2005.

29. This information has been found in many places, including the above, and was compiled in concise form in "The Democratic Reform Agenda for a Stronger America" from the Democratic Senatorial Campaign Committee, 2005.

30. From *60 Minutes* news program on the cost of drugs in Europe, broadcast June 5, 2005.

31. Maureen Dowd, "DeLay, Deny and Demagogue," *New York Times*, March 24, 2005.

32. Luke 12:34.

33. John Johnson, "Five Mainline Protestant Leaders Call Bush's 2006 Budget "unjust," from Worldwide Faith news archives, March 8, 2005.

34. Ibid.

35. Karl Barth, *The Epistle to the Romans*, trans. from 6th edition by Edwyn C. Hoskyns (London: Oxford University Press, 1933), p. 442.

36. William James, *Varieties of Religious Experience*, quoted in *Under the Banner of Heaven* by Jon Krakauer, New York: Anchor Books, 2004, p. 191. From "The Varieties of Religious Experience: a Study in Human Nature, Being the Gifford Lectures on Natural Religion" delivered at Edinburgh in 1901–1902, (New York: Modern Library, 1999).

Chapter 3:
Beautiful Savior, King of Creation

1. There are many passages; among them are Psalms 89:12, 148:5; Job 12:10, 14:15; Proverbs 8; John 1; Collosians 1:23; Revelation 4:11.
2. Numbers 32:22, 29; Jeremiah 34:11, 16; Esther 7:8; Nehemia 5:5. Also Theodore Hiebert, "Rethinking Dominion Theology," *Direction*, Fall 1996, p. 19.
3. Bennett J. Sims, *Servanthood: Leadership for the Third Millennium* (Cambridge, MA: Cowley Publications, 1997), p. 147.
4. Hiebert, "Rethinking Dominion Theology."
5. Sims, *Servanthood*, pp. 147–149. Also Hiebert, "Rethinking Dominion Theology," *Direction*, Fall 1996, p. 18.
6. Numbers 24:19, Leviticus 26:17, Isaiah 14:6. Also Hiebert, "Rethinking Dominion Theology," p. 18.
7. Psalms 104.
8. Walter Brueggemann, "King in the Kingdom of Things" from *The Christian Century*, September 10, 1969, p. 1166.
9. Sims, *Servanthood*, p. 149.
10. Hiebert, "Rethinking Dominion Theology," p. 21.
11. David Tobin Asselin, "The Notion of Dominion in Genesis 1–3," *The Catholic Biblical Quarterly*, vol. 16, p. 290.
12. Hiebert, "Rethinking Dominion Theology," p. 22. A similar interpretation is given by Dr. Phyllis Tribble, who taught a class I took at Immaculate Heart College Center. She talked a great deal about this word, *adamah*.
13. Genesis 2:15, 3:23
14. Genesis 12:16, Exodus 4:23.

15. Hiebert, "Rethinking Dominion Theology," p. 23.

16. Ibid.

17. Ibid., 24

18. Ibid.

19. Richard L. Means, from *Saturday Review*, December 2, 1967, quoted in "King in the Kingdom of Things" by Walter Brueggemann, from *The Christian Century*, Sept. 10, 1969, p. 1165.

20. Conrad Bonifazi, *A Theology of Things* (Philadelphia: Lippincott, 1967), quoted by Walter Brueggemann in his article, "King in the Kingdom of Things," p. 1165.

21. Brueggemann, "King in the Kingdom of Things," p. 1165.

22. Mark 10:42–44.

23. 1 Peter 5:2–3

24. Genesis 6, 7.

25. Proverbs 12:10.

26. Deuteronomy 22:4.

27. Deuteronomy 22:6–7.

28. Deuteronomy 22:10.

29. Deuteronomy 20:19–20.

30. Rev. Dr. David T. Williams, "Fill the Earth and Subdue It: Dominion to Exploit and Pollute?" *Scripturea* 44, 1993, p. 52.

31. Quoted by Matthew Fox, from *Original Blessings: A Primer in Creation Spirituality*, Jeremy P. Tarcher (New York: Putnam, 2000), p. 88. Originally published by Bear & Co., Inc., Santa Fe, New Mexico, 1983.

32. Quoted at Web page *www.henriettaaucc.org/PastorsPage/Sermon3.shtml*.

33. Fox, 90.

34. Ibid. 89.
35. Pierre Teilhard de Chardin, *Hymn of the Universe* (New York: Harper Torchbooks, 1961), p. 124.
36. Fox, 119.
37. Terry L. Anderson and Clay J. Landry, "Exporting Water to the World," published by Universities Council on Water Resources, USA Issue #118, January 2001.
38. Lester Brown, "'Plan B': The Rescue of a Planet and a Civilization," *Friends Journal*, October 2004.
39. Al Gore, *Earth in the Balance: Ecology and the Human Spirit* (New York: Plume Book, 1993), p. 264.
40. Ibid.
41. Ibid., 71.
42. Ibid., 73.
43. Ibid., 257.
44. Ibid., 262.
45. Christine Todd Whitman, *It's My Party Too: The Battle for the Heart of the GOP and the Future of America* (New York: Penguin Press, 2005), p. 153.
46. "Arctic Oil Search Moves to New Turf, New Controversies," by Yereth Rosen, *Christian Science Monitor*, May 16, 2005.
47. Whitman, *It's My Party Too*, pp. 151–152.
48. Ibid., 178.
49. Ibid., 172–173.
50. Ibid., 194.
51. Ibid.
52. Ibid., 164.
53. Ibid.
54. Ibid., 168.

55. Ibid., 163.

56. Andrew C. Revkin, "Bush Aide Edited Climate Reports," *New York Times*, June 8, 2005.

57. James Carney and John F. Dickerson, "The Rocky Rollout of Cheney's Energy Plan." Web interview, posted May 19, 2001, from *Time* online edition. Also discussed in Whitman, *It's My Party Too*, p. 182.

58. Whitman, *It's My Party Too*, p. 152.

59. "Senate Overwhelmingly Approves Energy Bill," July 29, 2005, CNN.com.

60. "Energy Bill Heads for Home," CBSNews.com, July 26, 2005.

61. "Energy Deal Cuts Conservation Support: Compromise on Measure Has Billions in Tax Breaks for Companies," Associated Press, August 1, 2005.

62. Andrew Server, "The Missing Energy Strategy," *New York Times*, April 19, 2005.

63. Ibid.

64. Kai M. A. Chan, "Heating the Political Climate: GW's Indefensible Position on Climate Change Deserves Widespread Moral Outrage," from DailyPrincetonian.com, April 19, 2001.

65. "Bush Rejects Kyoto-style G8 Deal," BBC News/UK edition, July 4, 2005. From BBC News Online, *http://news.bbc.co.uk/1/hi/world/americas/4647383.stm*.

66. Woods Hole Oceanographic Institution, "Abrupt Climate Change: Bigger Hurricanes: A Consequence of Climate Change?" by Ruth Gorski Curry, September 20, 2004, from Ocean and Climate Change Institution. Also see "Simulated Increase of Hurricane Intensities in a CO_2-

Warmed Climate" by Thomas R. Knutson, Robert E. Tuleya, Yhoshio Kurihara from *Science*, vol. 279, February 13, 1998, and "Warming World Blamed for More Strong Hurricanes" by Fred Pearce from NewScientist.com, September 15, 2005. Also see the *Time* magazine cover story from October 3, 2005. "Are We Making Hurricanes Worse?" as well as "Global Warming: The Culprit? Evidence Mounts that Human Activity Is Helping Fuel These Monster Hurricanes" by Jeffery Kluger, *Time*, October 3, 2005.

67. Jarrett Murphy, "Storm Front: In Global Warming's Kitchen, Hurricanes Love the Heat," *Village Voice*, September 27, 2005. The connection between hurricanes and global warming can be found in innumerable scientific articles, including several issues of *Science* magazine (Issues #279, #299) and *New Scientist* (June 25, 2005; September 15, 2005).

68. Quoted in David Remnick, "The White House Under Water," *The New Yorker*, September 12, 2005, pp. 36–37.

69. Sims, *Servanthood*, p. 142.

70. Barry Commoner, "Freedom and the Environment," in *Freedom in America: A 200 Year Perspective*, ed. Norman A. Graebner (University Park, PA: Pennsylvania State University Press, 1978), p. 243.

Chapter 4:
The Ethical Dilemma of Abortion

1. Matthew 5:32; also found in Luke 16:18 and Mark 10:11.
2. Psalm 100:3.

3. Isaiah 44:24; Job 31:15, 10:8–12; Psalm 139:13–16.

4. Isaiah 49:1, Jeremiah 1:5.

5. Exodus 21:22–25, Amos 1:13.

6. Exodus 4:11, Isaiah 45: 9–11, Romans 9:20.

7. 1 Corinthians 6:19–20, Psalm 127:3, Ezekiel 18:4.

8. Steven D. Levitt and Stephen J. Dubner, *Freakonomics: A Rogue Economist Explores the Hidden Side of Everything,* (New York: William Morrow, 2005), 118.

9. Ibid., 137.

10. Ibid., 137–138.

11. Ibid., 137.

12. Ibid., 144.

13. Ibid., 141.

14. Remarks by Senator Hillary Rodham Clinton to the NYS Family Planning Providers, January 24, 2005 in Albany, New York. Also Steven Ertelt, "Pro-life Group Seeks Meeting with Hillary Clinton to Discuss Abortion," Life-News.com, February 9, 2005, and Andrew Sullivan, "TRB from Washington: Life Lesson," *The New Republic* Online, January 27, 2005.

15. "Plan to Reduce the Number of Abortions," Press Release, April 21, 2005. From Democrats for Life, found at *www.democratsforlife.org/Press/95-10%20release.html.*

16. "The Changing Politics of Abortion," by Susan Page *USA Today*, May 1, 2005

17. Quote from Congressman Tim Roemer at the Democrats for Life of America Press Conference, which introduced the 95-10 Initiative that would try to reduce 95 percent of abortions within ten years, April 21, 2005.

18. United States House of Representatives Committee on Government Reform—Minority Staff Special Investigations Division, "The Content of Federally Funded Abstinence-Only Education Program," prepared by Rep. Henry A. Waxman, December 2004, 17–18. From Web site *www.democrats.reform.house.gov*, retrieved June, 2005.
19. Ibid., 3.

Chapter 5:
Homosexuals: Civil Rights? Civil Unions?

1. According to information supplied by the Lambda Legal Defense and Education Fund (external article) and American Civil Liberties Union (external article). From *http://en.wikipedia.org/wiki/Sodomy_laws-in-the-United-States*, retrieved July 2005.
2. Focus on the Family says it's about 2 to 3 percent; the Pikes Peak Gay and Lesbian Community Center uses 10 percent, including gays, lesbians, bisexual, and transgender.
3. Isaiah 45:9–13.
4. Romans 9:20.
5. Peter J. Gomes, *The Good Book: Reading the Bible with Mind and Heart,* HarperSanFrancisco, 1996, p. 171 (originally published by William Morrow in hardcover, 1996).
6. Focus on the Family, "Responding to Pro-Gay Theology, What Does the Bible Really Say?" 11.
7. Genesis 19:6–8.

8. Gray Temple, *Gay Unions: In the Light of Scripture, Tradition, and Reason* (New York: Church Publishing, 2004), p. 58.

9. Matthew 10:14–15, Luke 10:10–12.

10. Leviticus 20:9.

11. Leviticus 20:2.

12. Leviticus 20:10.

13. Leviticus 20:15.

14. Gomes, *The Good Book*, p. 153.

15. Ibid., p. 154.

16. Ibid.

17. From an interview with Dr. Gary Rendberg, May 2005.

18. Deuteronomy 22:50.

19. Gomes, *The Good Book*, p. 52.

20. Ibid.

21. Ibid.

22. Ibid.

23. 1 Samuel 18:1.

24. 1 Samuel 18:3.

25. 1 Samuel 18:4.

26. 1 Samuel 20:3, 41.

27. 2 Samuel, 1:26.

28. Catherine Griffith, "The Bible and Same-Sex Relationship," *Friends Journal at 50: Quaker Thought and Life Today*, January 2005, 14. Catherine Griffith was a pastor at Valley Mills (Indiana) Meeting; she holds a Ph.D. in Religious Ethics from the University of Virginia. Also see Gomes, *The Good Book*, 159.

29. Griffith, "The Bible and Same-Sex Relationship," 14.

30. 1 Corinthians 6, 7.

31. Temple, *Gay Unions*, 77.
32. Ibid., 78.
33. Ibid., 64–65.
34. Ibid., 70.
35. Ibid., 71–72.
36. Ibid., 72–73
37. Romans 2:1–4.
38. James 4:12.
39. Gomes, *The Good Book*, 158.
40. Temple, *Gay Unions*, 74.
41. Focus on the Family, "Responding to Pro-Gay Theology: What Does the Bible Really Say?" 28.
42. Ibid.
43. Timothy J. Dailey, Focus on the Family, "The Bible, the Church and Homosexuality," p. 34.
44. Ibid., 35.
45. Beth Stroud, "Methodist Panel Votes to Reinstate Lesbian Minister," *Colorado Springs Gazette*, April 30, 2005.
46. "HRC Releases Poll Data Showing Plurality of Americans Support or Accept Marriage Rights for Gay and Lesbian Couples: "Human Rights Campaign," August 1, 2003. From a poll by the Peter D. Hart Research Association, American Viewpoint, Civil Rights, Protections, Benefits. For another view, read "Jerry Falwell—Gay Rights' Activist?" by Terry Mattingly, found on his Religion column on Gospelcom.net, 9/28/05, at *http//tmatt.gospelcom.net/column/2005/09/28*.
47. "Religion and Gay Marriage, Pew Forum on Religion and Public Life," 2000–2005.

48. Sean Cahill, "Why We Need Same Sex Marriage," Testimony to the U.S. Senate Judiciary Committee, 9/4/03. Also published in *The W Effect: Sexual Politics in the Bush Years and Beyond*, edited by Laura Flanders (New York: Feminist Press at CUNY, 2004).

49. William Lee Adams, "Stats: Gay to Wed," *Newsweek*, May 23, 2005.

50. C. S. Lewis, *Mere Christianity* (HarperSanFrancisco, 2001), pp. 102–103.

51. Temple, *Gay Unions*, 111.

52. Lewis, *Mere Christianity*, 102.

Chapter 6:
War and Peace

1. William Durland, *God or Nations: Radical Theology for the Religious Peace Movement* (Baltimore: Fortkamp Publishing Company, 1989), p. 95.

2. Ibid., 94.

3. Ibid., 95.

4. Isaiah 2:4, Hosea 2:18, Micah 4:30.

5. Revelation 21:4.

6. The Church of the Brethren Witness for Peace from *www.brethren.org/genbd/witness/pcjus.htm*. The Quaker Witness of Peace from Durango Friends Meeting (Colorado), "A Call for Justice, Not Revenge," submitted by co-clerks Ross A. Worley and Kathryn Bowers, from Web site *http://members.aol.com/friendsbull/peacemakers.html*, August 1, 2005.

7. From an interview with Col. Paul E. Pirog, Department Head, Department of Law, U.S. Air Force Academy.

8. Col. Paul E. Pirog of U.S. Air Force Academy Law Department, JAG officer, talked about this in a panel discussion, "The Iraq War and Conscientious Objection," at Colorado College, Colorado Springs, Colorado, March 31, 2005. The panel discussion was set up by the Justice and Peace Commission of Colorado Springs.

9. "Bush Vows to Rid the World of Evil-doers," by Manuel Perez-Rivas, September 16, 2001, CNN.com.

10. "Terrorism and War: A Catholic Response, from Web-Exclusives, from Web site *www.americancatholic.org/News/JustWar.*

11. Robert A. Seeley, *Choosing Peace: A Handbook on War, Peace, and Your Conscience* (Philadelphia: Central Committee for Conscientious Objectors, 1994), p. 34.

12. From the 2004 Republican Party Platform.

13. From an interview with Dr. Norman Graebner, June 2005.

14. Seeley, *Choosing Peace*, 34.

15. Ibid.

16. Ibid.

17. Ibid.

18. Ibid.

19. From the Catechism of the Catholic Church.

20. Garry Wills, *Lincoln at Gettysburg: The Words that Remade America* (New York: Simon & Schuster, 1992), p. 179.

21. Ibid., 181.

22. From an interview with William Flavin, June 2005.

23. Seeley, *Choosing Peace*, 35.

24. From an interview with William Flavin, June 2005.

25. This is documented in many articles, among them: Dana Priest, "Jet Is an Open Secret in Terror War," *Washington Post*, December 27, 2004; Jane Mayer, "The Experiment," *The New Yorker*, July 11 and July 18, 2005, p. 60.

26. Thom Shanker and Joel Brinkley, "U.S. Is Set to Sell Jets to Pakistan; India Is Critical," *New York Times*, March 26, 2005.

27. Barry Schweid, "Bush Was Unready for Postwar Iraq, Panel Concludes," Associated Press, July 27, 2005. Also see Congressman Martin T. Meehan, press release, "Meehan: New Report Shows Mismanagement of Iraq War Is Weakening Military," July 22, 2004; Robert Parry, "Iraq War's Two Constants," consortiumnews.com, August 13, 2005; and Kelley Beaucar Vlahos, "Bush Supporters Question Iraq War Tactics," Foxnews.com, September 12, 2005.

28. Griff Witte, "Halliburton's Higher Bill: Rising Costs Reflect Growing Demand for Firm's Services," *Washington Post*, July 6, 2005.

29. Ibid.

30. John Connly Walsh, "Big Disappointments in Iraq," *The Spectator*, August 10, 2005.

31. "4 Halliburton Workers Die in Iraq Attack," Associated Press, December 22, 2004.

32. "Estimates Costs of Iraq War: War in Iraq Could Cost up to $9 Billion Monthly, says CBO," August 8, 2005. From Congressional Budget Office.

33. Dr. Rachel M. MacNair, "History Shows: Winning with Nonviolent Action," Xlibris Corporation, 2004, pp. 10, 17.

34. Romans 12:15–21.

35. Christian Aid, *Pocket Prayers for Peace and Justice* (London: Church House Publishing, 2004).

Chapter 7:
Confronting Terrorism and Fear

1. Matthew 24:7.
2. Luke 21:11.
3. 1 Peter 3:6.
4. 1 John 4:18.
5. Ibid.
6. Psalm 23.
7. Psalm 91.
8. Ibid.
9. Isaiah 51.
10. Ezekiel 11.
11. Psalm 128, Proverbs 14, Job 28.
12. Psalms 34, 55.
13. 1 John 4:18.
14. From the "Beyond War" seminars held in the 1980s and 1990s. I attended several of these seminars in Los Angeles, California, in the 1980s.

15. Psalm 23.
16. God came to earth as a little child. Other verses relating to this include Matthew 18:1–6, Luke 18:17.
17. Luke 10:29–37.
18. Luke 15:8–10.
19. Matthew 23:37, Luke 13:34.
20. Matthew 5:46–47.
21. Matthew 5:43–44; Luke 6:27, 6:35; Romans 12:20.
22. Koran 5.8, "The Dinner Table."
23. 1 Samuel 17.
24. John 9.
25. Matthew 12.
26. William Durland, *God or Nations: Radical Theology for the Religious Peace Movement* (Baltimore: Fortkamp Publishing Company, 1989), p. 163.
27. Ibid.
28. John 8.
29. Hosea 8:7, Galatians 6:7.
30. Matthew 6:26. Much of this is discussed in Durland, *God and Nations*, 165.
31. Durland, *God and Nations*, 166.
32. This theory is discussed in more detail in my book *Web-Thinking: Connecting Not Competing for Success* (Maui, Hawaii: Inner Ocean, 2002).
33. Bill Clinton, *My Life* (New York: Alfred A. Knopf, 2004), p. 717.
34. Ibid.

35. Quoted in *God's Politics: Why the Right Gets It Wrong and the Left Doesn't Get It* by Jim Wallis, HarperSanFrancisco, 2005, p. 88.
36. Ibid., 95.

Chapter 8:
Secrets, Lies, and Deceptions

1. Matthew 5:33–37.
2. Walter Hooper, ed., *The Business of Heaven: Daily Readings by C. S. Lewis* (San Diego: Harcourt Brace Jovanovich, 1984), p. 186.
3. From speech by George W. Bush on Monday, October 7, 2002. "President Bush Outlines Iraqi Threat," Remarks by the President on Iraq, Cincinnati Museum Center, Cincinnati Union Terminal, Cincinnati, Ohio, October 7, 2002.
4. "President Links Terrorist Attacks and Iraq during Speech" at Fort Bragg, NC, June 2005. Also from "President Addresses Nation, Discusses Iraq, War on Terror" from the White House News, October 14, 2005.
5. Matthew 23:23.

Chapter 9:
Crossing the Political Divide

1. Some of these verses include Romans 12, 1 Corinthians 12, 13.
2. Raymond Hernandez and Patrick D. Healy, "Oddly Hillary and, Yes, Newt Agree to Agree," *New York Times*, May 13, 2005; also "A Good Idea from the Odd Couple," from the Editorial Desk, *New York Times*, May 16, 2005.

Index